READING AND ATTENTION DISORDERS

CONFERENCE PARTICIPANTS

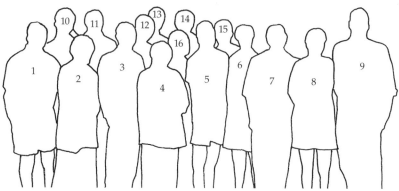

1. Steve Petersen
2. Ann Schulte
3. Bennett Shaywitz
4. Sally Shaywitz
5. Dan Geschwind
6. Marge Livingstone
7. Frank Wood
8. Paula Tallal

9. Will Baker
10. Tom West
11. Glenn Rosen
12. Katja Voeller
13. Stewart Anderson
14. Drake Duane
15. John DeFries
16. Maryanne Wolf

READING AND ATTENTION DISORDERS

Neurobiological Correlates

Edited by Drake D. Duane, M.D.

YORK PRESS   Baltimore, Maryland

This book was manufactured in the United States of America.

Typography by Type Shoppe II Productions Ltd.

Printing and binding by Data Reproductions Corp.

Cover design by Joseph Dieter, Jr.

Contents

Preface

In the summer of 1998, the National Dyslexia Research Foundation called together a group of eminent neuroscientists to update one another (and now this readership) on recent advances in the neurobiologic correlates between constitutional disorders of reading (dyslexia) and attentional disorders, particularly of the attention deficit disorder category of constitutional (childhood) onset. The cordiality of the investigators in their interaction equaled that of the environment on the big island of Hawaii where this small conference met.

To Colleen Osburn, conference coordinator, our gratitude for supervising the culinary aspects of the conference which were as nourishing as the intellectual content of the presentations. For financial aid, the Foundation and the participants are deeply grateful to the John Chany Trust, to the Sharon Lund Foundation, to Helen U. Baker, and to MCI for making this meeting possible.

This publication represents the second round of the series of periodic updates in the neurobiology, neuropsychology, and education pertinent to the field of reading disorder. The editor has provided a synopsis at the conclusion of each chapter to summarize key points. I am deeply indebted to Warner Stuart, B. A., who supervised the compilation of materials from the various authors; to Will Baker, Jr., for his foresight in creating the National Dyslexia Research Foundation in order to promote international scientific cross fertilization between the fields of neuroscience, psychology, and education; and to Elinor Hartwig and her staff for the rapid final preparation of this text so that it might be available prior to the close of the century, just over 100 years from the first clinical description of a student struggling to learn to read. This text attempts to clarify the issue of why it is that those with reading disorder may also be encumbered by difficulties in attention and vice versa. We have now a platform from which to launch the next century of investigation.

Drake D. Duane, M.D.
Scottsdale, Arizona 1999

Dedication

To Kazmiera Angela Duane who taught that childhood nurturance and familial bonding prepare for competence in adulthood.

Contributors

Stewart A. Anderson, M.D.
  Laboratory of Developmental
    Neurobiology
  Department of Psychiatry
  University of California San Francisco
  401 Parnassus Avenue
  San Francisco, California 94143

Kyle Boone, Ph.D.
  Department of Psychiatry and
    Behavioral Sciences
  UCLA School of Medicine
  Los Angeles, California

C. Keith Connors, Ph.D.
  Duke University Medical Center
  2200 West Main Street, Suite 230B
  Durham, North Carolina 27705

John C. DeFries, Ph.D.
  Institute for Behavioral Genetics
  Campus Box 447
  University of Colorado
  Boulder, Colorado 80309-0447

Drake D. Duane, M.D.
  Institute for Developmental Behavioral
    Neurology
  10210 North 92nd Street, Suite 300
  Scottsdale, Arizona 85258

Pauline Filipek, M.D.
  University of California Irvine Medical
    Center
  Departments of Pediatrics and
    Neurology
  UCI Medical Center, Route 81-4482
  101 City Drive South
  Orange, California 92868-3298

Christopher M. Filley, M.D.
  Departments of Neurology and
    Psychiatry
  University of Denver School of
    Medicine
  4200 East Ninth Avenue
  Denver, Colorado 80262

Daniel Geschwind, M.D., Ph.D.
  Department of Neurology
  UCLA School of Medicine
  Reed Neurological Pavilion, Room 1-145
  710 Westwood Plaza
  Los Angeles, California 90024

William M. Jenkins, Ph.D.
  Scientific Learning Corporation
  1995 University Avenue Suite 400
  Berkeley, California 94704-1074

Valerie S. Knopik, Ph.D.
  Institute for Behavioral Genetics
  Campus Box 477
  University of Colorado
  Boulder, Colorado 80309-0447

Margaret Livingstone, Ph.D.
  Harvard Medical School
  Department of Neurobiology
  220 Longwood Avenue
  Boston, Massachusetts 02115

Michael Merzenich, Ph.D.
  Keck Center for Integrative
    Neuroscience
  University of California San Francisco
  San Francisco, California

Steve L. Miller, Ph.D.
Scientific Learning Corporation
1995 University Avenue Suite 400
Berkeley, California 94704-1074

Susan S. Osborne, Ph.D.
Department of Curriculum and
Instruction
College of Education and Psychology
602 Poe Hall, Box 7801
North Carolina State University
Raleigh, North Carolina 27695-7801

Bruce F. Pennington, Ph.D.
Department of Psychology
University of Denver
2155 South Race Street
Denver, Colorado 80208

Ann C. Schulte, Ph.D.
Department of Psychology
640 Poe Hall, Box 7801
North Carolina State University
Raleigh, North Carolina 27695-7801

Bennett Shaywitz, M.D.
Department of Pediatrics
Yale University Medical School
New Haven, Connecticut 06510

Sally Shaywitz, M.D.
Department of Pediatrics
Yale University Medical School
New Haven, Connecticut 06510

Jack H. Simon, M.D., Ph.D.
University of Colorado Health Science
Center
4200 East 9th Avenue
Campus Box A034
Denver, Colorado 80262

Paula Tallal, Ph.D.
Center for Molecular and Behavioral
Neuroscience
Rutgers University, Newark
197 University Avenue
Newark, New Jersey 07102

Kytja Voeller, M.D.
Developmental Behavioral Neurology
Unit
Department of Psychiatry
University of Florida
Gainesville, Florida 32610

Sally J. Wadsworth, Ph.D.
Institute for Behavioral Genetics
Campus Box 447
University of Colorado
Boulder, Colorado 80309-0447

Thomas G. West
National Dyslexia Research Foundation
6622 32nd Street, N.W.
Washington, D.C. 20015

Frank B. Wood, Ph.D.
Section of Neuropsychology
Wake Forest University School of
Medicine
1 Medical Center Boulevard
Winston-Salem, North Carolina 27157-
1043

Dlx Genes, the Striatal Subventricular Zone, and the Development of Neocortical Interneurons

Stewart A. Anderson

Several lines of evidence indicate that developmental dyslexia may be caused by genetic abnormalities of forebrain development. For example, concurrence for dyslexia is higher in identical twins than in fraternal twins (DeFries, Fulker, and LaBuda 1987; Light, Defries, and Olson 1998). Recently, linkage analysis has implicated the involvement of specific regions of chromosomes 6 and 15 in distinct aspects of reading disorder (Grigorenko et al. 1997). In addition to the progress toward discovering a genetic etiology for dyslexia, studies using functional brain imaging are detecting abnormalities in increasingly specific forebrain regions, particularly within the cerebral cortex (Eden and Zeffiro 1998; Shaywitz et al. 1998). Evidence that some cases of dyslexia result from abnormalities in brain development has also been mounting. Some imaging studies have found an absence of the normal left-right brain asymmetry in the temporal lobes of some individuals with dyslexia (Gauger, Lombardino, and Leonard 1997). In addition, post-mortem studies suggest that some dyslexic individuals had disruptions of neuronal migration in the cerebral cortex occurring early in development (Galaburda et al. 1985; Humphreys, Kaufmann, and Galaburda, 1990).

Although no molecular etiologies of dyslexia have been found, advancements in the genetics of neurodevelopment make uncovering these etiologies an attainable goal. This chapter will begin with a brief overview of recent discoveries regarding the genetic control of forebrain development. A more detailed account of the role of two regulatory genes, Dlx-1 and Dlx-2, will follow. Finally, implications of the analysis of Dlx-1/Dlx-2 mutants for cerebral cortical development are presented. Although a specific link between the Dlx family of transcription factors and developmental dyslexia cannot currently be drawn, this chapter intends to demonstrate how the study of molecular neurogenetics is making inroads toward understanding the genetic regulation of forebrain development.

In the developing mammalian embryo, neurons are born along the inside of a tube of proliferating cells, the neural tube, then migrate into the wall of the tube where they mature (see figure 1). The processes involved are termed; (1) regional specification, whereby regions of the neural tube become specified to produce particular brain areas, (2) proliferation of neural precursor cells, (3) migration of these cells out of the proliferative zone, and (4) differentiation, whereby the cells attain their mature location, chemical attributes, and connectivity. This process, by which billions of neurons and glia develop in a highly orchestrated fashion to produce an organ of immense complexity, is regulated by hierarchies of transcription factors, proteins that bind specific DNA sequences to alter gene transcription.

Over the last two decades, a host of transcription factor genes has been identified, many of them through mutant screens in the fruit fly drosophila. Despite some 200 million years of intervening evolution, many key regulatory genes in the fly have mammalian homologues that share high levels of similarity in DNA sequence and expression pattern (Graham, Papalopulu, and Krumlauf 1989). For example, the drosophila gene *distaless* is expressed in the wing bud, central nervous system, and head (Cohen et al. 1989). In mouse and human, the distaless homologues, the Dlx gene family, are expressed in the limb buds, developing brain, and cranial neural crest (Stock et al. 1996). This high level of gene conservation across species allows experiments on gene function in mice (or, to a lesser extent, in worms and flies) to be highly relevant for human development. These experiments generally take the form of "knock-outs" where mouse mutants are generated that lack a given gene, or "knock-ins" in which mouse mutants have a given gene misexpressed in higher than normal levels or at altered developmental stages or locations.

Recent studies of knockout mice have begun to shed light on the genetic regulation of forebrain development. For example, the transcription factor gene Otx-2 appears to be involved in forebrain specifi-

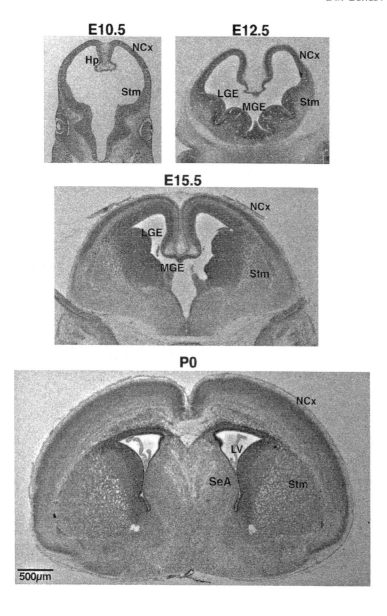

Figure 1. Development of the murine telencephalon. Shown are coronal sections through the mouse telencephalon stained with cresyl violet. E- embryonic day. P0- day of birth. Hp- hippocampal anlage. Ncx- neocortical anlage. Stm- striatal anlage. SeA- septal area. LGE- lateral ganglionic eminence. MGE- medial ganglionic eminence. LV- lateral ventricle.

cation, since null mutants essentially lack brain tissue rostral (toward the nose) to the hindbrain (Matsuo et al. 1995). On the other hand, mutants for the transcription factor BF-1 show abnormalities of proliferation in the rostral portion of the forebrain, the telencephalon (septal region, hippocampus, striatum, cerebral cortex, and olfactory bulb) (Xuan et al. 1995). Mutants for Dlx-1 and Dlx-2, described below, have abnormalities of both neuronal migration and differentiation in the telencephalon (Anderson et al. 1997).

Advances in mapping and sequencing the mouse and human genomes have aided in the identification of human transcription factor mutations. These mutations can have highly variable effects, even when the same gene is affected. For instance, the Emx-1 gene has been linked to schizencephaly, a condition in which abnormal clefts form in the cerebral cortex, possibly as a result of disruptions in neuronal proliferation (Boncinelli 1997). Depending on the extent of the gene's alteration, the effect on human brain development may vary from severe malformations and mental retardation, to relatively normal cognitive function but the development of seizures. Although it may seem that mutations in "master regulatory genes" such as Emx-1 would lead to major developmental abnormalities, this is not necessarily the case. Single base-pair mutations in coding sequences can result in a protein product with only a partial alteration in function. Alternatively, small mutations in regulatory sequences may alter the timing, location, or level of expression in subtle ways. Finally, many transcription factors exist as a group of closely related family members that have partially or wholly redundant expression domains and functions. These gene families are thought to form by duplication events over the course of evolution. They may allow useful gain of function alterations in one copy to occur without compromising the original function of the gene. Due to redundancy between gene family members, the loss of function of one family member can result in remarkably subtle abnormalities.

DLX-1 AND DLX-2 PARTICIPATE IN REGULATING THE DEVELOPMENT OF THE BASAL FOREBRAIN

In this section the effects of mutations of the transcription factors Dlx-1 and Dlx-2 are discussed. In addition to showing how a loss of function mutation in these genes results in abnormal forebrain development, this section and the one following illustrate how gene knockout experiments can shed light on developmental processes that extend beyond the direct influence of the disrupted genes.

In the developing telencephalon there are two populations of dividing cells. The first population to form lies within the ventricular zone (VZ) adjacent to the lateral ventricles (Boulder Committee 1970; Takahashi, Nowakowski, and Caviness 1993). A second proliferative population lies predominantly in the subventricular zone (SVZ), which is located between the VZ and the mantle zone, the region of differentiating cells (Bhide 1996; Takahashi, Nowakowski, and Caviness 1995) (see figure 2). Unlike cells of the VZ, the nuclei of dividing cells in the SVZ do not move to the ventricular surface to undergo mitosis (Smart 1961). While the telencephalic ventricular zone is known to produce neurons, the fate(s) of SVZ-derived cells is unclear. Postnatally, the SVZ gives rise to glia (Levison and Goldman 1993) and to interneurons of the olfactory bulb (Luskin 1993). The SVZ, however, begins to produce post-mitotic cells during the period of neurogenisis (approximately E12-E17 in the mouse). Specifically, the SVZ in more lateral portions of the neocortex develops at about E13.5

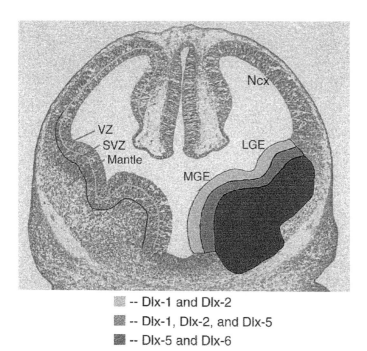

▓ -- Dlx-1 and Dlx-2

▓ -- Dlx-1, Dlx-2, and Dlx-5

▓ -- Dlx-5 and Dlx-6

Figure 2. Expression of Dlx-1, -2, -5 and -6 at embryonic day 12.5. At this age, all four genes have an expression pattern that is restricted to the basal telencephalon. Dlx-1 and -2 are expressed within the VZ, these two genes and Dlx-5 are expressed in the SVZ, and Dlx-5 and Dlx-6 are expressed in the mantle zone. This expression pattern suggests that the Dlx genes control the development of the same cell lineages at different stages of differentiation. VZ- ventricular zone. SVZ- subventricular zone. Ncx- neocortical anlage. LGE- lateral ganglionic eminence. MGE- medial ganglionic eminence.

(Takahashi, Nowakowski, and Caviness 1995), while that in the lateral ganglionic eminence (LGE, see figure 1), the primordia of the striatum, begins as early as E11.0 (Sheth and Bhide 1997). Since striatal neurons in the mouse are born approximately from E12.0- E17, this finding suggests that some striatal neurons are generated from the SVZ. The likelihood that both populations of dividing cells in the LGE give rise to striatal neurons raises the question of whether distinct neuronal subtypes are generated by each one.

The striatum is a collection of nuclei within the basal telencephalon. Much of the striatal input is highly processed information from all regions of the cerebral cortex. One striatal function may be to participate in the feedback loop by which the organism sequences and organizes action plans (thought or motor), and then compares the result of actions with their goal (Graybiel 1998). Among the multiple levels of organization of the striatum are two domains of cells— the patch and matrix domains. These groups of cells differ in their organization, connectivity, and chemical characteristics (Gerfen 1992). In addition, patch cells are generally "born" earlier than matrix cells (van der Kooy and Fishell 1986).

To investigate the genetic mechanisms controlling striatal development, genes were identified that are preferentially expressed in the developing basal telencephalon. A group of genes, the Dlx family, was identified that encode for putative transcription factors based on their encoding for a DNA binding domain common to many transcription factors. Four of the Dlx genes, Dlx-1, -2, -5 and -6, are expressed in the developing LGE (Liu et al. 1997). Their pattern of expression at E12.5 suggests that they have distinct functions in striatal development (figure 1). Although all four genes are initially restricted in their expression to the basal forebrain, Dlx-1 and -2 expression occurs primarily in the proliferative zones the ventricular zone (VZ) and subventricular zone (SVZ) (Bulfone et al.1993). Dlx-5 is expressed at highest levels within the SVZ and mantle zone, while Dlx-6 is expressed primarily in the mantle zone (Simeone et al. 1994; Liu et al. 1997). Thus Dlx-1 and -2 are expressed where they may control processes of specification, proliferation, and/or migration, whereas Dlx-5 may function mainly in cell migration and/or differentiation, and Dlx-6 may function mainly in differentiation.

To study the functions of Dlx-1 and Dlx-2 in forebrain development, three types of "knockout" mice were generated. None of the mutants was viable, as Dlx-2 and Dlx-1/Dlx-2 homozygous mutants died shortly after birth (P0) and Dlx-1 homozygous mutants died within the first month of life (Qiu et al. 1995; Qiu et al. 1997). Death appeared to be due to craniofacial and/or enteric nervous system defects related to Dlx-1 and -2 expression in the cranial neural crest.

Mutants for either Dlx-1 or Dlx-2 were essentially normal in terms of striatal development, although the Dlx-2 mutant had a subtle abnormality involving interneurons of the olfactory bulb. In contrast, histological analysis of mutants lacking functional copies of both Dlx-1 and Dlx-2 revealed an enlarged region of undifferentiated cells within the LGE (Anderson et al. 1997). Lateral to this region was a small area of striatum-like cells.

Further analysis of the Dlx-1 and -2 mutants revealed a number of interesting details. First, generation, migration, and differentiation of patch neurons appeared grossly normal. This was determined by the presence of markers for patch neurons within the mutant striatal mantle, as well as cell birth dating experiments that indicated a predominance of early-born cells (E11.5 and E12.5) in the mutant striatal mantle. In addition, migration from the LGE proliferative zone to the mantle zone in slice cultures from E12.5 mutant animals was normal. On the other hand, later born cells that should give rise mainly to the striatal matrix appeared to accumulate in the undifferentiated region close to the lateral ventricle. Interestingly, although the later-born mutant cells were unable to migrate out of the striatal proliferative zone (LGE), they did undergo partial differentiation as evidenced by their expression of MAP2 protein, a marker of postmitotic neurons.

Several lines of evidence suggest that the Dlx-1 and -2 mutation primarily effects cells from the proliferative population within the SVZ. The timing of the onset of migrational abnormalities out of the LGE coincides with the period when the SVZ would normally become the dominant proliferative population in the LGE (Sheth and Bhide 1997). Several transcription factors, including Dlx-5, are absent from the mutant SVZ region (although they are present initially in the mutant striatal mantle, where they may be affecting the differentiation of the early born, striatal patch cells). Finally, one of the derivatives of the SVZ, the interneurons of the olfactory bulb, are virtually undetectable in the Dlx-1 and -2 mutants.

In sum, analysis of the Dlx-1,-2, and double mutants has begun to shed light on the genetic regulation of striatal development. As has been found in a number of other systems, functional redundancy between Dlx-1 and Dlx-2 occurs in such a way that mice that lack either one have grossly normal striatal development, although the double mutants are severely affected. The two genes are not equivalent, however, as the single mutants differ considerably in their phenotypes within the cranial bones and the olfactory bulb (Qiu et al. 1997).

Although the molecular functions of Dlx-1 and -2 in striatal development remain to be determined, the relatively selective effect of the double mutant on migration and/or differentiation of cells derived from the SVZ of the LGE raises a hypothesis regarding striatal development. Earlier born neurons may arise from the ventricular zone (VZ), migrate through the SVZ, and differentiate into patch cells in a process that is independent of Dlx-1 and Dlx-2. A separate lineage of later-born cells arising from the SVZ may differentiate into the striatal matrix in a Dlx-1 and -2 dependent process. Induction of Dlx-5 in the SVZ by Dlx-1 and Dlx-2 may be part of this process. This hypothesis is one of the few to link transcription factor genes to the development of a neuronal subpopulation in the forebrain. Teasing out the roles of specific genes in the formation of specific neuronal subtypes is a key aspect of attaining a molecular understanding of neural development and related human disorders.

A POPULATION OF NEOCORTICAL INTERNEURONS MAY ORIGINATE WITHIN THE BASAL TELENCEPHALON.

In addition to shedding light on Dlx gene function in striatal development, the Dlx-1 and -2 mutant mice provide opportunities to investigate the derivatives of the SVZ (up to P0, when the double mutants die). One such derivative, as noted above, is the interneuron population of the olfactory bulb. Based on further examination of the Dlx-1 and -2 mutant, as well as work from several other laboratories, it appears that the basal telencephalon also gives rise to interneurons in the neocortex.

There are two general classes of neocortical neurons, the excitatory pyramidal neurons that send their axons to distant targets, and the inhibitory (GABAergic) interneurons that form only local synaptic connections. The excitatory neurons compose 70% to 85% of all neocortical neurons (Meinecke and Peters 1987; Parnavelas, Lieberman, and Webster 1977). Despite their lower number, the inhibitory neurons play a vital role in modulating neocortical output.

Neocortical neurons have generally been thought to derive from the proliferative zone of the dorsal telencephalon. Thus cells born in the dorsal VZ migrate along radial glial fibers into the neocortical mantle (Rakic 1988). This schema has important implications for research into the genetic causes of disorders of neuronal migration. For example, the search for dysfunctional genes involved in the formation of neocortical neuronal migration disorders could be restricted to those genes that are expressed in the dorsal telencephalon.

Although tangential migration of neurons in the neocortex has been reported (O'Rourke et al. 1995; Rakic 1995; and see figure 2 of Boulder Committee 1970), evidence from slice culture experiments had suggested that these cells are dorsally generated because tangentially migrating cells in the VZ do not cross the boundary between the neocortical and striatal primordia (Fishell, Mason, and Hatten 1993). However, recent studies of neuronal migration in vitro raised the possibility that cells migrate from the LGE into the neocortex via the striatal SVZ and/or mantle zone. De Carlos, Lopez-Mascarague, and Valberde (1996) used an elegant whole-mount culture technique to make focal tracer injections into the LGE of rat embryos. Although most of the cell migration from the LGE appeared to be directed radially toward the striatal mantle and the ventrally located primary olfactory cortex, some cells migrated tangentially/dorso-medially into the neocortex. Tamamaki (1997) used both cultures of rostral telencephalon and in utero injections into E16 rat embryos to demonstrate that a robust cell migration occurs from the LGE into the neocortex. Brunstrom et al. (1997) applied neurotrophin-4 to E16 forebrain slice cultures and found that heterotopias developed in the neocortical marginal zone. Since evidence indicated that the abnormal cells were neither derived from the neocortical ventricular zone, nor born within the heterotopia itself, the authors hypothesized that NT4 had increased tangential migration from the basal forebrain into the neocortical marginal zone.

Although both in vitro and in vivo studies have found that cells migrate tangentially from the basal forebrain into the neocortex (see also Anderson et al. 1997), the fate of the migrating cells has remained unclear. Several lines of evidence suggest that it includes one or more populations of GABA-ergic interneurons. First, GABA immunoreactive cells can be found in the lateral striatal mantle and the intermediate zone of the neocortex fairly early in telencephalic development (mouse E12.5: DeDiego, Smith-Fernandez, and Fairen 1994; Del Rio, Soriano, and Ferrer 1992). Many of these cells have a morphology and orientation that suggests they may be migrating dorso-medially from the LGE into the neocortex. Second, a retroviral lineage study reported that, unlike clones of projection neurons, which tend to be arranged in columnar clusters extending radially through the neocortical layers, clones of GABA-containing interneurons frequently are distributed widely across the neocortex (Mione et al. 1997). This pattern would be consistent with a tangentially migrating mitotic precursor, or with tangential migration of the interneurons after their final division. Recently, a second lineage analysis has further supported the notion that radially oriented neocortical clones tend to contain projection neurons and are clonally distinct from tangentially dispersed clones, which tend to contain interneurons (Tan et al. 1998).

Clearly, evidence that some clonally related groups of interneurons are tangentially dispersed in the neocortex is consistent with tangential migration of these cells, but does not address their origin. Two recent reports have presented evidence that some neocortical GABA-ergic cells indeed originate in the basal telencephalon. Brunstrom and coworkers (1997) found that many of the cells in the NT4-induced heterotopias were GABA-ergic. Subsequent work by the same group found that in slice cultures, cell tracer placed in the LGE subsequently labeled NT4-induced heterotopias in the neocortex that included GABA-immunoreactive cells (Brunstrom, Gray-Swain, and Pearlman 1998). The authors conclude that a population of GABA-ergic subpial granule cells are stimulated by NT4 to migrate into the neocortex in vivo.

Interneurons in the deeper neocortical layers may also originate in the basal telencephalon. Anderson et al. (1997) combined an organotypic slice culture preparation with the analysis of the Dlx-1 and -2 mutant mice to demonstrate that many neocortical GABA-containing interneurons derive from the basal forebrain. First, LGE cells were labeled with DiI prior to incubation of mouse E12.5 forebrain slices. After cells had migrated into the neocortex sections, they were fixed, resectioned, and then stained for GABA immunohistochemistry. Some of the LGE-derived neocortical cells were GABA positive. Furthermore, mechanical separation of the neocortex from the LGE in slices resulted in a major reduction of neocortical GABA positive cells. Finally, slices from the Dlx-1 and -2 mutant did not have basal forebrain to neocortical migration, and staining of forebrain sections from P0 mutants revealed a 75% reduction in neocortical GABA immunoreactive cells.

In sum, it appears that the neocortex in rodents is composed of cells from both the dorsal and the basal telencephalic proliferative zones. At least some of the neocortical cells derived from the basal telencephalon are interneurons, but a number of key questions remain. For example, the basal forebrain contains two invaginations of proliferative neuroepithelium, the medial (MGE) and the lateral (LGE) ganglionic eminences. Crystals of the lipophilic tracer DiI label cells moving into the neocortex from both the LGE and from the MGE (Anderson and Rubenstein, unpublished observations). It remains to be determined whether different subpopulations of GABA-ergic neurons originate in these regions. The fact that several transcription factors are differentially expressed in the MGE and LGE, and that the important signaling molecule Sonic Hedgehog differentially affects these regions (Kohtz et al. 1998) suggests that they may give rise to different cell types that migrate into the neocortex.

Some neurons traverse several millimeters of tissue as they migrate from basal forebrain to neocortex. Given this fact, the question arises as to how this migration is guided. Any combination of intrinsic programming, extrinsic guidance by secreted factors, or factors located on cortical axons could affect the tangential migration. During the early postnatal period, the rostral septal region appears to secrete

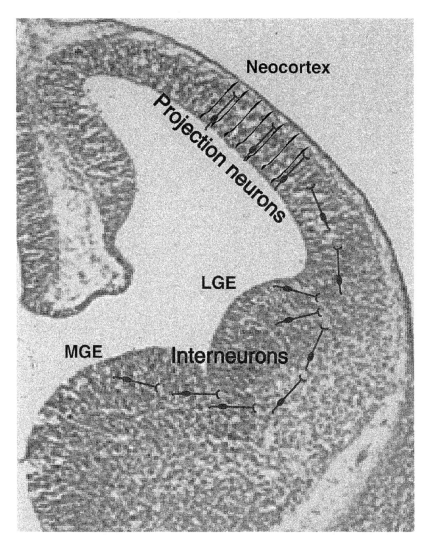

Figure 3. Migration of neocortical cells during embryonic development. This schema presents the hypothesis that, although projection neurons in the neocortex migrate radially from the neocortical ventricular zone, many neocortical interneurons migrate into the neocortex tangentially from the MGE and LGE. In this scenario, regulatory genes that have expression patterns restricted to the subcortical telencephalon can influence the development of cells fated to reside within the neocortex. LGE- lateral ganglionic eminence. MGE- medial ganglionic eminence.

a chemorepellant factor that drives a population of subventricular neurons to migrate toward the olfactory bulb (Hu and Rutishauser 1996). However, preliminary results using explants of neocortex, LGE, MGE, or forebrain floorplate in collagen gels failed to demonstrate any chemorepulsive or attractive activity for migrating cells. Instead, cell migration into the collagen from the MGE or LGE explants was not affected by neocortical, MGE, or forebrain floorplate placed nearby (Anderson and Rubenstein, unpublished results). It should be noted that a negative result from such experiments by no means rules out the possibility that some chemotrophic activity for these regions exists in vivo.

Dlx-1 and Dlx-2 may themselves play important roles in regulating tangential migration. As noted above, cells in the embryonic striatal subventricular zone express high levels of these genes, and there is an abnormal accumulation of postmitotic cells in this region in the Dlx-1 and -2 mutants. Moreover, in normal mice the proteins encoded by these genes continue to be present in at least some of the tangentially migrating cells in the neocortical intermediate zone and in layer I (Anderson et al. 1997 and unpublished results). Current studies are attempting to identify genes whose transcription is affected by the Dlx-1 and -2 proteins.

Finally, despite the close homologies between mammals (i.e. between rodents and humans) in nearly every aspect of brain development, it remains to be demonstrated that basal forebrain to neocortical migration occurs in humans. Gadissex et al. (1992), using immunohistochemistry and electron microscopy in human fetal tissue, have reported the presence of GABA-containing neurons with an orientation and morphology that is consistent with ganglionic eminence to neocortical migration. This migration is reported to occur at the rostral end of the ganglionic eminence, just caudal to the olfactory bulb, and to involve neurons migrating into layer I of the neocortex. Other studies in human and non-human primates have demonstrated that tangentially oriented, and in some instances GABA positive, neurons are present in several layers of the developing human and monkey neocortex (Schwartz and Meinecke 1992; Yan, Zheng, and Garey 1992). However, the origin of these cells is not known.

Advances in the neurogenetics of forebrain development are filling in the gap between gene function at the molecular level and gene function at the tissue level. At the same time, gene knockout experiments that affect specific brain regions are providing new insights into interactions between forebrain regions during development, such as cell migration and axonal connectivity. As sequencing the human genome (and thus the identification of all human genes) becomes a reality, mouse neurogenetics will play a vital role in determining the functions of these genes, and the roles they play in human disorders of neurodevelopment.

EDITOR'S COMMENTS

Why is it that one in three of those with reading disorders appear to have coexistent difficulty with attention? Contrari-wise, why is there so high a percentage of those who present with attention disorders also exhibiting difficulty in decoding script? If the work of Kemper and Galaburda in 1979 and since suggest that there is a cortical morphologic characteristic that distinguishes those with dyslexia, then perhaps there is a similar morphologic characteristic in attention disorder co-occurring with reading disorder. Furthermore, if indeed this is a disorder of genetic origin, how is it that a gene mechanism may induce cortical malformation and specifically that region of the cortex currently felt to be germane to attention, namely the frontal cortex and its connections to the deep structures known as the basal ganglia?

Dr. Anderson provides us with a potential explanation. Nerve cells on the surface of the frontal cortex appear to have a genetic origin that embryonically arises from deep structures as demonstrated in his elegant experiments using the Dlx-1, 2 model. At a neurochemical level, that these neurons should be pertinent to the gamma amino butyric acid (GABA) system is all the more pertinent based on the work of Frank Wood and his colleagues presented elsewhere in this book. One should also bear in mind that these studies, although currently bound together in a text on reading and attention, may have broader biologic implications for behavior, including that most serious of psychiatric states, schizophrenia, which, as a biologically oriented psychiatrist, is one of Dr. Anderson's chief fields of inquiry. Likewise, the clinical observation of coexistent obsessive-compulsive disorder with reading and attention disorders may reflect frontal and mesial frontal (cingulum) cortical dysmorphogenesis. Readers who are members of the International Dyslexia Association (formerly the Orton Dyslexia Society) should bear in mind that Samuel T. Orton was a neuropsychiatrist, a collaborative clinical science only recently reunited.

—DDD

REFERENCES

Anderson, S. A., Qiu, M.-S., Bulfone, A., Eisenstat, D. D., Meneses, J. R. P, and Rubenstein, J. L. R. 1997. Mutations of the homeobox genes Dlx-1 and Dlx-2 disrupt the striatal subventricular zone and differentiation of late-born striatal neurons. *Neuron* 19(1):27–37.

Bhide, P. G. 1996. Cell Cycle Kinetics in the Embryonic Mouse Corpus Striatum. *Journal of Comparative Neurology* 374:506–22.

Boncinelli, E. 1997. Homeobox genes and disease. *Current Opinion in Genetics and Development* 7(3):331–7.

Boulder Committee. 1970. Embryonic vertebrate central nervous system: Revised terminology. *Anatomical Record* 166:257–61.

Brunstrom, J.E., Gray-Swain, M. R., Osborne, P. A., and Pearlman, A. L. 1997. Neuronal heterotopias in the developing cerebral cortex produced by neurotrophin-4. *Neuron* 18(3):505–17.

Brunstrom, J. E., Gray-Swain, M. R., and Pearlman, A. L. 1998. *Neurotophin-4 Influences the Migration and Differentiation of Early Cortical Neurons.* Cold Spring Harbor, New York. Cold Spring Harbor Laboratory.

Bulfone, A., Kim, H. J., Puelles, L., Porteus, M. H., Grippo, J. F., and Rubenstein, J. L. R. 1993. The mouse Dlx-2 (Tes-1) gene is expressed in spatially restricted domains of the forebrain, face and limbs in midgestation mouse embryos. *Mechanisms of Development* 40:129–40.

Cohen, S. M., Bronner, G., Kuttner, F., Jurgens, G., and Jackle, H. 1989. Distalless encodes a homeodomain protein required for limb development in Drosophila. *Nature* 338:432–34.

de Carlos, J. A., Lopez-Mascaraque, L., and Valverde, F. 1996. Dynamics of cell migration from the lateral ganglionic eminence in the rat. *Journal of Neuroscience* 16(19):6146–56.

DeDiego, I., Smith-Fernandez, A., and Fairen, A. 1994. Cortical cells that migrate beyond area boundaries: Characterization of an early neuronal population in the lower intermediate zone of prenatal rats. *European Journal of Neuroscience* 6(6):983–97.

DeFries, J. C., Fulker, D. W., and LaBuda, M. C. 1987. Evidence for a genetic aetiology in reading disability of twins. *Nature* 329(6139):537–39.

Del Rio, J. A., Soriano, E., and Ferrer, I. 1992. Development of GABA-immunoreactivity in the neocortex of the mouse. *Journal of Comparative Neurology* 326(4):501–26.

Eden, G. F., and Zeffiro, T. A. 1998. Neural systems affected in developmental dyslexia revealed by functional neuroimaging. *Neuron* 21(2):279–82.

Fishell, G., Mason, C. A., and Hatten, M. E. 1993. Dispersion of neural progenitors within the germinal zones of the forebrain. *Nature* 362:636–38.

Gadisseux, J. F., Goffinet, A. M., Lyon, G., and Evrard, P. 1992. The human transient subpial granular layer: An optical, immunohistochemical, and ultrastructural analysis. *Journal of Comparative Neurology* 324(1):94–114.

Galaburda, A. M., Sherman, G. F., Rosen, G. D., Aboitiz, F., and Geschwind, N. 1985. Developmental dyslexia: Four consecutive patients with cortical anomalies. *Annals of Neurology* 18(2):222–33.

Gauger, L. M., Lombardino, L. J., and Leonard, C. M. 1997. Brain morphology in children with specific language impairment. *Journal of Speech, Language, and Hearing Research* 40(6):1272–84.

Gerfen, C. R. 1992. The neostriatal mosaic: Multiple levels of compartmental organization. *Trends in Neurosciences* 15:133–39.

Graham, A., Papalopulu, N., and Krumlauf, R. 1989. The murine and Drosophila homeobox gene complexes have common features of organization and expression. *Cell* 57:367–78.

Graybiel, A. M. 1998. The basal ganglia and chunking of action repertoires. *Neurobiology of Learning and Memory* 70(1-2):119–36.

Grigorenko, E. L., Wood, F. B., Meyer, M. S., Hart, L. A., Speed, W. C., Shuster, A., and Pauls, D. L. 1997. Susceptibility loci for distinct components of developmental dyslexia on chromosomes 6 and 15. *American Journal of Human Genetics* 60(1):27–39.

Hu, H., and Rutishauser, U. 1996. A septum-derived chemorepulsive factor for migrating olfactory interneuron precursors. *Neuron* 16(5):933–40.

Humphreys, P., Kaufmann, W. E., and Galaburda, A. M. 1990. Developmental dyslexia in women: Neuropathological findings in three patients. *Annals of Neurology* 28(6):727–38.

Kohtz, J. D., Baker, D. P., Corte, G., and Fishell, G. 1998. Regionalization within the mammalian telencephalon is mediated by changes in responsiveness to Sonic Hedgehog. *Development* 125:5079–89.

Levison, S. W., and Goldman, J. E. 1993. Both oligodendrocytes and astrocytes develop from progenitors in the subventricular zone of postnatal rat forebrain. *Neuron* 10:201–12.

Light, J. G., Defries, J. C., and Olson, R. K. 1998. Multivariate behavioral genetic analysis of achievement and cognitive measures in reading-disabled and control twin pairs. *Human Biology* 70(2):215–37.

Liu, J. K, Ghattas, I., Liu, S., Chen, S., and Rubenstein, J. L. 1997. Dlx genes encode DNA-binding proteins that are expressed in an overlapping and sequential pattern during basal ganglia differentiation. *Developmental Dynamics* 210(4):498–512.

Luskin, M. B. 1993. Restricted proliferation and migration of postnatally generated neurons derived from the forebrain subventricular zone. *Neuron* 11:173–89.

Matsuo, I., Kuratani, S., Kimura, C., Takeda, N., and Aizawa, S. 1995. Mouse Otx2 functions in the formation and patterning of rostral head. *Genes and Development* 9(21):2646–58.

Meinecke, D. L., and Peters, A. 1987. GABA immunoreactive neurons in rat visual cortex. *Journal of Comparative Neurology* 261(3):388–404.

Mione, M. C., Cavanagh, J. F. R., Harris, B., and Parnavelas, J. G. 1997. Cell fate specification and symmetrical/asymmetrical divisions in the developing cerebral cortex. *Journal of Neuroscience* 17(6):2018–29.

Morgan, A. E., and Hynd, G. W. 1998. Dyslexia, neurolinguistic ability, and anatomical variation of the planum temporale. *Neuropsychology Review* 8(2):79–93.

O'Rourke, N. A., Sullivan, D. P., Kaznowski, C. E., Jacobs, A. A., and McConnell, S. K. 1995. Tangential migration of neurons in the developing cerebral cortex. *Development* 121(7):2165–76.

Parnavelas, J. G., Lieberman, A. R., and Webster, K. E. 1977. Organization of neurons in the visual cortex, area 17, of the rat. *Journal of Anatomy* 124(2): 305–22.

Qiu, M., Bulfone, A., Ghattas, I., Meneses, J. J., Christensen, L., Sharpe, P. T., Presley, R., Pedersen, R. A., and Rubenstein, J. L. 1997. Role of the Dlx homeobox genes in proximodistal patterning of the branchial arches: Mutations of Dlx-1, Dlx-2, and Dlx-1 and -2 alter morphogenesis of proximal skeletal and soft tissue structures derived from the first and second arches. *Developmental Biology* 185(2):165–84.

Qiu, M., Bulfone, A., Martinez, S., Meneses, J., Shimamura, K., Pedersen, R. A., and Rubenstein, J. L. R. 1995. Null mutation of Dlx-2 results in abnormal morphogenesis of proximal first and second branchial arch derivatives and abnormal differentiation in the forebrain. *Genes and Development* 9:2523–38.

Rakic, P. 1988. Specification of cerebral cortical areas. *Science* 241(4862): 170–176.

Rakic, P. 1995. Radial versus tangential migration of neuronal clones in the developing cerebral cortex. *Proceedings of the National Academy of Sciences of the United States of America* 92(25):11323–7.

Schwartz, M. L., and Meinecke, D. L. 1992. Early expression of GABA-containing neurons in the prefrontal and visual cortices of rhesus monkeys. *Cerebral Cortex* 2(1):16–37.

Semrud-Clikeman M. 1997. Evidence from imaging on the relationship between brain structure and developmental language disorders. *Seminars in Pediatric Neurology* 4(2):117–24.

Shaywitz, S. E., Shaywitz, B. A., Pugh, K. R., Fulbright, R. K., Constable, R. T., Mencl, W. E., Shankweiler, D. P., Liberman, A. M., Skudlarski, P., Fletcher, J. M., and others.1998. Functional disruption in the organization of the brain for reading in dyslexia. *Proceedings of the National Academy of Sciences of the United States of America* 95(5):2636–41.

Sheth, A. N., and Bhide, P. 1997. Concurrent cellular output from two proliferative populations in the early embryonic mouse corpus striatum. *Journal of Comparative Neurology* 383(2):220–30.

Simeone, A., Acampora, D., Pannese, M., D'Esposito, M., Stornaiuolo, A., Gulisano, M., Mallamaci, A., Kastury, K., Druck, T., Huebner, K., and others. 1994. Cloning and characterization of two members of the vertebrate Dlx gene family. *Proceedings of the National Academy of Sciences of the United States of America* 91:2250–4.

Smart, I. 1961. The subependymal layer of the mouse brain and its cell production as shown by autoradiagraphy after thymidine-H3 injection. *Journal of Comparative Neurology* 116:325–48.

Stock, D. W., Ellies, D. L., Zhao, Z., Ekker, M., Ruddle, F. H., and Weiss, K. M. 1996. The evolution of the vertebrate Dlx gene family. *Proceedings of the National Academy of Sciences of the United States of America* 93(20):10858–63.

Takahashi, T., Nowakowski, R. S., and Caviness, V. S. 1993. Cell cycle parameters and patterns of nuclear movement in the neocortical proliferative zone of the fetal mouse. *Journal of Neuroscience* 13:820–33.

Takahashi, T., Nowakowski, R. S., and Caviness, V. S. J. 1995. Early ontogeny of the secondary proliferative population of the embryonic murine cerebral wall. *Journal of Neuroscience* 15(9):6058–68.

Tamamaki, N., Fujimori, E., and Takauji, R. 1997. Origin and route of tangentially migrating neurons in the developing neocortical intermediate zone. *Journal of Neuroscience* 17:8313–23.

Tan, S. S., Kalloniatis, M., Sturm, K., Tam, P. P., Reese, B. E, and Faulkner-Jones, B. 1998. Separate progenitors for radial and tangential cell dispersion during development of the cerebral neocortex. *Neuron* 21(2):295–304.

van der Kooy, D., and Fishell, G. 1986. Neuronal birthdate underlies the development of striatal compartments. *Brain Research* 401:155–61.

Xuan, S., Baptista, C. A., Balas, G., Tao, W., Soares, V. C., and Lai, E. 1995. Winged helix transcription factor BF-1 is essential for the development of the cerebral hemispheres. *Neuron* 14(6):1141–52.

Yan, X. X., Zheng, D. S., and Garey, L. J. 1992. Prenatal development of GABA-immunoreactive neurons in the human striate cortex. Brain Research. *Developmental Brain Research* 65(2):191–204.

Chapter • 2

Colorado Twin Study of Reading Disability

*J. C. DeFries, Valerie S. Knopik,
and Sally J. Wadsworth*

Results obtained from family studies (Hallgren 1950; Finucci 1978; DeFries and Decker 1982; Pennington et al. 1991; Wolff and Melngailis 1994) and previous twin studies (DeFries and Light 1996) suggest that reading difficulties are due, at least in part, to genetic influences. In order to test the hypothesis of a genetic etiology for reading disability more rigorously, a new twin study (Decker and Vandenberg 1985) was initiated in 1982 as part of a program project (DeFries 1985) supported by the National Institute of Child Health and Human Development (NICHD). Recent results obtained from this ongoing study, now supported by the NICHD-funded Colorado Learning Disabilities Research Center (DeFries et al. 1997), provide compelling evidence for the heritable nature of reading deficits (DeFries and Alarcón 1996). Moreover, the sample of twins is now sufficiently large to test hypotheses of differential etiology as a function of variables such as gender, IQ, and age more adequately than was possible in our previous studies. For example, although results obtained from previous analyses suggested that reading deficits of girls may be more heritable than those of boys, our most recent test of this hypothesis indicates little or no gender difference in etiology (Wadsworth, Knopik and DeFries in press). However, we have recently obtained evidence that reading deficits in children with higher IQ levels are more heritable than those in children with lower IQ

(Wadsworth et al. in press), and that the genetic etiologies of reading and spelling difficulties may change differentially as a function of age (DeFries, Alarcón, and Olson 1997).

In the present chapter, recent results obtained from the Colorado Twin Study of Reading Disability are reviewed. First, the sample of twins is described and a multiple regression analysis of twin data is outlined. Results obtained from recent applications of this methodology to assess the etiology of reading difficulties in the present twin sample and to test for differential etiology as a function of gender, IQ, and age, are then summarized. Finally, previous efforts to localize the individual genes that may cause reading disability are briefly reviewed and results of recent genetic linkage analyses employing an adaptation of the multiple regression analysis of twin data are presented.

TWIN SAMPLE

In the Colorado Twin Study of Reading Disability, identical (monozygotic, MZ) and fraternal (dizygotic, DZ) twins in which at least one member of each pair manifests a positive school history of reading difficulties, and a comparison group of twins with a negative school history, are tested using an extensive battery of tests that includes the WISC-R (Wechsler 1974) or the WAIS-R (Wechsler 1981), the Peabody Individual Achievement Test (PIAT; Dunn and Markwardt 1970), and various other psychometric and experimental tests (DeFries et al. 1997). In order to minimize the possibility of referral bias (Vogel 1990), twin pairs are systematically ascertained through 27 cooperating school districts in Colorado. School administrators identify all twin pairs in a school, and then permission is sought from the parents of these twins to review the school records of both members of each pair. Twin pairs in which at least one member has a school history of reading difficulties (e.g., low reading achievement test scores or referral to a reading therapist because of poor reading performance) are invited to complete an extensive battery of tests in the laboratories of J. C. DeFries and R. K. Olson at the University of Colorado, Boulder, and in B. F. Pennington's laboratory at the University of Denver.

Data from the PIAT Reading Recognition, Reading Comprehension and Spelling subtests are then used to compute a discriminant function score for each child, employing discriminant coefficients estimated from an analysis of PIAT data obtained from an independent sample of 140 nontwin children with reading disabilities and 140 children with no reading difficulties tested during an early stage of the program project (DeFries 1985). Twin pairs are included in the proband (reading disability) sample if at least one member of the pair with a positive school history of reading difficulties is also classified as affected by the discriminant score and has a Verbal or Performance IQ score of at least 90, no serious neurological, emotional or behavioral problems, and no uncorrected visual or auditory acuity deficits. Control twins are matched to probands on the basis of age, gender, and zygosity, having a negative school history of reading problems, and being classified as unaffected by the discriminant score.

Selected items from the Nichols and Bilbro (1966) twin questionnaire are used for zygosity testing. In doubtful cases, zygosity is confirmed by genotyping DNA markers from blood or buccal cell samples. All twin pairs in the sample were reared in English-speaking, primarily middle-class homes and ranged in age from 8 to 20 years (mean age = 11.82 years) at the time of testing.

As of February 28, 1998, a total of 209 MZ twin pairs and 278 DZ pairs (160 same-sex and 118 opposite-sex) met our criteria for inclusion in the proband sample. In addition, 209 MZ twin pairs and 217 DZ pairs (132 same-sex and 85 opposite-sex) are included in the control sample.

Although referred or clinic samples of children with reading difficulties typically include three or four times as many boys as girls (Vogel 1990), the gender ratio in our proband sample does not deviate substantially from 1:1. For example, the current sample of MZ and same-sex DZ twins includes 265 male probands and 242 female probands, a gender ratio of 1.10:1. However, because female MZ twin pairs tend to be overrepresented in twin studies (Lykken, Tellegen, and DeRubeis 1978), this relatively low gender ratio in probands from our twin sample may be due in part to a differential volunteer rate for male and female MZ twin pairs. In accordance with this expectation, the gender ratio in our sample of MZ probands is 0.95:1, whereas that for DZ probands is 1.38:1. However, both of these gender ratios are substantially lower than those typically reported in referred or clinic samples. These results are highly consistent with those of a previous study by Shaywitz et al. (1990) in which the gender ratio in a research-identified sample of nontwin children with reading disabilities was found to be substantially lower than that in a referred sample (1:36:1 vs. 3.19:1). Although James (1992) noted a slightly higher gender ratio (1.7:1) in the affected siblings of probands with various speech and language disorders, these results all suggest that the preponderance of males in referred and clinic samples of children with reading difficulties is due at least in part to a referral bias (Finucci and Childs 1981; Vogel 1990).

The probandwise concordance rate (DeFries and Alarcón 1996) for reading disability in the 209 MZ twin pairs included in the present sample is 0.66, whereas that for the 160 same-sex DZ pairs is 0.36, a highly significant difference ($p < 10^{-7}$). It is also interesting to note that the concordance rate for the opposite-sex DZ twin pairs (0.33) is highly similar to that for the same-sex DZ pairs, suggesting that the etiology of reading deficits may not differ substantially in boys and girls. Thus, in agreement with results obtained from previous family and twin studies, the difference between the concordance rates of MZ and both same- and opposite-sex DZ twin pairs tested in the Colorado Twin Study strongly indicates that reading disability is due in part to heritable influences.

MULTIPLE REGRESSION ANALYSIS OF TWIN DATA

For categorical variables (e.g., presence or absence of a disease state), a comparison of concordance rates in MZ and DZ twin pairs can provide prima facie evidence for a genetic etiology. However, reading disability in the Colorado Twin Study is diagnosed on the basis of a discriminant function score, a composite measure of reading performance. Transformation of this quantitative measure into a categorical variable (reading disability versus normal reading performance) obviously results in a loss of important information about the continuum of variation in reading performance. In contrast, the multiple regression analysis of twin data (DeFries and Fulker 1985, 1988) employs a comparison of MZ and DZ co-twin means to test for the genetic etiology of proband deficits.

When MZ and DZ probands have been ascertained because of deviant scores on a continuous measure such as reading performance, the scores of their co-twins are expected to regress toward the mean of the unselected population. However, to the extent that the average deficit of the probands is due to genetic influences, this regression toward the population mean should differ for their MZ and DZ co-twins. Because members of MZ twin pairs are genetically identical, whereas DZ pairs share only about one-half of their segregating genes on average, the scores of DZ co-twins should regress more toward the control mean than those of MZ co-twins if the deviant scores of the probands are due at least in part to heritable influences. Therefore, if the MZ and DZ proband means are approximately equal, a simple t-test of the difference between the means of the MZ and DZ co-twins could be used as a test for genetic etiology. However, the multiple regression analysis of such twin data provides a more general and statistically more powerful test.

In the basic multiple regression model (DeFries and Fulker 1985, 1988), each co-twin's score is predicted from the proband's score and their coefficient of relationship (1.0 for MZ twin pairs and 0.5 for DZ pairs) as follows:

$$C = B_1 P + B_2 R + A, \qquad (1)$$

where C symbolizes the co-twin's score, P is the proband's score, R is the coefficient of relationship and A is the regression constant. When this model is fitted to twin data in which at least one member of each pair (the proband) has a deviant score, the partial regression of the co-twin's score on the proband's score (B_1) provides a measure of average MZ and DZ twin resemblance. Of greater interest, B_2 estimates twice the difference between the means of the MZ and DZ co-twins after co-variance adjustment for any difference between the scores of MZ and DZ probands. Consequently, B_2 provides a direct test for genetic etiology that is more general and statistically powerful than a comparison of MZ and DZ concordance rates (DeFries and Fulker 1988).

Fitting the regression model in equation 1 to selected twin data can also be used to quantify the relative extent to which the average proband deficit is due to genetic influences (h_g^2). When data from twin pairs are transformed by expressing each score as a deviation from the mean of the unselected population and then dividing by the selection differential (i.e., the difference between the proband and control means), $B_2 = h_g^2$ (DeFries and Fulker 1988).

Distributions of discriminant function scores (the composite measure of reading performance) for the probands, MZ co-twins, and same-sex DZ co-twins in the Colorado Twin Study of Reading Disability are depicted in figure 1. From this figure it may be seen that the scores of the MZ and DZ co-twins have regressed differentially toward the mean of the control twin sample. The average discriminant scores of the MZ probands, same-sex DZ probands, and their co-twins, expressed as standardized deviations from the control mean, are presented in table I. Because truncate selection (DeFries and Gillis 1991) was employed to ascertain this sample of affected twins, data from concordant pairs have been double-entered for all analyses in a manner analogous to that used for the computation of probandwise concordance rates, and computer-generated tests of statistical significance have been adjusted accordingly (Stevenson et al. 1993). From table I it may be seen that the average discriminant scores of the MZ and DZ probands are highly similar and over 2.5 standard deviations below the mean of the controls. Moreover, it may be seen that the

Table I. Mean discriminant function scores ($\pm$ *SD*) of 209 pairs of identical twins and 160 pairs of same-sex fraternal twins in which at least one member of each pair (the proband) is reading-disabled

Zygosity	Probands	Co-twins
Identical	$-2.65 \pm .82$	-2.44 ± 1.08
Fraternal	$-2.59 \pm .85$	-1.66 ± 1.34

Note: Discriminant function scores are expressed in standard deviation units from the mean of 852 control twins. When equation 1 was fitted to these data, $B_2 = -1.47 \pm .22$, $p < 10^{-10}$.

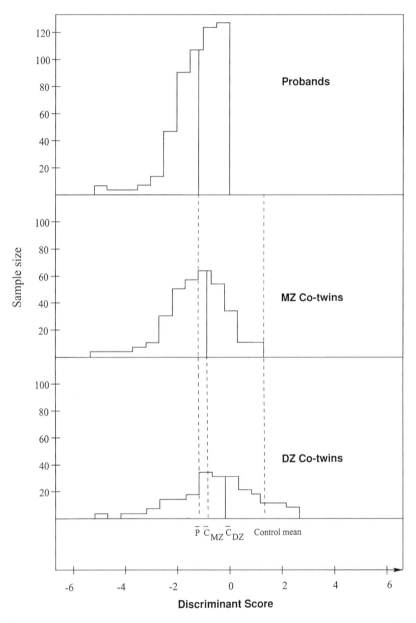

Figure 1.   Discriminant function score distributions of probands with reading disability, and their identical (MZ) and fraternal (DZ) co-twins.

scores of the DZ co-twins have regressed 0.93 standard deviation units on the average toward the control mean, whereas those of the MZ co-twins have regressed only 0.21 standard deviation units on average.

Thus, when the model in equation 1 was fitted to these data, $B_2 = -1.47$ ($p < 10^{-10}$).

The means of the transformed MZ and DZ proband and co-twin scores are presented in table II. When selected twin data are transformed in this manner (expressing each twin's score as a deviation from the mean of the unselected population and dividing by the corresponding MZ or DZ selection differential), the MZ and DZ proband mean scores are equated to unity and the difference between the average scores of the MZ and DZ co-twins ($0.92 - 0.64 = 0.28$) directly estimates $0.5\ h_g^2$. Thus, as expected, when the basic regression model (equation 1) is fitted to the transformed data, $B_2 = h_g^2 = 0.56$ ($p < 10^{-10}$). The magnitude of this highly significant genetic parameter estimate indicates that slightly more than half of the reading performance deficit of probands, on average, is due to heritable influences.

DIFFERENTIAL GENETIC ETIOLOGY

The multiple regression analysis of twin data (DeFries and Fulker 1985, 1988), sometimes referred to as DF analysis (Plomin and Rende 1991; Rodgers, Rowe and Li 1994; Waller 1994), is a highly versatile method. In addition to testing hypotheses regarding the etiology of group deficits, it can also be used to assess differences in etiology as a function of dichotomous variables such as gender (DeFries, Gillis, and Wadsworth 1993) or continuous covariates such as age (Wadsworth et al. 1989).

In order to test for differential etiology in two different groups (e.g., gender), the following extension of the basic regression model (equation 1) can be fitted to data from twin pairs from both groups simultaneously:

$$C = B_1P + B_2R + B_3G + B_4PG + B_5RG + A, \quad (2)$$

where G is a dummy code for group (e.g., -0.5 and $+0.5$ for males and females, respectively). Because interactions are represented by products of variables in hierarchical multiple regression models (Cohen and Cohen 1975), the B_4 regression coefficient tests for differential twin resemblance as a function of group membership, and B_5 tests for

Table II. Mean transformed discriminant function scores ($\pm SD$) of 209 pairs of identical twins and 160 pairs of same-sex fraternal twins in which at least one member of each pair (the proband) is reading-disabled

Zygosity	Probands	Co-twins
Identical	$1.00 \pm .31$	$.92 \pm .41$
Fraternal	$1.00 \pm .33$	$.64 \pm .52$

Note: When equation 1 was fitted to these data, $B_2 = h_g^2 = 0.56 \pm .08$, $p < 10^{-10}$.

differential h_g^2. When equation 2 is fitted to twin data including continuous covariates such as IQ or age, these interactions test for differential etiology as a linear function of the covariate.

Because our sample of twins is now substantially larger than it was when our previous tests of differential etiology were undertaken, we have recently employed DF analysis to test more rigorously hypotheses concerning the possible differential etiology of reading disability as a function of gender, IQ level, and age.

Gender

In a commentary for the proceedings of a conference on "Sex Differences in Dyslexia," Geschwind (1981) asked, "Why should one study sex differences?" He then answered this rhetorical question as follows: ". . . the arguments for studying the problem are powerful ones. In the first place, this type of investigation can have a useful impact on research. For example, the strikingly uneven proportion of males and females raises the possibility that the nature of dyslexia may not be uniform and that different retraining techniques may be necessary. Furthermore, the unequal sex ratio can suggest research approaches that may lead to better knowledge of the biological substrates of dyslexia and therefore lead to better prevention or treatment. Obviously, the possibilities for differences in sex ratio are many. Thus, it is conceivable that girls are less affected by certain environmental influences, such as the quality of teaching, social class differences, or outside pressures within society" (p. xiv).

Although the gender ratio for reading disability may not be as disproportionate as Geschwind (1981) surmised at that time, the possibility of a differential etiology in boys and girls is still tenable. In order to test Geschwind's hypothesis, DeFries et al. (1993) subjected discriminant function score data from 99 MZ and 73 same-sex DZ pairs participating in the Colorado Twin Study to multiple regression analysis. Resulting estimates of h_g^2 were 0.42 for males and 0.48 for females. Although the direction of this difference in h_g^2 estimates is consistent with Geschwind's hypothesis that genetic influences may be more important as a cause of reading difficulties in girls than in boys, the magnitude of the difference is relatively small and non-significant ($p > .50$). Consequently, DeFries et al. (1993) concluded that ". . . a larger sample of twins will be required to test more rigorously the hypothesis of differential etiology as a function of gender" (p. 200).

Because the Colorado Twin Study sample is now approximately twice as large as that previously analyzed by DeFries et al. (1993), we recently undertook a more powerful test of Geschwind's hypothesis (Wadsworth, Knopik, and DeFries in press). Discriminant function score data from 206 pairs of identical twins and 159 pairs of same-sex fraternal twins, in which at least one member of each pair met our criteria for reading disability, were again subjected to DF analysis. Resulting estimates of h_g^2 in boys and girls in this much larger sample were nearly identical (0.58 and 0.59, $p > .90$). Thus, results of this most recent analysis provide little or no evidence for the hypothesis that reading difficulties are more heritable in girls than in boys. In contrast, as discussed below, we have recently obtained evidence for a significant differential etiology of reading disability as a function of both IQ and age.

IQ Level

Children with specific reading disability (i.e., those with reading difficulties, but IQ scores within the normal range) are assumed to have a cognitive deficit that is independent of general cognitive ability (Stanovich 1986). In contrast, the reading deficits of children with a low IQ (the "garden-variety readers") are presumed to be due to their impaired general cognitive ability. However, within the past decade, the specificity assumption has been seriously challenged (e.g., Fletcher et al. 1989; Siegel 1989; Lyon 1995).

Although previously accepted definitions of reading disability were based on a discrepancy with measured intelligence (Stanovich 1989), Siegel (1989, 1998) has argued that IQ test scores are irrelevant. Children with learning disabilities have deficits in various skills measured by IQ tests, including expressive language abilities, short-term memory, speed of processing information, speed of responding, and knowledge of specific facts. Thus, rather than being a result of impaired general cognitive ability, reading problems could conceivably cause lower IQ scores. Furthermore, Siegel (1998) has marshaled evidence that the reading deficits of children with low IQ may not differ fundamentally from those of children with an IQ score within the normal range. Such lack of support for the specificity assumption clearly raises a serious problem for the use of IQ-reading discrepancy definitions (Lyon 1995).

We agree that reading difficulties may cause lower IQ and, consequently, do not routinely employ discrepancy scores (either difference scores or regression-deviation scores) in our genetic analyses. However, because reading disability has historically been defined by significant difficulty in reading that is not due to mental retardation (Kirk and Bateman 1962), we usually employ a cut-off score of 90 to ensure that our probands have general cognitive ability levels within the normal range. On the other hand, we have recently included some twin pairs with lower IQ scores (range of 59–139) in an augmented sample in order to assess the IQ-relevance issue (DeFries and Light 1996; Olson et al. in press; Wadsworth et al. in press).

As first noted by Olson et al. (1991), the multiple regression analysis of twin data facilitates an alternative test of the specificity assumption. If the cognitive processes of children with specific reading disability differ from those of children with reading difficulties and low IQ, then the etiology of reading deficits may vary as a function of IQ level.

In order to test the hypothesis that the genetic etiology of reading disability differs as a function of IQ level, we recently subjected discriminant function score data from 223 pairs of MZ twins and 169 pairs of same-sex DZ twins with reading difficulties to multiple regression analysis (Wadsworth et al. in press). For these analyses, full-scale IQ scores were averaged so that double-entry of concordant pairs would not result in the same pairs being represented in different groups. When the basic regression model (equation 1) was fitted to data from twin pairs with average full-scale IQ scores below 100, the resulting estimate of h^2_g was 0.43. In contrast, when the same model was fitted to data from twin pairs with IQ scores of 100 or above, $h^2_g = 0.72$. In order to test the significance of this difference in h^2_g estimates, the IQ data were first dichotomously coded using -0.5 for twin pairs with average IQ below 100, and $+0.5$ for twin pairs with average IQ scores of 100 or above. When equation 2 was then fitted to data from both groups simultaneously, $B_5 = 0.29$ ($p < .03$, one-tailed test). It is interesting to note that when the two groups are dichotomously coded in this manner, the B_5 coefficient exactly equals the difference in the two h^2_g estimates, viz., $0.72 - 0.43 = 0.29$.

We also tested for differential genetic etiology of reading disability as a linear function of IQ by fitting equation 2 to reading performance data from the combined sample, but using the average IQ score of both members of each twin pair as a continuous measure. As expected, the resulting B_5 estimate in this case was even more significant ($p < .007$, one-tailed). However, no evidence was obtained for differential genetic etiology of reading disability as a quadratic function of IQ (Wadsworth et al. in press). Similar results were also obtained when reading-IQ discrepancy scores were subjected to DF analysis, suggesting that our finding of a differential etiology of reading disability as a function of IQ may generalize to alternative reading-performance measures. Thus, although the specificity hypothesis has been seriously challenged in recent years, the results of the Wadsworth et al. (in press) study indicate that environmental influences are more salient as a cause of reading difficulties in children with low IQ.

Age

In a previous twin study of reading disability, Stevenson et al. (1984, 1987) administered the Schonell Graded Word Reading and Spelling

Tests (Schonell and Schonell 1960), the Neale Analysis of Reading Ability (Neale 1967), and the WISC-R to 285 pairs of 13-year-old twins ascertained from primary schools in the London area or by screening hospital records in five London boroughs. These standardized test scores were then used to diagnose the twins for reading or spelling "backwardness" (i.e., reading or spelling age more than 18 months below chronological age) and reading or spelling "retardation" (18 months or more below the expected reading or spelling age predicted by both IQ and chronological age). Employing these various diagnostic criteria, the sample included 14 to 19 pairs of MZ twins and 27 to 43 pairs of DZ twins in which at least one member of each pair had a reading or spelling disability. The corresponding probandwise concordance rates for the MZ and DZ twin pairs were as follows: reading backward (Neale), 38% and 54%; reading backward (Schonell), 50% and 43%; reading retarded (Neale), 33% and 29%; reading retarded (Schonell), 35% and 31%; spelling backward, 59% and 41%; and spelling retarded, 50% and 33%. Because the differences between the MZ and DZ concordance rates were smaller for the reading measures than for spelling, Stevenson et al. (1987) hypothesized a possible developmental dissociation between reading and spelling deficits. Although genetic factors may be important as a cause of reading disability at younger ages, spelling difficulties may be more heritable at 13 years of age: "In particular, the emergence of spelling as the most clearly genetically influenced literary skill may well be due to developmental changes that would not have been found at an earlier age" (Stevenson et al. 1987, p. 243).

Wadsworth et al. (1989) first conducted a preliminary test of the Stevenson et al. (1987) hypothesis of a developmental dissociation between reading and spelling difficulties by fitting the basic regression model (equation 1) separately to PIAT Reading Recognition, Reading Comprehension, and Spelling subtest scores of twin pairs tested in the Colorado Twin Study of Reading Disability. The sample included 99 pairs of MZ twins and 73 pairs of same-sex DZ twins in which at least one member of each pair was diagnosed as being reading disabled based upon school history and the discriminant function score criterion. Although the tests for differential genetic etiology as a function of age were nonsignificant for each of these measures, differences in h_g^2 estimated from data of younger (< 11.5 years) and older (11.5–20.2 years) twin pairs were somewhat larger for word recognition (0.57 vs. 0.36, respectively) and reading comprehension (0.68 vs. 0.31) than for spelling (0.63 vs. 0.52). In general, these results tended to support the hypothesis of Stevenson et al. (1987) that genetic factors may be more salient as a cause of spelling difficulties than of reading deficits in older children. However, estimates of h_g^2 for a given measure should be obtained from samples in which at least one member of each twin pair has a deviant score for that particular measure (DeFries and Fulker 1985, 1988); thus, more appropriate estimates of h_g^2 would have been obtained if the samples had been selected for deficits in the PIAT sub-test measures and not for the composite discriminant function score.

Because the sample of twins tested in the Colorado Twin Study is now substantially larger, we recently retested the hypothesis that the genetic etiologies of reading and spelling deficits may change differ-entially as a function of age (DeFries, Alarcón, and Olson 1997). Peabody Individual Achievement Test data from 195 pairs of MZ twins and 145 pairs of same-sex DZ twins in which at least one mem-ber of each pair had a positive school history for reading difficulties were subjected to DF analysis. In order to obtain separate estimates of h_g^2 for Reading Recognition, Reading Comprehension, and Spelling, three non-independent samples of probands were selected with scores at least 1.5 standard deviations below the mean of the controls for the relevant measure. All other ascertainment criteria were the same as those used to select the sample diagnosed using discriminant function score data, and the age cut-off was the same as that em-ployed by Wadsworth et al. (1989), viz., < 11.5 years versus 11.5 to 20.2 years.

A comparison of the resulting estimates of h_g^2 for the three mea-sures in the older and younger groups revealed a possible differential developmental change in etiology as a function of age. The estimate of h_g^2 for Reading Recognition was higher in the younger group than in the older group (0.64 vs. 0.47), but the converse pattern occurred for Spelling (0.52 vs. 0.68). In contrast, little or no change in h_g^2 was evi-dent for Reading Comprehension (0.40 vs. 0.39). When equation 2 was fitted to data from the younger and older groups simultaneously, but separately for each of the three measures, the test for differential h_g^2 as a linear function of age was marginally significant for Reading Recog-nition ($p < .10$, one-tailed) and Spelling ($p < .16$), but not for Reading Comprehension ($p < .27$). Nevertheless, this pattern of results supports the hypothesis of Stevenson et al. (1987) that spelling deficits are more heritable than reading deficits in older children.

The basic regression model (equation 1) was also fitted to data for an experimental measure of Time-Limited Word Recognition (TLWR) that requires a correct response within 2 seconds (Olson et al. 1994), and to data for the Wide Range Achievement Test (WRAT; Jastak and Jastak 1978) of spelling production. The resulting estimates of h_g^2 in the younger and older groups were 0.64 versus 0.48 for TLWR, and 0.58 versus 0.75 for WRAT. Although these age differences in h_g^2 were not significant for either measure, their contrasting developmental pattern was similar to that for the PIAT reading and spelling subtests. Thus, the differential developmental changes in genetic etiology replicate across both timed and untimed measures of word recognition and both recognition and production measures of spelling (DeFries, Alarcón, and Olson 1997). Such a developmental dissociation between reading and spelling difficulties could have important implications for future research. If spelling does in fact become the most genetically influenced literacy skill during early adolescence (Stevenson et al. 1987), future twin studies and genetic linkage analyses of reading disability in older children and adults should focus primarily upon spelling deficits.

GENETIC LINKAGE ANALYSES

Obtaining evidence that reading difficulties are due, at least in part, to genetic influences is only the first step toward a more comprehensive genetic analysis. If reading deficits are caused by one or more major genes or quantitative trait loci (QTL), it should be possible to determine their location on specific chromosomes using recent advances in molecular genetics and genetic linkage analysis (Gelderman 1975; Lander and Botstein 1989; Smith, Pennington, and DeFries 1996). Subsequent cloning and sequencing of these genes could provide potentially important information pertaining to the disorder's primary cause and developmental sequelae (Kidd 1991).

If genes are closely linked on the same chromosome, they tend to be transmitted together from one generation to the next. In contrast, genes that are either far apart on the same chromosome or are located on different chromosomes are inherited independently. Therefore, a gene can be localized to a specific chromosomal region by comparing its transmission pattern to those of marker genes whose locations are already known. Observed co-transmission between a condition and a marker suggests that a gene for the condition and the marker are in the same chromosomal region.

The first evidence that a putative gene for reading disability may be linked to a specific chromosome was reported by Smith et al. (1983). Data were obtained from 84 individuals who were members of nine extended families in which reading disability had apparently been transmitted in an autosomal dominant manner (i.e., at least one parent of each affected child was also affected, and about half of the children of an affected parent were also affected). A psychometric test battery was administered to diagnose reading deficits and to ensure that the disability was specific to reading and spelling problems. Diagnostic criteria for reading disability in children included a reading level at least two years below the expected grade level and a full scale IQ greater than 90. For adults, self reports were used for diagnosis if there was a discrepancy between test results and a history of reading problems.

Observed co-transmission between reading disability and a marker on chromosome 15 in these nine families yielded a total logarithm of the odds (LOD) score of 3.2, a value that provides significant evidence for linkage in complex inheritance (Morton 1998). However, about 70% of this total LOD score was contributed by only one family, and data from another family yielded a large negative score. Therefore, the results obtained from this first genetic linkage analysis of reading disability clearly suggest that the condition is genetically heterogeneous.

Smith et al.(1990) subsequently conducted genetic linkage analyses of data from an augmented sample that included 250 individuals in 21 families. In addition to the routine genotyping markers and chromosomal heteromorphisms used in their previous study, DNA markers were used for the first time to conduct a linkage analysis for reading disability. However, when data from this substantially larger sample were analyzed, the total LOD score for linkage to chromosome 15 decreased to 1.33, a nonsignificant result.

Results of these previous analyses suggested that most cases of heritable reading disability are caused by one or more genes at chromosomal locations other than 15, or possibly by the combined effects of several genes. Other studies by Smith and her colleagues (see DeFries et al. 1991, for a review) are using markers on chromosome 6 to search for other possible linkage relationships. Results of preliminary analyses of these data suggested apparent linkage in some families to chromosome 6, but not to 15. Because the markers used for chromosome 6 are near the human leucocyte antigen (HLA) region, this very tentative result suggested a possible relationship between reading disability and genes that affect the immune system in a subgroup of affected individuals (DeFries and Gillis 1991).

Some limited evidence that yet another gene may cause reading disability was reported by Rabin et al. (1993). Results of analyses of data from nine three-generation families suggested that a putative gene for reading disability may be linked to chromosome 1, but not to markers on chromosome 15. However, the maximum total LOD score for linkage to chromosome 1 in these families was only 2.33; thus, it will be important to confirm this tentative result in an independent study.

Linkage analyses of complex characters such as reading disability in extended families have serious limitations. For example, it must be assumed that the condition is caused by a single gene with a specified mode of inheritance. However, complex characters such as reading disability are probably genetically heterogeneous and influenced by genes at several different chromosomal locations. Moreover, a diagnosis must be applied to each family member. Thus, accurate diagnosis is necessary across a wide age range and for family members from different generations.

An alternative approach to linkage analysis uses diagnostic data only from sibling pairs (Haseman and Elston 1972). In contrast to pedigree linkage analysis, this approach does not require that a specific mode of inheritance be assumed, and phenotypic data from only one generation are required. However, because sib-pair analysis is statistically less powerful than linkage analysis using extended pedigrees, data from more individuals may be necessary with sib-pair linkage analysis to achieve statistical significance.

The logic of sib-pair linkage analysis is elegantly simple. If a gene that causes reading disability is closely linked to a given chromosomal marker, then pairs of siblings that are concordant for reading disability will also tend to be concordant for the marker. In order to determine if a marker carried by two siblings was inherited from the same parent, i.e., the markers are "identical by descent" (ibd), the parents of the siblings should also be genotyped for the markers. These genotypic data can then be used to estimate the proportion (π) of the alleles (alternative forms of a gene) that the two siblings share that are ibd at the marker locus. A pair of siblings can share either zero, one or two alleles for a marker, with corresponding π values of 0.0, 0.5, and 1.0. The sib-pair linkage analysis of Haseman and Elston (1972) relates the square of the difference between phenotypic scores of siblings for a continuous measure to the π value at each marker locus.

Smith, Kimberling, and Pennington (1991) applied this method to reanalyze data from siblings included in their extended family study. Two different diagnostic criteria were used: (1) a dichotomous diagnosis that they had employed in their previous family study; and (2) the continuous discriminant function score used in our Colorado Twin Study of Reading Disability. Although the two different diagnostic criteria yielded somewhat different results, results of the sib-pair linkage analyses again provided evidence for possible linkage to markers on chromosomes 6 and 15.

Fulker et al. (1991) subsequently proposed a new sib-pair linkage analysis that employs a simple extension of the DeFries and Fulker (1985) multiple regression method to localize QTLs to specific chromosomal regions. Instead of using the coefficient of relationship (R) in equation 1, π is used to quantify ibd status at various marker loci. Fulker et al. (1991) employed this method to reanalyze reading performance data from sib pairs in the Smith, Kimberling, and Pennington (1991) family study, and also obtained evidence for linkage of a putative gene for reading disability to markers on chromosome 15.

Subsequently, Cardon et al. (1994, 1995) used interval mapping to localize a possible QTL for reading disability on chromosome 6. For this analysis, ibd status was estimated at small (one centimorgan) intervals between adjacent markers from ibd information at the markers and known distances between them. In a sample of 126 sib pairs from 19 extended families previously analyzed by Smith, Kimberling, and Pennington (1991), four markers located on the short arm (p) of chromosome 6 were genotyped. In addition, polymerase chain reaction was used to genotype more informative DNA markers in the same region for a subset (114 pairs) of the kindred sibships and for an independent sample of 46 DZ twin pairs tested in the Colorado Twin Study of Reading Disability. Results obtained from interval DF analysis of reading performance data from the sibling sample localized a possible QTL for reading disability to a two-centimorgan region on the short arm of chromosome 6 near the HLA complex ($p < .01$ and .05 for the two different sets of markers). Analyses of data from the independent sample of DZ twin pairs provided confirmatory evidence for linkage ($p < .01$) to the same chromosomal region.

More recently, Grigorenko et al. (1997) obtained evidence for the linkage of susceptibility loci for reading-related difficulties to the same region of chromosome 6, as well as to markers on chromosome 15. Six extended families with at least four affected members were genotyped for chromosomal markers on 6p, 15, and 16. Five phenotypic measures were analyzed: (1) phonological awareness; (2) phonological decoding; (3) rapid automatized naming; (4) single-word reading; and (5) discrepancy between IQ and reading performance. Two-point and multipoint allele-sharing analyses yielded evidence for significant ($p < .000001$) linkage of phonological awareness to five DNA markers on chromosome 6p, and some evidence for linkage of single-word reading to markers in the same region was also obtained ($p < .005$). Moreover, a significant LOD score of 3.15 was obtained for linkage of single-word reading to a DNA marker on chromosome 15, but results for phonological awareness were negative for this region. Linkage analyses with chromosome 16 markers were negative for all measures. Thus, the results of this study provide important confirmatory evidence for the presence of susceptibility loci for reading-related difficulties on both chromosomes 6 and 15.

Gayan et al. (1999) have recently conducted a linkage analysis of data from an independent sample of DZ twin pairs, their sibs, and sibs of MZ twins in the Colorado Twin Study of Reading Disability to identify the specific reading-related component skills that may be most strongly influenced by a QTL on chromosome 6. In addition to the PIAT subtests (Reading Recognition, Reading Comprehension, and Spelling), data for measures of phonological decoding (the oral reading of pronounceable nonwords), orthographic decoding (viz., Orthographic Choice, choosing the word in word-pseudohomophone pairs; and Homonym Choice, choosing the correct homophone to fit the meaning of a sentence), and phoneme awareness (Phoneme

Transposition, a "pig-Latin"game; and Phoneme Deletion, the removal of specified phonemes from nonwords) were analyzed. The sample of 126 sib pairs for this study (twins and siblings from 79 families in the Colorado Twin Study) was completely independent of the sample previously analyzed by Cardon et al. (1994, 1995). Subjects were genotyped for eight informative DNA markers on chromosome 6p, and their data were analyzed using a multipoint sib-pair method that estimates ibd status at small intervals between markers from information on all markers simultaneously (Fulker, Cherny, and Cardon 1995). This method, also an extension of the DF regression model, is a powerful method for linkage analysis because it exploits the selected nature of the sample (Wijsman and Amos 1997). Although this sample of twins was preselected for a positive school history of reading difficulties, not all subjects had low scores on all measures. Consequently, probands were reselected for each measure using a cut-off score of two standard deviations below the control mean.

As shown in figure 2, the results obtained by Gayan et al. (1999) confirm the presence of a QTL on chromosome 6p that influences reading-related difficulties, especially for Orthographic Choice and Phonological Decoding. With more extreme selection of affected individuals, even

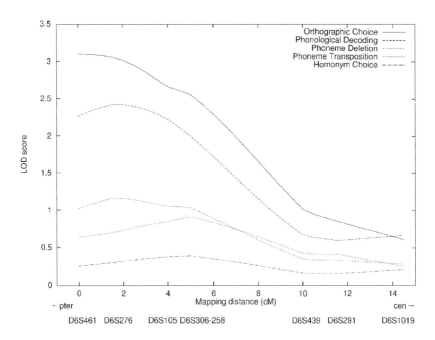

Figure 2. Results of multipoint sib-pair linkage analyses for seven DNA markers on the short arm of chromosome 6 and measures of orthographic and phonological processing (After Gayan et al. 1999; courtesy of Javier Gayan).

larger LOD scores were obtained for Orthographic Choice (3.51 for a 2.25 SD cut-off) and Phoneme Deletion (4.35 for a 2.5 SD cut-off). Of special interest, the evidence obtained for linkage in this study varies substantially among the various reading-related measures. In contrast to the results obtained in our previous analyses (e.g., Gayan et al. 1995), evidence for linkage of word-recognition measures was not significant in this sample.

Gayan et al. (1999) located the putative QTL to a region within several centimorgans on the short arm of chromosome 6, very near the region tentatively identified by Cardon et al. (1994, 1995) in their independent sample. Recent analyses in the United Kingdom of data from 181 sib pairs selected on the basis of a dyslexic proband revealed the presence of a QTL that affects both phonological and orthographic skills in exactly the same chromosomal region (Fisher et al. 1999). The QTL localized by Grigorenko et al. (1997) is in an overlapping region. Although the genetic map used by Gayan et al. (1999) and Fisher et al. (1999) does not correspond perfectly with that used by Grigorenko et al. (1997), genetic linkage analyses of data from five independent samples (two in the study by Cardon et al. 1994 and 1995; Grigorenko et al. 1997; Fisher et al. 1999; and Gayan et al. 1999) have each provided evidence for a QTL for reading-related difficulties in a relatively small region on the short arm of chromosome 6. Moreover, in a recent immunogenetic study, Warren et al. (1996) found that subjects with reading disability had an increased frequency of the null allele for one of the genes (C4B) in the major histocompatibility complex, also located in the same general region on the short arm of chromosome 6. Thus, this first independent confirmation of linkage for a complex behavioral character (Pennington 1997) appears to be robust.

CONCLUDING REMARKS

Results obtained from our most recent analyses of data from the Colorado Twin Study of Reading Disability provide compelling evidence that reading difficulties are due at least in part to heritable influences. In our current sample of 209 MZ, 160 same-sex DZ, and 118 opposite-sex DZ twin pairs, the probandwise concordance rate for members of MZ twin pairs (0.66) is substantially higher than those for both same-sex and opposite-sex DZ twin pairs (0.36 and 0.33, respectively). Moreover, when discriminant function score data from the same-sex twin pairs were subjected to multiple regression analysis (DeFries and Fulker 1985, 1988), the resulting estimate of h_g^2 indicated that over half (0.56, $p < 10^{-10}$) of the reading performance deficit of probands, on average, was due to genetic influences.

The multiple regression analysis of twin data is a highly versatile methodology. In addition to providing an index of the extent to which the deficit of probands is due to heritable factors, it can also be used to test for differential etiology as a function of dichotomous variables such as gender or continuous covariates such as IQ and age. Our sample of twin pairs with reading difficulties is now sufficiently large to conduct rigorous tests of these hypotheses. For example, although results obtained from previous analyses had suggested that genetic influences may be somewhat more important as a cause of reading deficits in girls than in boys, our most recent results (Wadsworth, Knopik, and DeFries in press) indicate that h_g^2 estimates for males and females are nearly identical (0.58 and 0.59, respectively). However, results of corresponding analyses employing IQ as a covariate indicate that the genetic etiology of reading deficits differs substantially as a function of IQ level (Wadsworth et al. in press). Moreover, we have also recently reported evidence for differential developmental changes in the etiology of reading and spelling deficits as a function of age (DeFries, Alarcón, and Olson 1997). Whereas deficits in word recognition are somewhat more heritable in younger children (< 11.5 years) than in an older sample (11.5 to 20.2 years), the converse pattern occurs for spelling deficits.

The multiple regression analysis of twin data can also be used to test hypotheses of relevance to other current issues in the field of learning disabilities (DeFries and Light 1996). For example, it can be used to test the hypothesis that the etiology of deviant scores differs from that of individual differences within the normal range of variation (DeFries and Alarcón 1996; Shaywitz et al. 1992), and bivariate applications may be employed to assess the etiology of comorbidity for conditions such as reading and mathematics disabilities (Knopik, Alarcón, and DeFries 1997) or ADHD symptoms (Stevenson et al. 1993). Thus, in addition to providing a statistically powerful test of genetic etiology, the multiple regression analysis of twin data may be employed to test hypotheses that are relevant to a number of other important current issues in the field.

As noted in this chapter, the multiple regression analysis of twin data has even been adapted to find the chromosomal location of a gene or quantitative trait locus (QTL) that may cause reading difficulties (Cardon et al. 1994, 1995). This initial report of the localization of a QTL for reading-related difficulties to a small region on the short arm (p) of chromosome 6 was subsequently confirmed by Grigorenko et al. (1997), and we have recently conducted a linkage analysis of data from other children tested in the Colorado Twin Study of Reading Disability to identify the reading-related component skills that may be most strongly influenced by this 6p QTL (Gayan et al. 1999). We are also continuing to obtain psychometric test data from additional DZ twin and sibling pairs, and to type additional markers to determine more precisely the location of the gene (Smith et al. 1998). Once the gene is located to a somewhat smaller region (less than one centimorgan), additional molecular genetic methods will be employed to find the gene. For example, it may eventually be possible to identify mutations in candidate genes in the region that have a functional relationship to reading difficulties. In addition to providing important information about the disorder's primary cause and neurobiological basis, such findings could be used to identify children who are at risk for reading disability, thereby facilitating preschool intervention in children with affected parents or siblings prior to the manifestation of reading deficits, and also could possibly aid in making diagnoses at later ages. Thus, a concerted effort to find the susceptibility loci for reading-related difficulties is clearly warranted.

ACKNOWLEDGMENTS

The Colorado Learning Disabilities Research Center is supported in part by program project and center grants from the National Institute of Child Health and Human Development (HD-11681 and HD-27802). During the preparation of this manuscript, V. S. Knopik was supported by NIMH training grant MH-16880. The invaluable contributions of the staff members of the many school districts from which our sample of twins was ascertained, and of the hundreds of families of twins who participated in our study, are gratefully acknowledged. We also thank Ms. Kathy Huckfeldt for providing secretarial services.

EDITOR'S COMMENTS

Since early in the twentieth century, reports of multiple affected family members with reading disability have raised the possibility that reading disorders might have a familial, perhaps genetic, component. The work reported by Drs. DeFries, Knopik, and Wadsworth shows that during the last two decades, a series of investigations using identical and non-identical twins, both with and without reading disability, have verified that, indeed, there is a heritable factor among reading disorders.

Several points in these studies clarify confusing prior issues. First, early reports had suggested a higher rate of occurrence of reading disorders among males than females. In these twin investigations, however, it is clear that in this form of familial reading disorder, gender risk is almost equal among males and females. The second is the notion that the heritability of reading disorder is influenced by intelligence as measured by IQ tests. Thus, those with an average or above average IQ score have a greater probability that their reading disorder will have a heritable genetic characteristic. Finally, the heritability of spelling disorder, a characteristic that clinicians have noted for years, is the most persistent trait of those with early-in-life reading disorder, intensifying with increased age.

That what was speculated on less than 100 years ago as a potential familial factor should now be brought to a specific gene level is truly a scientific wonder. To pinpoint the short arm of chromosome 6, as well as chromosome 15 and possibly chromosome 1, as gene sites related to specific behavioral deficits creates the possibility of identifying individuals at risk for reading disorder based on their genetics, and the possibility of changing the educational environment to optimize their mastery of script.

—DDD

REFERENCES

Cardon, L. R., Smith, S. D., Fulker, D. W., Kimberling, W. J., Pennington, B. F., and DeFries, J. C. 1994. Quantitative trait locus for reading disability on chromosome 6. *Science* 266:276–79.

Cardon, L. R., Smith, S. D., Fulker, D. W., Kimberling, W. J., Pennington, B. F., and DeFries, J. C. 1995. Quantitative trait locus for reading disability: A correction. *Science* 268:5217.

Cohen, J., and Cohen, P. 1975. *Applied Multiple Regression/Correlation Analysis for the Behavioral Sciences.* Hillsdale, NJ: Lawrence Erlbaum Associates.

Decker, S. N., and Vandenberg, S. G. 1985. Colorado twin study of reading disability. In *Biobehavioral Measures of Dyslexia*, eds. D. B. Gray and J. F. Kavanagh. Parkton, MD: York Press.

DeFries, J. C. 1985. Colorado Reading Project. In *Biobehavioral Measures of Dyslexia*, eds. D.B. Gray and J. F. Kavanagh. Parkton, MD: York Press.

DeFries, J. C., and Alarcón, M. 1996. Genetics of specific reading disability. *Mental Retardation and Developmental Disabilities Research Reviews* 2:39–47.

DeFries, J. C., Alarcón, M., and Olson, R. K. 1997. Genetic aetiologies of reading and spelling deficits: Developmental differences. In *Dyslexia: Biology, Cognition and Intervention*, eds. C. Hulme and M. Snowling. London: Whurr Publishers, Ltd.

DeFries, J. C., and Decker, S. N. 1982. Genetic aspects of reading disability: A family study. In *Reading Disorders: Varieties and Treatments*, eds. R. N. Malatesha and P. G. Aaron. New York: Academic Press.

DeFries, J. C., Filipek, P. A., Fulker, D. W., Olson, R. K., Pennington, B. F., Smith, S. D., and Wise, B. W. 1997. Colorado learning disabilities research center. *Learning Disabilities* 8:7–19.

DeFries, J. C., and Fulker, D. W. 1985. Multiple regression analysis of twin data. *Behavior Genetics* 15:467–73.

DeFries, J. C., and Fulker, D. W. 1988. Multiple regression analysis of twin data: Etiology of deviant scores versus individual differences. *Acta Geneticae Medicae et Gemellologiae* 37:205–16.

DeFries, J. C., and Gillis, J. J. 1991. Etiology of reading deficits in learning disabilities: Quantitative genetic analysis. In *Advances in the Neuropsychology of Learning Disabilities: Issues, Methods and Practice*, eds. J. E. Obrzut, and G. W. Hynd. Orlando, FL: Academic Press.

DeFries, J. C., Gillis, J. J., and Wadsworth, S. J. 1993. Genes and genders: A twin study of reading disability. In *Dyslexia and Development: Neurobiologic Aspects of Extra-Ordinary Brains*, ed., A. M. Galaburda. Cambridge, MA: Harvard University Press.

DeFries, J. C., and Light, J. G. 1996. Twin studies of reading disability. In *Language, Learning, and Behavior Disorders: Developmental, Biological, and Clinical Perspectives*, eds. J. H. Beitchman, N. J. Cohen, M. M. Konstantareas and R. Tannock. New York: Cambridge University Press.

DeFries, J. C., Olson, R. K., Pennington, B. F., and Smith, S. D. 1991. Colorado Reading Project: An update. In *The Reading Brain: The Biological Basis of Dyslexia*, eds. D. D. Duane and D. B. Gray. Parkton, MD: York Press.

Dunn, L. M., and Markwardt, F. C. 1970. *Examiner's Manual: Peabody Individual Achievement Test*. Circle Pines, Minn.: American Guidance Service.

Finucci, J. M. 1978. Genetic considerations in dyslexia. In *Progress in Learning Disabilities*, ed. H. R. Myklebust. New York: Grune and Stratton.

Finucci, J. M., and Childs, B. 1981. Are there really more dyslexic boys than girls? In *Sex Differences in Dyslexia*, eds. A. Ansara, N. Geschwind, A. Galaburda, M. Albert and N. Gartrell. Towson, MD: Orton Dyslexia Society.

Fisher, S. E., Marlow, A. J., Lamb, J., Maestrini, E., Williams, D. F., Richardson, A. J., Weeks, D. E., Stein, J. F., and Monaco, A. P. 1999. A quantitative-trait locus on chromosome 6p influences different aspects of developmental dyslexia. *American Journal of Human Genetics* 64:146–56.

Fletcher, J. M., Espy, K. A., Francis, D. J., Davidson, K. C., Rourke, B. P., and Shaywitz, S. E. 1989. Comparisons of cutoff and regression-based definitions of reading disabilities. *Journal of Learning Disabilities* 22:334–8.

Fulker, D. W., Cardon, L. R., DeFries, J. C., Kimberling, W. J., Pennington, B. F., and Smith, S. D. 1991. Multiple regression analysis of sib pair data on reading to detect quantitative trait loci. *Reading and Writing: An Interdisciplinary Journal* 3:299–313.

Fulker, D. W., Cherny, S. S., and Cardon, L. R. 1995. Multipoint interval mapping of quantitative trait loci, using sib pairs. *American Journal of Human Genetics* 56:1224–33.

Gayan, J., Olson, R. K., Cardon, L. R., Smith, S. D., Fulker, D. W., Kimberling, W. J., Pennington, B. F., and DeFries, J. C. 1995. Quantitative trait locus for different measures of reading disability. *Behavior Genetics* 25:266.

Gayan, J., Smith, S. D., Cherny, S. S., Cardon, L. R., Fulker, D. W., Brower, A. M., Olson, R. K., Pennington, B. F., and DeFries, J. C. 1999. Quantitative trait locus for specific language and reading deficits on chromosome 6p. *American Journal of Human Genetics* 64:157–64.

Gelderman, H. 1975. Investigations on inheritance of quantitative characters in animals by gene markers: I. Methods. *Theoretical and Applied Genetics* 46:319–30.

Geschwind, N. 1981. A reaction to the conference on sex differences in dyslexia. In *Sex Differences in Dyslexia*, eds. A. Ansara, N. Geschwind, A. Galaburda, M. Albert and N. Gartrell. Towson, MD: The Orton Dyslexia Society.

Grigorenko, E. L., Wood, F. B., Meyer, M. S., Hart, L. A., Speed, W. C., and Shuster, A. 1997. Susceptibility loci for distinct components of developmental dyslexia on chromosomes 6 and 15. *American Journal of Human Genetics* 60:27–39.

Hallgren, B. 1950. Specific dyslexia: A clinical and genetic study. *Acta Psychiatrica et Neurologica Scandinavica* 65 (Supplement):1–287.

Haseman, J. K., and Elston, R. C. 1972. The investigation of linkage between a quantitative trait and a marker locus. *Behavior Genetics* 2:3–19.

James, W. H. 1992. The sex ratios of dyslexic children and their sibs. *Developmental Medicine and Child Neurology* 34:530–33.

Jastak, J. F., and Jastak, S. 1978. *The Wide Range Achievement Test: Manual of Instructions.* Wilmington, DE: Jastak Associates, Inc.

Kidd, K. K. 1991. Trials and tribulations in the search for genes causing neuropsychiatric disorders. *Social Biology* 38:163–78.

Kirk, S. A, and Bateman, B. 1962. Diagnosis and remediation of learning disabilities. *Exceptional Children* 29:73–78.

Knopik, V. S., Alarcón, M., and DeFries, J. C. 1997. Comorbidity of mathematics and reading deficits: Evidence for a genetic etiology. *Behavior Genetics* 27:447–53.

Lander, E. S., and Botstein, D. 1989. Mapping Mendelian factors underlying quantitative traits using RFLP linkage maps. *Genetics* 121:185–199.

Lykken, D. T., Tellegen, A., and DeRubeis, R. 1978. Volunteer bias in twin research: The rule of two-thirds. *Social Biology* 25:1–9.

Lyon, G. R. 1995. Toward a definition of dyslexia. *Annals of Dyslexia* 45:3–27.

Morton, N. E. 1998. Significance levels in complex inheritance. *American Journal of Human Genetics* 62:690–7.

Neale, M. D. 1967. *Neale Analysis of Reading Ability.* London: Macmillan.

Nichols, R. C., and Bilbro, W. C., Jr. 1966. The diagnosis of twin zygosity. *Acta Genetica Medicae et Gemellologiae* 16:265–75.

Olson, R. K., Datta, H., Gayan, J., and DeFries, J. C. (in press). A behavioral-genetic analysis of reading disabilities and component processes. In *Converging Methods for Understanding Reading and Dyslexia*, eds. R. M. Klein and R. A. McMullen. Cambridge, MA: MIT Press.

Olson, R. K., Forsberg, H., Wise, B., and Rack, J. 1994. Measurement of word recognition, orthographic, and phonological skills. In *Frames of Reference for the Assessment of Learning Disabilities: New Views on Measurement Issues*, ed. G. R. Lyon. Baltimore: Paul H. Brookes Publishing Co.

Olson, R. K., Rack, J. P., Conners, F. A., DeFries, J. C., and Fulker, D. W. 1991. Genetic etiology of individual differences in reading disability. In *Subtypes of Learning Disabilities: Theoretical Perspectives and Research*, eds. L. V. Feagans, E. J. Short and L. J. Meltzer. Hillsdale, NJ: Lawrence Erlbaum Associates.

Pennington, B. F. 1997. Invited editorial: Using genetics to dissect cognition. *American Journal of Human Genetics* 60:13–6.

Pennington, B. F., Gilger, J. W., Pauls, D., Smith, S. A., Smith, S. D., and DeFries, J. C. 1991. Evidence for major gene transmission of developmental dyslexia. *Journal of the American Medical Association* 266:1527–34.

Plomin, R., and Rende, R. 1991. Human behavioral genetics. *Annual Review of Psychology* 42:161–90.

Rabin, M., Wen, X. L., Hepburn, M., Lubs, H. A., Feldman, E., and Duara, R. 1993. Suggestive linkage of developmental dyslexia to chromosome 1p34–p36. *Lancet* 342:178.

Rodgers, J. L., Rowe, D. C., and Li, C. 1994. Beyond nature versus nurture: DF analysis of nonshared influences on problem behavior. *Developmental Psychology* 30:374–84.

Schonell, F. J., and Schonell, P. E. 1960. *Diagnostic and Attainment Testing.* Edinburgh: Oliver and Boyd.

Shaywitz, S. E., Escobar, M. D., Shaywitz, B. A., Fletcher, J. M., and Makuch, R. 1992. Evidence that dyslexia may represent the lower tail of a normal distribution of reading ability. *New England Journal of Medicine* 326:144–50.

Shaywitz, S. E., Shaywitz, B. A., Fletcher, J. M., and Escobar, M. D. 1990. Prevalence of reading disability in boys and girls. *Journal of the American Medical Association* 264:998–1002.

Siegel, L. S. 1989. IQ is irrelevant to the definition of learning disabilities. *Journal of Learning Disabilities* 22:469–78.

Siegel, L. S. 1998. The discrepancy formula: Its use and abuse. In *Specific Reading Disability: A View of the Spectrum*, eds. B. K. Shapiro, P. J. Accardo, and A. J. Capute. Timonium, MD: York Press.

Smith, S. D., Brower, A. M., Cardon, L. R., and DeFries, J. C. 1998. Genetics of reading disability: Further evidence for a gene on chromosome 6. In *Specific Reading Disability: A View of the Spectrum*, eds. B. K. Shapiro, P. J. Accardo and A. J. Capute. Timonium, MD: York Press.

Smith, S. D., Kimberling, W. J., and Pennington, B. F. 1991. Screening for multiple genes influencing dyslexia. *Reading and Writing: An Interdisciplinary Journal* 3:285–98.

Smith, S. D., Kimberling, W. J., Pennington, B. F., and Lubs, H. A. 1983. Specific reading disability: Identification of an inherited form through linkage analysis. *Science* 219:1345–7.

Smith, S. D., Pennington, B. F., and DeFries, J. C. 1996. Linkage analysis with complex behavioral traits. In *Toward a Genetics of Language*, ed. M. L. Rice. Mahwah, NJ: Lawrence Erlbaum Associates.

Smith, S. D., Pennington, B. F., Kimberling, W. J., and Ing, P. S. 1990. Familial dyslexia: Use of genetic linkage data to define subtypes. *Journal of the American Academy of Child and Adolescent Psychiatry* 29:204–13.

Stanovich, K. E. 1986. Cognitive processes and the reading problems of learning-disabled children: Evaluating the assumption of specificity. In *Psychological and Educational Perspectives on Learning Disabilities*, eds. J. K. Torgesen and B. Y. L. Wong. Orlando, FL: Academic Press.

Stanovich, K. E. 1989. Various varying views on variation. *Journal of Learning Disabilities* 22:366–9.

Stevenson, J., Graham, P., Fredman, G., and McLoughlin, V. 1984. The genetics of reading disability. In *The Biology of Human Intelligence*, eds. C. J. Turner and H. B. Miles. Nafferton: Nafferton Books Limited.

Stevenson, J., Graham, P., Fredman, G., and McLoughlin, V. 1987. A twin study of genetic influences on reading and spelling ability and disability. *Journal of Child Psychology and Psychiatry* 28:229–47.

Stevenson, J., Pennington, B. F., Gilger, J. W., DeFries, J. C., and Gillis, J. J. 1993. Hyperactivity and spelling disability: Testing for shared genetic aetiology. *Journal of Child Psychology and Psychiatry* 34:1137–52.

Vogel, S. A. 1990. Gender differences in intelligence, language, visual-motor abilities, and academic achievement in students with learning disabilities: A review of the literature. *Journal of Learning Disabilities* 23:44–52.

Wadsworth, S. J., Gillis, J. J., DeFries, J. C., and Fulker, D. W. 1989. Differential genetic aetiology of reading disability as a function of age. *The Irish Journal of Psychology* 10:509–20.

Wadsworth, S. J., Knopik, V. S., and DeFries, J. C. (in press). Reading disability in boys and girls: No evidence for a differential genetic etiology. *Reading and Writing.*

Wadsworth, S. J., Olson, R. K., Pennington, B. F., and DeFries, J. C. (in press). Differential genetic etiology of reading disability as a function of IQ. *Journal of Learning Disabilities.*

Waller, N. G. 1994. A DeFries and Fulker regression model for genetic nonadditivity. *Behavior Genetics* 24:149–53.

Warren, R. P., Singh, V. K., Averett, R. E., Odell, J. D., Maciulis, A., Burger, R. A., Daniels, W. W., and Warren, W. L. 1996. Immunogenetic studies in autism and related disorders. *Molecular and Chemical Neuropathology* 28:77–81.

Wechsler, D. 1974. *Examiner's Manual: Wechsler Intelligence Scale for Children— Revised.* New York: The Psychological Corporation.

Wechsler, D. 1981. *Examiner's Manual: Wechsler Adult Intelligence Scale— Revised.* New York: The Psychological Corporation.

Wijsman, E. M., and Amos, C. I. 1997. Genetic analysis of simulated oligogenic traits in nuclear and extended pedigrees: Summary of GAW10 contributions. *Genetic Epidemiology* 14:719–35.

Wolff, P. H., and Melngailis, I. 1994. Family patterns of developmental dyslexia: Clinical findings. *American Journal of Medical Genetics* (Neuropsychiatric Genetics) 54:122–31.

Chapter • 3

Structural and Functional Neuroanatomy in Reading Disorder

*Pauline A. Filipek, Bruce F. Pennington,
Jack H. Simon, Christopher M. Filley, and
John C. DeFries*

The structural and functional deficits underlying developmental dyslexia or reading disorder (RD) have been researched by numerous investigators using postmortem analyses or in vivo neuroimaging techniques. This chapter focuses on RD studies of hemispheric asymmetries, corpus callosum, deep gray nuclei, and perisylvian regions, including temporal lobes, planum temporale, and insula. Differing criteria for the diagnosis of dyslexia, the matching of controls, variable ages spanning from childhood through adulthood, variable methods of magnetic resonance (MR) image acquisition and subsequent image analysis, and various image-based anatomic definitions for these structures provide the basis for the divergence of the early studies. Despite many early contradictory findings, the most recent studies point to structural and functional abnormalities in bilateral perisylvian regions, as would be predicted by traditional localization theories. Until replicated by larger, homogeneous, and matched study populations, the individual findings discussed in this review cannot yet be considered as characteristic in RD.

INTRODUCTION

Between 3% and 10% of the population is affected by developmental dyslexia or reading disorder (RD), in which an underlying phonological deficit alters the normal development of reading and spelling skills (Shaywitz, Fletcher, and Shaywitz 1995; Shaywitz 1998). Reading Disorder affects approximately 5% of the population, with a gender ratio (male to female) of approximately 1.5:1 (Shaywitz et al. 1990; Wadsworth et al. 1992). Despite the numerous neuroimaging and postmortem studies performed in RD, we currently know more about the genetics and behavioral phenotype than we do its neuroanatomic basis (Filipek 1995; Filipek 1999; Fulbright et al. 1997; Hynd and Semrud-Clikeman 1989). Dyslexia has been linked to genetic markers on both chromosome 6 (Cardon et al. 1994; Gayan et al. 1999) and chromosome 15 (Grigorenko et al. 1997; Smith et al. 1983). The two different loci are proposed possibly to represent two distinct RD phenotypes, reflecting different levels in the hierarchy of reading skills: phonological awareness on chromosome 6 and single word reading on chromosome 15 (Grigorenko et al. 1997). Presumably these, and possibly other genes, subtly affect the brain during development, resulting in the characteristic cognitive deficits observed in RD.

None of the developmental disorders, including RD, has been associated with characteristic discrete focal lesions or recognized encephaloclastic processes. Most, if not all, of the reported imaging and pathology cases in RD have appeared normal at the level of gross anatomy, with a few isolated exceptions (Cohen, Campbell, and Yaghmai 1989; Jackson and Plante 1996; Landau, Goldstein, and Kleffner 1960; Preis et al. 1998a). Therefore, routine clinical imaging is not indicated in RD or any other developmental disorder.

Prior imaging and pathology studies focused on hemispheric asymmetries, the corpus callosum, thalamus, and the perisylvian regions, including planum temporale and insula. The samples in most of these studies were small and usually highly selected, and both anatomic definitions and methods of image acquisition varied across studies (Beaton 1997; Filipek 1995; Filipek 1999; Semrud-Clikeman 1997). The collective studies point to both anomalous structure and function of the traditional perisylvian "language regions" of the brain, including primary auditory and auditory association cortices in the temporal and adjacent posterior parietal regions of the brain.

Hemispheric Asymmetries

The early computerized tomographic (CT) studies in RD examined hemispheric widths and lengths using linear measurements on single selected slices. In general, these studies produced conflicting findings of hemispheric symmetry or reversal of the expected anterior (right-larger-than-left) or posterior (left-larger-than-right) asymmetry in RD. Hynd and Semrud-Clikeman (1989) provided a detailed meta-analysis of these early neuroimaging studies in developmental dyslexia.

Two more recent magnetic resonance imaging (MRI) studies also report opposite findings relative to anterior (frontal) and posterior (temporo-parietal-occipital junction) hemispheric symmetry differences in RD. Hynd et al. (1990) measured hemispheric linear widths on a single 5 mm axial (horizontal) MRI slice in dyslexic children; three of the RD children also had psychiatric co-diagnoses. They reported normal posterior widths, but smaller right anterior widths, which produced frontal symmetry instead of the expected asymmetry. Duara et al. (1991) divided each hemisphere into six regions on a single axial (horizontal) slice, and reported the ratio of the area of each region to the total area of both hemispheres combined. In contrast to Hynd et al. (1990), Duara et al. (1991) noted a reversal of the expected left-larger-than-right posterior asymmetry in RD adults, with normal right-larger-than-left anterior asymmetry.

The Corpus Callosum

Several recent MRI studies have focused on measurements of the corpus callosum in RD. The underlying hypotheses were that previously reported findings of frontal and/or temporal-parietal reversed asymmetry in dyslexics may be related to anomalous interhemispheric pathways through the callosum to the known language regions. The collective studies were performed on subjects in differing age ranges, using differing measurements, and differing methods of reporting the resulting data.

The total area of the corpus callosum in RD appears to be similar to control subjects in most studies (Duara et al. 1991; Hynd et al. 1995; Larsen, Høien, and Ödegaard 1992; Pennington et al. in press; Rumsey et al. 1996), although it is thinner in its mid-callosal width (Witelson 1989) in RD (Pennington et al. in press). One study reported significantly larger total areas in RD males, particularly the anterior half (Robichon and Habib 1998). The posterior portion of the corpus callosum has been reported to be larger in RD males (Hynd et al. 1995; Rumsey et al. 1996), and reported as both larger (Duara et al. 1991) and smaller (Pennington et al. in press) in RD males and females with co-morbid Attention-Deficit Hyperactivity Disorder (RD-ADHD). The anterior callosum has also been noted to be smaller anteriorly in RD (Hynd et al. 1995) and larger anteriorly in female RD-ADHD (Duara et al. 1991). Each of these studies used a different definition for dividing the callosum into subregions, which most likely accounts for the divergent findings. In addition, co-morbid ADHD was not routinely controlled across the collective studies, and smaller posterior regions of the corpus callosum have been reported in ADHD alone (Semrud-Clikeman et al. 1994). Pennington et al. (in press) found that those with

RD-ADHD accounted for smaller posterior callosal areas, which were not found in RD alone. The interested reader is referred to recent reviews of the role of the callosum in RD for more comprehensive discussions (Beaton 1997; Filipek 1995; Hynd and Semrud-Clikeman 1989).

Perisylvian Regions

The planum temporale, a major focus of investigation in RD, is not a distinct structure, but rather is a triangular landmark located on the superior surface of the temporal lobe just posterior to Heschl's gyrus. The left planum has been associated with language comprehension because of its location adjacent to primary auditory cortex and because it includes part of Wernicke's area. The plana were first studied in detail by Geschwind and Levitsky (1968), who evaluated planum asymmetry in a large normal postmortem population. They found that the left planum is larger than the right in approximately 65% of the population, the left and right plana are symmetric in 24%, and the right is larger than the left ("reversed" asymmetry) in 11%.

Not only are the boundaries of the planum not obvious, but there is also considerable dispute concerning the definitions of the boundaries, particularly the anterior and posterior borders (Shapleske et al. 1999). In spite of this inconsistency, the planum temporale is the most commonly measured brain region in RD, both *in vivo* and *in vitro* (Filipek 1995; Filipek 1999; Galaburda 1988; Galaburda 1993c; Morgan and Hynd 1998; Shapleske et al. 1999). Galaburda (1988; 1993b; 1994) and Humphreys, Kaufmann, and Galaburda (1990) performed the only comprehensive postmortem studies to date in five brains from severe dyslexics obtained from The Orton Dyslexia Society. Although this was a small sample, the right planum temporale area was larger than the left in 100% of cases (relative to 11% in normals); a finding thought to result from reduced programmed cell death in the right hemisphere. Based on these findings, the investigators hypothesized that normally asymmetric plana temporale (left > right) may be necessary for the development of normal phonologic awareness, the core deficit in RD (Galaburda 1988; Galaburda 1993b; Galaburda 1994; Humphreys, Kaufmann, and Galaburda 1990). There was also a very high frequency of microdysgenesis, particularly in the left frontal and temporal opercula (Galaburda 1988; Humphreys, Kaufmann, and Galaburda 1990). Taken together, the postmortem findings suggest anomalous brain development during the late stages of corticogenesis in at least these severe dyslexics, potentially producing abnormally improved neuronal survival in the right hemisphere, subsequent redefinition of cortical architecture in the left hemisphere, and anomalous asymmetry (Galaburda 1988; Galaburda 1992).

Accurate definition of the planum boundaries is extremely difficult with neuroimaging methods (Filipek 1995; Filipek 1999; Shapleske et al. 1999) and sometimes even on postmortem examination (Galaburda 1988). Because of this "structural" ambiguity, neuroimaging measures have varied from unidimensional lengths or widths to areas or volumes of often disparate "plana" or temporal lobes. Therefore, despite the popularity of the planum temporale and posterior temporal "language" regions in neuroimaging studies of RD, direct comparisons cannot be made at present across the available studies (Dalby, Elbro, and Stødkilde-Jørgensen 1998; Gauger, Lombardino, and Leonard 1997; Hynd et al. 1990; Jernigan et al. 1991; Kushch et al. 1993; Larsen, Høien, and Ödegaard 1990; Leonard et al. 1993; Preis et al. 1998b; Rumsey et al. 1997a; Schultz et al. 1994), which are summarized in table I (Filipek 1999). Therefore, there is currently insufficient evidence to confirm anomalous asymmetry in all dyslexic individuals based on neuroimaging studies. Figure 1 demonstrates the results of the different anatomic definitions used in two of the studies. This topic is extensively discussed in two recent comprehensive reviews of the planum temporale in RD (Beaton 1997; Shapleske et al. 1999).

In contrast to the planum temporale, measures of the insula have been more concordant across collective structural and functional neuroimaging studies. Hynd et al. (1990) first reported bilaterally shorter insula lengths in ten dyslexic children. In a cohort of 75 monozygotic

Table I.   The Planum Temporale (PT) and Temporal Lobe (TL) in Reading/Language Disorder

Study	Measurement	Finding in RD	Lateralization
Galaburda (1993a)	surface area of PT	symmetry	larger right
Hynd et al. (1990)	length of PT	right ≥ left	shorter left
Larsen et al.(1992)	length of PT	symmetry	longer right
Jernigan et al. (1991)	volume of posterior TL	smaller L (bilateral in RH)	—
Kushch et al. (1993)	superior surface area of TL	smaller L	—
Leonard et al.(1993)	length of PT	—	—
Schultz et al. (1994)	convolutional surface area of PT	left >right	normal
Rumsey et al. (1997a)	surface area of PT	left > right	normal
Gauger, Lombardino and Leonard (1997)	length of PT	left > right	smaller left
Dalby, Elbro, Stødkilde-Jørgensen et al. (1998)	*coronal* cross sectional area of TL	right ≥ left	smaller left
Preis et al. (1998b)	surface area of PT	left > right	normal

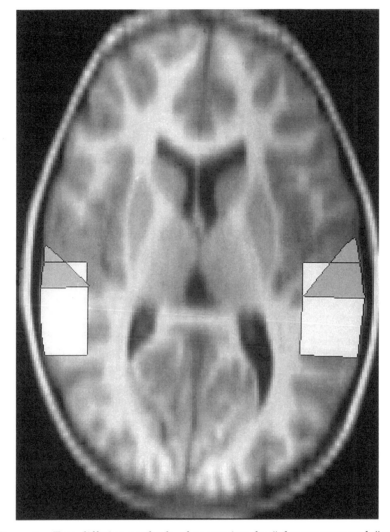

Figure 1.   Two differing methods of measuring the "planum temporale" superimposed on a horizontal magnetic resonance imaging scan (taken from Galaburda 1993c; Larsen, Høien, and Ödegaard 1990). Note that, although the two "plana" overlap, there is considerable difference in the surface area as specified by the two definitions.

and dizygotic twin pairs with RD, Pennington et al. (in press) noted that the insula was the only structure that differed significantly in the RD twins, and was bilaterally smaller in volume than in the 22 control twins. Total cerebral, neocortical (including the temporal lobes) and subcortical volumes (including basal ganglia and thalamus) were similar, although the frontal regions were only slightly smaller. Using positron emission tomography (PET), Paulesu et al. (1996) found that left temporoparietal regions were activated during a phonologic memory task and Broca's area was activated during a rhyming task in RD, however, each was activated independently rather than in the expected sequential pattern. None of the expected intermediary activation occurred in the left insula, suggesting that RD may be a disconnection syndrome due to a dysfunctional left insula.

Other functional neuroimaging studies also implicate the perisylvian areas in the pathogenesis of RD. Although Gross-Glenn et al. (1991) reported decreased glucose metabolism in the left perisylvian region using PET during oral reading tasks, Hagman et al. (1992) noted increased metabolism in the left medial temporal lobe during a syllable discrimination task, relative to controls. Rumsey et al. (1992; 1994b) found that dyslexics failed to activate left temporoparietal regions using PET during a phonologic task (rhyme detection). Horwitz, Rumsey, and Donohue (1998) reported that normal readers demonstrate a functional connectivity between the left angular gyrus and occipital and temporal lobe regions during single word reading using PET, which is missing in dyslexic adults. Rae et al. (1998) also noted biochemical differences in the left temporal-parietal lobe by [1]Hydrogen magnetic resonance spectroscopy. Using magnetoencephalography during a word recognition task in RD individuals, Salmelin et al. (1996) noted failure of activation or a slowly increasing late response in the left inferior temporo-occipital region, leading to the conclusion that perception of words as specific units appears to be impaired in dyslexics. These collective functional studies indicate significant dysfunction of left posterior language regions in RD.

Right hemispheric involvement has also been implicated in RD, however. Rumsey et al. (1997c) found reduced activation and unusual deactivation in bilateral posterior temporal and left inferior parietal cortices, with essentially normal activation of left inferior frontal cortex, during word recognition and phonologic processing tasks. In addition, tonal memory tasks in RD do not produce the expected increase in regional cerebral blood flow in the right perisylvian regions (Rumsey et al. 1994a).

Shaywitz et al. (1998) performed a sophisticated hierarchy of language-based activation tasks designed to make progressively increasing phonologic demands using functional MRI (fMRI) in dyslexic adults. There was underactivation of the left posterior perisylvian and occipital regions (Wernicke's area, the angular gyrus, and striate cortex) and overactivation to even the simple phonologic task in both left anterior (inferior frontal gyrus) and right posterior perisylvian regions. This study further supports the bilateral posterior perisylvian localization of anomalous brain structure and function in RD.

The Central Gray Nuclei

In addition to a primary phonologic deficit in RD, some studies implicate deficits in the perception of rapid, high contrast, *visual* information as critical to RD (Eden et al. 1995; Eden et al. 1996b; Greatrex and Drasdo 1995; Stein and Walsh 1997; Tallal, Miller, and Fitch 1993; Tallal et al. 1996). The ventral magnocellular layers of the lateral geniculate nuclei are highly sensitive to rapidly presented, moving stimuli of low contrast with lower spatial resolution, while the dorsal parvocellular layers are color coded with higher spatial resolution and low contrast sensitivity. Livingstone et al. (1991) and Galaburda and Livingstone (1993) studied the geniculate bodies from the five postmortem RD specimens noted previously. In the RD brains, the magnocellular layers were disorganized, with 27% smaller cell bodies, which were variable in size and shape, relative to controls. There were no differences noted in the size of the parvocellular neurons, nor in the layers of primary visual cortex that receive input from magnocellular and parvocellular neurons. Although the medial geniculate bodies consisted of neurons of similar size, the RD sample showed a relative lack of larger neurons, with an apparent excess of smaller neurons. In addition, the normal controls had a greater number of larger neurons in the left medial geniculate, although the RD had more large neurons in the right.

Eden et al. (1996a; 1998) and Demb, Boynton, and Heeger (1998) reported that the presentation of moving stimuli failed to activate the magnocellular visual subsystem in RD with fMRI appropriately. In contrast, presentation of stationary patterns did produce the expected activation in the parvocellular innervated cortex in both RD and controls (Eden et al. 1996a; Eden and Zeffiro 1998). These functional neuroimaging studies therefore support the presence of a magnocellular visual deficit in dyslexia.

WHY THE DIVERGENT FINDINGS?

The collective results of recent neuroimaging studies, in any of the developmental disorders, approaches a collection of loosely related "apples and oranges." To answer the question posed above, one must consider multiple variables, including the definition of subject and control cohorts, the scanning protocols, the image analysis methods, and, for the functional imaging studies, the activation paradigms, used across the collective studies in RD (Filipek 1995; Filipek 1996; Filipek, Kennedy, and Caviness 1992).

Who is studied? What is the comparison group?

Developmental dyslexia is only behaviorally defined at present, a fact that contributes to the, sometimes heterogeneous, cohorts studied in these disorders. Additional factors for consideration include age, gender, IQ, handedness, neuropsychological and behavioral parameters, and the uniformity of matching of controls. Early neuroimaging studies often used medical controls with "normal" MRI scans obtained for clinical reasons, including seizures, instead of normal controls (i.e., "normal" scans, not normal subjects).

How were they scanned?

The collective studies represent vastly differing scanning protocols, with variable slice thickness, orientation, and position. The two-dimensional MRI slices can range from one to ten mm in thickness. The anatomy seen on any given two-dimensional slice represents the anatomy *averaged* through the thickness of that slice (e.g., *volume averaging*), rather than the surface anatomy alone, as seen with an actual postmortem brain slice. Therefore, three contiguous 3 mm slices will more accurately represent the true neuroanatomy than will a single 9 mm slice. Some older scanning procedures produced variable *interslice gaps*, where the brain *was not imaged*, although more recent studies use pulse sequences that produce thin contiguous slices. The slice orientation (e.g., coronal or axial or sagittal) and the angle at which the slices were obtained also contributed to the neuroanatomic variability. This was particularly relevant for unidimensional or two-dimensional measurements of structures or regions performed on single selected slices, where the given slice may significantly differ across subjects. For example, positional variability could result in significantly different "midsagittal" planes for measurement of corpus callosum across subjects. Current technology permits volumetric pulse sequences, and any current and future scanning protocols will be able to utilize this capability to obtain thin contiguous slices approximately one mm thick. These pulse sequences produce in essentially isotropic voxels (volume picture elements) and permit accurate image reconstruction (e.g., for positional normalization) within three-dimensional space.

What was measured? How was it measured?

The collective studies represent a combination of qualitative and quantitative image analysis methods, without uniform anatomic definitions. It is not surprising, therefore, that the collective combination in any given developmental disorder of unidimensional or two-dimensional measures of length, width, or area on a single selected slice, three-dimensional volume interpolated through interslice gaps, and three-dimensional volumes on thin contiguous slices, all performed with variable anatomic definitions, have produced heterogeneous results that often appear conflicting. In reality, they cannot be directly compared.

What cognitive process was tested?

This emerges as yet another crucial element with the increased availability of functional neuroimaging techniques. Not all phonologic tasks are equal, for example. Although a given activation task may indeed involve phonologic processing, it may also activate other functional neural systems interdependently, which may compromise the specificity of the paradigm. An informed reader must tease out the individual components of any given paradigm to understand accurately the results.

THE FUTURE

Despite these inexact results, the current findings endorse continued use of quantitative neuroimaging in RD to identify the underlying pathogenesis, which clearly will be subtle. To avoid the conglomeration of the "apples and oranges" phenomenon, however, future neuroimaging studies must be performed with state-of-the-art methodology (Rumsey et al. 1997b). Structural MRI methods will focus on three-dimensional measures obtained on isotropic scans, as uni- (e.g., linear) or two-dimensional (e.g., areas) measurements on individual slices can now be considered obsolete. Computerized MRI-based morphometric methods with objective mathematical approaches have replaced subjective hand-drawn methods, and traditional planimetric analyses are virtually antiquated. It is now a routine capability to reformat three-dimensional MRI data into any plane, which allows positional normalization of the entire brain regardless of the original position of the head in the scanner (Alpert et al. 1990; Filipek, Kennedy, and Caviness 1991; Filipek et al. 1994). These techniques produce essentially identical image planes across subjects for accurate cross-scan comparisons. Although some anatomic resolution may be compromised with positional normalization methods (Courchesne, Yeung-Courchesne, and Egaas 1994), the superior quality of reformatted images resulting from conventional MRI pulse sequences negates this argument.

The scope of future analyses includes any of the neural systems associated with RD and language function (Filipek 1996; Filipek 1999). The older hemispheric en bloc methods included regions subserving differing neuropsychological functions, and often divided functional regions across subdivisions. Methods of cortical (e.g., Kennedy et al. 1998; Kennedy et al. 1994; Rademacher et al. 1992; Steinstrater and

Lutkenhoner 1998), and subcortical (Makris et al. 1999; Meyer et al. 1999) mapping, although still approximate and based on the extremely variable surface topology of the human brain, have improved the accuracy of functional localization using traditional brain-behavior nomenclature (Damasio and Frank 1992; Damasio and Damasio 1989; Heilman and Valenstein 1985; Mesulam 1985). As an example, consider the specificity of reported morphometric or functional differences "in primary auditory and auditory association cortices" instead of "in the posterior temporal region." Functional imaging methods conventionally have relied upon anatomic atlases for localization, because of the inherent poor anatomic specificity of these methods. The recent availability of methods of cortical parcellation now permit more precise anatomic localization with functional imaging modalities, providing direct correlations between a subject's own MRI template and functional imaging scan.

Measurements of developmental trajectories in normal children can now be performed, not only to compare with measures of children under study, but also to increase our understanding of the *in vivo* normal variability of brain development (Filipek 1996; Filipek, Kennedy, and Caviness 1992; Rumsey et al. 1997b). With larger studies in the pediatric population, including normal and developmentally disordered children, age-appropriate structural parameters may be included within the traditional adult model, based on actual structural-functional correlation data (Filipek 1995; Filipek, Kennedy, and Caviness 1992; Rumsey et al. 1997b). These collective approaches can now accommodate the challenge and help establish secure brain-behavior correlations in the developing brain (Filipek 1996; Filipek 1999; Filipek, Kennedy, and Caviness 1992).

ACKNOWLEDGMENTS

This work was supported in part by HD 27802, HD 04024, HD 28202, and HD 35458 from the National Institute of Child Health and Human Development, NS 35896 from the National Institute of Neurological Disorders and Stroke, and by MH 00419 and MH 38820 from the National Institute of Mental Health; National Institutes of Health, Bethesda, MD, USA.

EDITOR'S COMMENTS

In the mid-1970s, imaging of the living brain became possible. Using computed tomography (CT), crude, oval, gray-black-white thick slices of the brain were generated; and within the decade, magnetic resonance imaging (MRI) provided much more clearly delineated two-dimensional shades of gray-black-white images of the brain. These included images of cortical/subcortical gray and white matter, with sagittal views that provided images of the lower part of the brain, brainstem, and cerebellum. In 1968, Geschwind and Levitsky, and in 1979, Kemper and Galaburda, showed that symmetry between the two halves of the brain rather then the asymmetry usually seen at post mortem, was the rule in people with dyslexia.

Attempts to visualize clearly in life, the back roof of the temporal lobe lying nestled within the cleft called the sylvian fissure, have been met with difficulty, although it has been observed post mortem. Dr. Filipek demonstrates why such replication, even with today's sophisticated three-dimensional imaging techniques, is not easy even if the original observation is valid. Three factors confound comparing post mortem to in vivo observations: study variations in the technology employed for imaging, definition of what constitutes reading disorder, and age of the subject.

Bear in mind that the anatomy underlying reading disorder has been determined prebirth, but the specific regions involved in language processing within a given individual are apt to be influenced by environmental factors such as the language to be learned, the method of instruction in the script of the language, and the extent to which the individual has had auditory exposure to the sound of the language system. Consequently, the functional or physiological anatomy of reading and reading disorder (fMRI, PET) are apt to vary in their coherence with each other, and in comparison with purely anatomic studies.

Educators, physicians, speech and language clinicians, and treating psychologists should, however, not be dismayed by these observations of an anatomic substrate to reading disorder. These explanations do not necessarily bode for incapability of improvement in reading as clinical experience and education verified studies sponsored by the National Institute of Child Health and Human Development in Florida as well as the work with piracetam as a pharmacotherapy for reading and spelling disorders suggests that the skeletal superstructure of the brain has within it a chemistry and physiology malleable and improvable if properly managed.

—DDD

REFERENCES

Alpert, N. M., Bradshaw, J. F., Kennedy, D. N., and Correia, J. A. 1990. The principle axis transformation- A method for image registration. *Journal of Nuclear Medicine* 31:1717–17.

Beaton, A. A. 1997. The relation of planum temporale asymmetry and morphology of the corpus callosum to handedness, gender, and dyslexia: A review of the evidence. *Brain and Language* 60:255–322.

Cardon, L. R., Smith, S. D., Fulker, D. W., Kimberling, W. J., Pennington, B. F., and DeFries, J. C. 1994. Quantitative trait locus for reading disability on chromosome 6. *Science* 266:276–79.

Cohen, M., Campbell, R., and Yaghmai, F. 1989. Neuropathological abnormalities in developmental dysphasia. *Annals of Neurology* 25:567–70.

Courchesne, E., Yeung-Courchesne, R., and Egaas, B. 1994. Methodology in neuroanatomic measurement (editorial). *Neurology* 44:203–208.

Dalby, M. A., Elbro, C., and Stødkilde-Jørgensen, H. 1998. Temporal lobe asymmetry and dyslexia: An in vivo study using MRI. *Brain and Language* 62:51–69.

Damasio, A. R., and Frank , R. 1992. Three-dimensional in vivo mapping of brain lesions in humans. *Archives of Neurology* 49:137–43.

Damasio, H., and Damasio, A. R. 1989. *Lesion Analysis in Neuropsychology.* New York: Oxford University Press.

Demb, J. B., Boynton, G. M., and Heeger, D. J. 1998. Functional magnetic resonance imaging of early visual pathways in dyslexia. *Journal of Neuroscience* 18:6939–51.

Duara, R., Kushch, A., Gross-Glenn, K., Barker, W. W., Jallad, B., Pascal, S., Loewenstein, D. A., Sheldon, J., Rabin, M., Levin, B., and Lubs, H. 1991. Neuroanatomic differences between dyslexic and normal readers on magnetic resonance imaging scans. *Archives of Neurology* 48:410–16.

Eden, G. F., Stein, J. F., Wood, H. M., and Wood, F. B. 1995. Temporal and spatial processing in reading disabled and normal children. *Cortex* 31:451–68.

Eden, G. F., VanMeter, J. W., Rumsey, J. M., Maisog, J. M., Woods, R. P., and Zeffiro, T. A. 1996a. Abnormal processing of visual motion in dyslexia revealed by functional brain imaging. *Nature* 382:66–9.

Eden, G. F., VanMeter, J. W., Rumsey, J. M., and Zeffiro, T. A. 1996b. The visual deficit theory of developmental dyslexia. *Neuroimage* 4:S108–17.

Eden, G. F., and Zeffiro, T. A. 1998. Neural systems affected in developmental dyslexia revealed by functional neuroimaging. *Neuron* 21:279–82.

Filipek, P. A. 1995. Neurobiological correlates of developmental dyslexia-What do we know about how the dyslexics' brains differ from those of normal readers? *Journal of Child Neurology* 10 (Suppl 1):S62–69.

Filipek, P. A. 1996. Structural variations in measures of developmental disorders. In *Developmental Neuroimaging: Mapping the Development of Brain and Behavior*, eds. R. W. Thatcher, G. R. Lyon, J. Rumsey and N. Krasnegor. San Diego, CA: Academic Press.

Filipek, P. A. 1999. Neuroimaging in the developmental disorders: The state of the science. *Journal of Child Psychology and Psychiatry* 40:113–28.

Filipek, P. A., Kennedy, D. N., and Caviness, V. S., Jr. 1991. Volumetric analysis of central nervous system neoplasm based on MRI. *Pediatric Neurology* 7:347–51.

Filipek, P. A., Kennedy, D. N., and Caviness, V. S., Jr. 1992. Neuroimaging in child neuropsychology. In *Handbook of Neuropsychology. Volume 6: Child Neuropsychology*, eds. I. Rapin and S. Segalowitz. Amsterdam: Elsevier Science Publishers.

Filipek, P. A., Richelme, C., Kennedy, D. N., and Caviness, V. S. 1994. The young adult human brain: An MRI-based morphometric analysis. *Cerebral Cortex* 4:344–60.

Fulbright, R. K., Shaywitz, S. E., Shaywitz, B. A., Pugh, K. R., Skudlarski, P., Constable, R. T., Fletcher, J. M., Liberman, A. M., Shankweiler, D. P., Katz, L., Lacadie, C., Bronen, R. A., Marchione, K. E., and Gore, J. C. 1997. Neuroanatomy of reading and dyslexia. *Child and Adolescent Psychiatric Clinics of North America* 6:431–45.

Galaburda, A. M. 1988. The pathogenesis of childhood dyslexia. *Research Publications-Association for Research in Nervous and Mental Disease* 66:127–38.

Galaburda, A. M. 1992. Neurology of developmental dyslexia. *Current Opinion in Neurology and Neurosurgery* 5:71–6.

Galaburda, A. M. 1993a. Neuroanatomic basis of developmental dyslexia. *Neurology Clinics of North America* 11:161–73.

Galaburda, A. M. 1993b. Neurology of developmental dyslexia. *Current Opinion in Neurobiology* 3:237–42.

Galaburda, A. M. 1993c. The planum temporale (editorial). *Archives of Neurology* 50:457.

Galaburda, A. M. 1994. Developmental dyslexia and animal studies: at the interface between cognition and neurology. *Cognition* 50:133–49.

Galaburda, A. M., and Livingstone, M. 1993. Evidence for a magnocellular defect in developmental dyslexia. *Annals of the New York Academy of Science* 682:70–82.

Gauger, L. M., Lombardino, L. J., and Leonard, C. M. 1997. Brain morphology in children with specific language impairment. *Journal of Speech, Language, and Hearing Research* 40:1272–84.

Gayan, J., Smith, S. D., Cherny, S. S., Cardon, L. R., Fulker, D. W., Brower, A. M., Olson, R. K., Pennington, B. F., and DeFries, J. C. 1999. Quantitative-trait locus for specific language and reading deficits on chromosome 6p. *American Journal of Human Genetics* 64:157–64.

Geschwind, N., and Levitsky, W. 1968. Human brain: Left-right asymmetry in temporal speech region. *Science* 161:186–87.

Greatrex, J. C., and Drasdo, N. 1995. The magnocellular deficit hypothesis in dyslexia: A review of reported evidence. *Ophthalmic and Physiological Optics* 15:501–506.

Grigorenko, E. L., Wood, F. B., Meyer, M. S., Hart, L. A., Speed, W. C., Shuster, A., and Pauls, D. L. 1997. Susceptibility loci for distinct components of developmental dyslexia on chromosomes 6 and 15. *American Journal of Human Genetics* 60:27–39.

Gross-Glenn, K., Duara, R., Barker, W. W., Loewenstein, D., Chang, J. Y., Yoshii, F., Apicella, A. M., Pascal, S., Boothe, T., Sevush, S., Jallad, B. J., Novoa, L., and Lubs, H. A. 1991. Positron emission tomographic studies during serial word reading by normal and dyslexic adults. *Journal of Clinical and Experimental Neuropsychology* 13:531–44.

Hagman, J. O., Wood, F., Buchsbaum, M. S., Tallal, P., Flowers, L., and Katz, W. 1992. Cerebral brain metabolism in adult dyslexic subjects assessed with positron emission tomography during performance of an auditory task. *Archives of Neurology* 49:734–9.

Heilman, K. M., and Valenstein, E., eds. 1985. *Clinical Neuropsychology*. New York: Oxford University Press.

Horwitz, B., Rumsey, J. M., and Donohue, B. C. 1998. Functional connectivity of the angular gyrus in normal reading and dyslexia. *Proceedings of the National Academy of Science* USA 95:8939–44.

Humphreys, P., Kaufmann, W. E., and Galaburda, A. M. 1990. Developmental dyslexia in women: Neuropathological findings in three patients. *Annals of Neurology* 28:727–38.

Hynd, G. W., Hall, J., Novey, E. S., Eliopulos, D., Black, K., Gonzalez, J. J., Edmonds, J. E., Riccio, C., and Cohen, M. 1995. Dyslexia and corpus callosum morphology. *Archives of Neurology* 52:32–8.

Hynd, G. W., and Semrud-Clikeman, M. 1989. Dyslexia and brain morphology. *Psychological Bulletin* 106:447–82.

Hynd, G. W., Semrud-Clikeman, M., Lorys, A. R., Novey, E. S., and Eliopulos, D. 1990. Brain morphology in developmental dyslexia and attention deficit disorder/hyperactivity. *Archives of Neurology* 47:919–26.

Jackson, T., and Plante, E. 1996. Gyral morphology in the posterior Sylvian region in families affected by developmental language disorder. *Neuropsychology Review* 6:81–94.

Jernigan, T. L., Hesselink, J. R., Sowell, E., and Tallal, P. A. 1991. Cerebral structure on magnetic resonance imaging in language- and learning-impaired children. *Archives of Neurology* 48:539–45.

Kennedy, D. N., Lange, N., Makris, N., Bates, J., Meyer, J., and Caviness, V. S., Jr. 1998. Gyri of the human neocortex: an MRI-based analysis of volume and variance. *Cerebral Cortex* 8:372–84.

Kennedy, D. N., Meyer, J. W., Filipek, P. A., and Caviness, V. S., Jr. 1994. MRI-based topographic segmentation. In *Functional Neuroimaging: Technical Foundations.* eds. R. W. Thatcher, M. Hallet, T. A. Zeffiro, E. R. John and J. M. Huerta. San Diego, CA: Academic Press, Inc.

Kushch, A., Gross-Glenn, K., Jallad, B., Lubs, H., Rapin, M., Feldman, E., and Duara, R. 1993. Temporal lobe surface area measurements on MRI in normal and dyslexic readers. *Neuropsychologia* 31:811–21.

Landau, W., Goldstein, R., and Kleffner, F. 1960. Congenital aphasia: A clinicopathologic study. *Neurology* 10:915–21.

Larsen, J. P., Høien, T., and Ödegaard, H. 1990. MRI evaluation of the size and symmetry of the planum temporale in adolescents with developmental dyslexia. *Brain and Language* 39:289–301.

Larsen, J. P., H ien, T., and ôdegaard, H. 1992. Magnetic resonance imaging of the corpus callosum in developmental dyslexia. *Cognitive Neuropsychology* 9:123–34.

Leonard, C. M., Voeller, K. K. S., Lombardino, L. J., Morris, M. K., Hynd, G. W., Alexander, A. W., Andersen, H. G., Garofalakis, M., Honeyman, J. C., Mao, J., Agee, O. F., and Staab, E. V. 1993. Anomalous cerebral structure in dyslexia revealed with magnetic resonance imaging. *Archives of Neurology* 50:461–69.

Livingstone, M. S., Rosen, G. D., Drislane, F. W., and Galaburda, A. M. 1991. Physiological and anatomical evidence for a magnocellular defect in developmental dyslexia. *Proceedings of the National Academy of Science* USA 88:7943–7.

Makris, N., Meyer, J. W., Bates, J. F., Yeterian, E. H., Kennedy, D. N., and Caviness, V. S. 1999. MRI-Based topographic parcellation of human cerebral white matter and nuclei. *Neuroimage* 9:18–45.

Mesulam, M.-M. 1985. Patterns in behavioral neuroanatomy: Association areas, the limbic system, and hemispheric specialization. In *Principles of Behavioral Neurology*, ed. M.-M. Mesulam. Philadelphia: FA Davis Company.

Meyer, J. W., Makris, N., Bates, J. F., Caviness, V. S., and Kennedy, D. N. 1999. MRI-Based topographic parcellation of human cerebral white matter. *Neuroimage* 9:1–17.

Morgan, A. E., and Hynd, G. W. 1998. Dyslexia, neurolinguistic ability, and anatomical variation of the planum temporale. *Neuropsychology Review* 8:79–93.

Paulesu, E., Frith, U., Snowling, M., Gallagher, A., Morton, J., Frackowiak, R. S., and Frith, C. D. 1996. Is developmental dyslexia a disconnection syndrome? Evidence from PET scanning. *Brain* 119:143–57.

Pennington, B. F., Filipek, P. A., Churchwell, J., Kennedy, D. N., Lefly, D., Simon, J. H., Filley, C. M., Galaburda, A. M., and DeFries, J. C. 1999. Brain morphometry in reading-disabled twins. *Neurology 53:723–29.*

Preis, S., Engelbrecht, V., Huang, Y., and Steinmetz, H. 1998a. Focal grey matter heterotopias in monozygotic twins with developmental language disorder. *European Journal of Pediatrics* 157:849–52.

Preis, S., Jancke, L., Schittler, P., Huang, Y., and Steinmetz, H. 1998b. Normal intrasylvian anatomical asymmetry in children with developmental language disorder. *Neuropsychologia* 36:849–55.

Rademacher, J., Galaburda, A. M., Kennedy, D. N., Filipek, P. A., and Caviness, V. S. 1992. Human cerebral cortex: localization, parcellation, and morphometry with magnetic resonance imaging. *Journal of Cognitive Neuroscience* 4:352–74.

Rae, C., Lee, M. A., Dixon, R. M., Blamire, A. M., Thompson, C. H., Styles, P., Talcott, J., Richardson, A. J., and Stein, J. F. 1998. Metabolic abnormalities in developmental dyslexia detected by 1H magnetic resonance spectroscopy. *The Lancet* 351:1849–52.

Robichon, F., and Habib, M. 1998. Abnormal callosal morphology in male adult dyslexics: relationships to handedness and phonological abilities. *Brain and Language* 62:127–46.

Rumsey, J. M., Andreason, P., Zametkin, A. J., Aquino, T., King, A. C., Hamburger, S. D., Pikus, A., Rapoport, J. L., and Cohen, R. M. 1992. Failure to activate the left temporoparietal cortex in dyslexia. An oxygen 15 positron emission tomographic study. *Archives of Neurology* 49:527–34.

Rumsey, J. M., Andreason, P., Zametkin, A. J., King, A. C., Hamburger, S. D., Aquino, T., Hanahan, A. P., Pikus, A., and Cohen, R. M. 1994a. Right frontotemporal activation by tonal memory in dyslexia, an O15 PET Study. *Biological Psychiatry* 36:171–80.

Rumsey, J. M., Casanova, M., Mannheim, G. B., Patronas, N., De Vaughn, N., Hamburger, S. D., and Aquino, T. 1996. Corpus callosum morphology, as measured with MRI, in dyslexic men. *Biological Psychiatry* 39:769–75.

Rumsey, J. M., Donohue, B. C., Brady, D. R., Nace, K., Giedd, J. N., and Andreason, P. 1997a. A magnetic resonance imaging study of planum temporale asymmetry in men with developmental dyslexia. *Archives of Neurology* 54:1481–89.

Rumsey, J. M., Filipek, P. A., Kennedy, D. N., Lange, N., Reiss, A. L., Evans, A. C., Giedd, J. N., Bookheimer, S. Y., Cohen, M. S., Horwitz, B., and Simpson, G. 1997b. Tools for Pediatric Neuroimaging Workshop: Report of the Working Groups. Vienna, VA: Inter-Institute Group for Pediatric Neuroimaging: NIMH, NINDS, NICHD.

Rumsey, J. M., Nace, K., Donohue, B., Wise, D., Maisog, J. M., and Andreason, P. 1997c. A positron emission tomographic study of impaired word recognition and phonological processing in dyslexic men. *Archives of Neurology* 54:562–73.

Rumsey, J. M., Zametkin, A. J., Andreason, P., Hanahan, A. P., Hamburger, S. D., Aquino, T., King, A. C., Pikus, A., and Cohen, R. M. 1994b. Normal activation of frontotemporal language cortex in dyslexia, as measured with oxygen 15 positron emission tomography. *Archives of Neurology* 51:27–38.

Salmelin, R., Service, E., Kiesila, P., Uutela, K., and Salonen, O. 1996. Impaired visual word processing in dyslexia revealed with magnetoencephalography. *Annals of Neurology* 40:157–62.

Schultz, R. T., Cho, N. K., Staib, L. H., Kier, L. E., Fletcher, J. M., Shaywitz, S. E., Shankweiler, D. P., Katz, L., Gore, J. C., Duncan, J. S., and Shaywitz, B. A. 1994. Brain morphology in normal and dyslexic children: The influence of sex and age. *Annals of Neurology* 35:732–42.

Semrud-Clikeman, M. 1997. Evidence from imaging on the relationship between brain structure and developmental language disorders. *Seminars in Pediatric Neurology* 4:117–24.

Semrud-Clikeman, M., Filipek, P. A., Biederman, J., Steingard, R., Kennedy, D. N., Renshaw, P., and Bekken, K. 1994. Attention-deficit hyperactivity disorder: Magnetic resonance imaging morphometric analysis of the corpus callosum. *Journal of the American Academy of Child and Adolescent Psychiatry* 33:875–81.

Shapleske, J., Rossell, S. L., Woodruff, P. W., and David, A. S. 1999. The planum temporale: A systematic, quantitative review of its structural, functional and clinical significance. *Brain Research. Brain Research Reviews* 29:26–49.

Shaywitz, B. A., Fletcher, J. M., and Shaywitz, S. E. 1995. Defining and classifying learning disabilities and attention-deficit/hyperactivity disorder. *Journal of Child Neurology* 10 (Suppl 1):S50–57.

Shaywitz, S. E. 1998. Dyslexia. *New England Journal of Medicine* 338:307–312.

Shaywitz, S. E., Shaywitz, B. A., Fletcher, J. M., and Escobar, M. D. 1990. Prevalence of reading disability in boys and girls. Results of the Connecticut Longitudinal Study. *Journal of the American Medical Association* 264:998–1002.

Shaywitz, S. E., Shaywitz, B. A., Pugh, K. R., Fulbright, R. K., Constable, R. T., Mencl, W. E., Shankweiler, D. P., Liberman, A. M., Skudlarski, P., Fletcher, J. M., Katz, L., Marchione, K. E., Lacadie, C., Gatenby, C., and Gore, J. C. 1998. Functional disruption in the organization of the brain for reading in dyslexia. *Proceedings of the National Academy of Science USA* 95:2636–41.

Smith, S. D., Kimberling, W. J., Pennington, B. F., and Lubs, H. A. 1983. Specific reading disability: Identification of an inherited form through linkage analysis. *Science* 219:1345–47.

Stein, J., and Walsh, V. 1997. To see but not to read: The magnocellular theory of dyslexia. *Trends in Neurosciences* 20:147–52.

Steinstrater, O., and Lutkenhoner, B. 1998. Three-dimensional reconstruction of the auditory cortical areas from magnetic resonance images. *Audiology and Neuro-Otology* 3:265–78.

Tallal, P., Miller, S., and Fitch, R. H. 1993. Neurobiological basis of speech: a case for the preeminence of temporal processing. *Annals of the New York Academy of Science* 682:27–47.

Tallal, P., Miller, S. L., Bedi, G., Byma, G., Wang, X., Nagarajan, S. S., Schreiner, C., Jenkins, W. M., and Merzenich, M. M. 1996. Language comprehension in language-learning impaired children improved with acoustically modified speech. *Science* 271:81–4.

Wadsworth, S. J., DeFries, J. C., Stevenson, J., Gilger, J. W., and Pennington, B. F. 1992. Gender ratios among reading-disabled children and their siblings as a function of parental impairment. *Journal of Child Psychology and Psychiatry* 33:1229–39.

Witelson, S. F. 1989. Hand and sex differences in the isthmus and genu of the human corpus callosum: A postmortem morphological study. *Brain* 112: 799–835.

Chapter • 4

Klinefelter's Syndrome: A Genetic Model for Learning Disabilities in the Verbal and Frontal-Attentional Domains

Daniel H. Geschwind and Kyle Boone

Klinefelter's syndrome (KS) patients present a potentially powerful genetic model for the study of learning difficulties associated with verbal-linguistic and executive-attentional domains. Despite having a normal or near normal IQ, subjects with KS manifest signs of verbal learning disabilities throughout their lives and show persistent developmental difficulties with fine motor coordination that are reminiscent of non-aneuploidic children with developmental dyslexia. Adolescents and adults with KS also demonstrate frontal-executive dysfunction similar to that observed in non-aneuploidic adults with a history of attention-deficit disorder (ADD). Both the frontal-attentional and the verbal learning difficulties are likely to be due to the presence of an extra X chromosome in patients with KS. Although it is clear that non-sex linked loci are likely to have more significant contributions to dyslexia and ADD in the general population, the putative X chromosomal locus or loci acting in KS provide one point of entry for the study of the genetic and biological basis of these traits. Furthermore, although frontal-attentional dysfunction and verbal learning problems are present in the population of subjects with KS, they are separable in individual KS patients. Thus, one does not cause the other, nor is their biological basis neatly overlapping.

In addition to specific learning disabilities, patients with KS also manifest anomalous cerebral dominance and thus provide a genetic model for the study of cerebral laterality. How cerebral laterality contributes to, or is associated with, KS patients' cognitive phenotypes, especially dyslexia, is unknown, but is an area of great interest. We are in the early stages of applying DNA microarray technology and other genetic approaches to begin to correlate various aspects of the KS cognitive phenotype with specific chromosomal regions.

DYSLEXIA IS A COMPLEX GENETIC TRAIT

A large number of family, twin, and genetic linkage studies support the assertion that reading ability and developmental reading disabilities have an underlying genetic component (DeFries, this volume). Twin studies indicate that the heritability of reading-related phenotypes is between 0.5 and 0.6, consistent with a significant genetic predisposition, but that reading is also modifiable by environmental factors (for example, see DeFries, this volume). These twin studies and genetic linkage studies also demonstrate that developmental dyslexia is a genetically heterogeneous condition. This genetic heterogeneity is entirely consistent with the undoubtedly complex neural circuits presumed to underlie reading.

Reading is not an isolated cognitive ability. The capability to read relies on a complex set of interacting cognitive functions that are tied to the development of language abilities. Functional brain imaging and studies of patients with brain damage due to stroke or other causes have elucidated some of our knowledge of the overlapping anatomy of the brain regions involved in expressive and receptive language functions (Habib, Demonet, and Frackowiak 1996; Hinke et al. 1993; Klein et al. 1995; Warburton et al. 1996). These studies reveal a parallel distributed network that is centered in the left hemisphere of most right-handers, and that spans multiple brain regions, using a multitude of neurotransmitters, receptors, and other cellular machinery. Thus, the notion that the genetics of reading or any facet of language function would be complex is self-evident. It then follows that the developmental and molecular genetic pathways to reading disability would be similarly complex. This, of course, does not eliminate the potential existence of major gene influences, or single gene, reading-related phenotypes that segregate in certain populations or families.

FRAMING DYSLEXIA IN THE BROADER CONTEXT OF LANGUAGE AND CEREBRAL ASYMMETRY

It is most likely that genes that contribute to reading disability are involved broadly in language functions or perhaps have even more pleiomorphic effects on human cognition. The assertion that specific genes dedicated specifically to reading are unlikely to exist is supported by several lines of reasoning. The first is that genes do not directly contribute to behavior or cognition, but to neural structures both fixed and dynamic, structural and chemical, that are involved in cognitive and behavioral functioning. An appropriate analogy would be the assumption that there is a gene for basketball talent. The genes that may contribute to talent in basketball actually underlie structural factors such as height (bone size), various components of the musculature and perhaps synaptic function, rather than specific aspects of behavior observed in basketball games. Modern neuroscience has revealed that brain regions serve many functions by acting within partially overlapping, parallel distributed neural systems. Any gene that alters the structure, chemistry, or physiology of a given brain region or regions is likely to affect many brain functions. Secondly, from a purely evolutionary standpoint, a specific genetic contribution to reading is improbable. It is unlikely that evolutionary forces could have exerted a large influence on reading, because, on a population level, humans have been reading for less than 1000 years. In contrast, the ability to use spoken language to communicate is likely a fundamental evolutionary event that gave the species with this ability a significant survival advantage (Corballis 1997). Third, children with developmental dyslexia are rarely found to have pure reading disability. Other aspects of spoken language, motor skills, or cognition are typically involved (Denckla 1985; Denckla, Rudel, and Broman 1981; Denckla et al. 1985). Therefore, most genes and brain structures that underlie reading are likely to be heavily intertwined and dependent on those involved in other language processes, and perhaps other functions that are unrelated to language. For this reason, the neurobiologic substrate of reading may eventually be best understood in the broader context of language, as well as the other sensory and motor processing and integrating systems necessary for reading.

Because language function is associated with structural asymmetries of the human brain, one of our approaches to learn more about language development and evolution has been to identify genes that may contribute to cerebral hemispheric asymmetry. Language is localized in a distributed system centered around the left perisylvian region in 97% to 99% of right-handers (Alexander and Annett 1996; Bogen 1993; Geschwind 1978; Geschwind and Galaburda 1985). This relationship of language lateralization to handedness is somewhat different in left-handers. Left-handers show either left-hemisphere (50%) or bilateral (40-45%) language, and less frequently, right-hemisphere (5-10%) language (Geschwind and Galaburda 1985; Hécaen and Consoli 1973). This functional asymmetry for language is correlated with structural asymmetry of the planum temporale of the posterior superior temporal gyrus, which is larger on the left than on the right in most right-handers (Galaburda et al. 1978; Geschwind and Galaburda 1985; Geschwind and Levitsky 1968). This anatomical asymmetry develops prior to the completion of cortical neurogenesis, and thus likely provides the neural substrate on which behaviors such as hand preference and language develop (Chi, Dooling, and Gilles 1976; Witelson and Pallie 1973). As mentioned above, left-handers often diverge from the usual patterns of functional and anatomical asymmetry seen for language in right-handers by demonstrating either reduced asymmetry or loss of asymmetry, a condition that has been termed anomalous dominance (Annett 1985; Foundas, Leonard, and Heilman 1995; Geschwind and Galaburda 1985).

Pathological conditions involving developmental disturbances in language, namely developmental reading disability (dyslexia) and stuttering, have also been associated with altered dominance patterns in humans. Several studies have demonstrated a significantly increased incidence of left-handedness among stutterers and people with dyslexia (Geschwind and Behan 1982; Tonnessen et al. 1993). Post-mortem anatomical and in vivo imaging analysis of dyslexic brains have also demonstrated a loss of the typical leftward asymmetry of the planum temporale, similar to what has been observed in left-handers (Duara et al. 1991; Galaburda 1993; Kushch et al. 1993; Larsen et al. 1990). Both dyslexia and left-handedness have significant genetic components (Annett 1985; Cardon et al. 1994; McManus 1991; Pennington et al. 1992).

However, the heritability of dyslexia and left-handedness deduced from twin studies and family data are different, and we have not found strong evidence for linkage of left-handedness to the published dyslexia loci on chromosome 6 or 15, although the possibility cannot be eliminated (D. Geschwind, unpublished results). This is consistent with the notion that alterations in hand dominance, and perhaps other features of brain asymmetry may explain some of the predisposition to dyslexia in certain populations, but that most genetic factors that contribute to dyslexia susceptibility may not have an impact on cerebral asymmetry in a manner that alters handedness. Still, because of the associations discussed above, the study of human populations manifesting anomalous dominance patterns (left-handers and those with developmental language disabilities) presents a unique opportunity to study human cerebral asymmetry and its pathologic associations.

GENETIC HETEROGENEITY POSES A CHALLENGE
FOR GENETIC STUDIES OF DYSLEXIA AND LATERALITY

Classic genetic approaches, such as linkage analysis of left-handedness, are hampered by the low sibling relative risk (λ_s = 1.5), because a large number of individuals need to be genotyped at very high marker density to attain reasonable power (Lander and Kruglyak 1995; Risch 1990). If left-handedness is not due to a single major gene as is often assumed, this power is even lower. Although a number of compelling single-gene models have been proposed for handedness (Annett 1985; McManus 1991), there is no a priori certainty that a single gene exists for hand preference. Furthermore, none of these models offers plausible a priori predictions of all of the twin and family data. This is further affirmed by segregation analysis that cannot differentiate between dominant, recessive, or polygenic modes of inheritance (Risch and Pringle 1985).

The situation for developmental dyslexia is considerably better than handedness, but still has required massive genotyping to detect genetic linkage to a chromosomal region (λ_s = 6 to 15). The genetic linkage approach has yielded positive results, and at least two chromosomal loci have been identified, one on chromosome 6 and potentially another on chromosome 15 (Cardon et al. 1994; Grigorenko et al. 1997; Pennington 1990; Pennington et al. 1992). However, these results have not been universally confirmed, and the chromosomal regions linked to dyslexia in published reports remain wide, making a search for causal genes somewhat daunting (e.g., Field and Kaplan 1998). It is primarily the significant genetic and clinical heterogeneity of dyslexia and the problems with its definition that underlie the difficulties uncovering genes contributing to dyslexia (Cardon et al. 1994; Pennington 1990; Pennington et al. 1992). Although some specific dyslexic subtypes breed true within families, many do not (Pennington 1990). Compounding the issue of genetic and clinical heterogeneity is the observation that dyslexia is not typically pure (Denckla, Rudel, and Broman 1981; Denckla et al. 1985; Galaburda 1993). The subdivision of dyslexia by its underlying neurocognitive phenotype, (e.g., phonological awareness) may avoid some loss in power caused by the clinical heterogeneity (Grigorenko et al. 1997), but does not directly address the issue of genetic heterogeneity.

CIRCUMVENTING GENETIC HETEROGENEITY

One approach that attempts to circumvent the issues of genetic heterogeneity is the study of dyslexia in Finland, a relative genetic isolate.

The study of dyslexia in the Finnish population offers two major advantages over other populations. First, Finnish is a phonetic language, with every written syllable (grapheme) corresponding to only one phoneme (unit of pronunciation). This is in contrast to English, where the context often alters grapheme to phoneme conversion. This heterogeneity of the English language creates diverse pathways to reading, leading to great potential for clinical variability. Given the uniformity of the language, it is not surprising that linguists and neuropsychologists have demonstrated a relatively uniform phonologic deficit in Finnish dyslexic children. Secondly, the ability to study relative genetic isolates significantly increases our ability to find and narrow loci that contribute to complex cognitive traits (Hastbacka et al. 1992; Lander and Kruglyak 1995; Lander and Schork 1994). A relevant example is the lack of strongly positive reproducible findings of linkage to most putative schizophrenia loci despite the genotyping of over 500 sibling pairs in the United States and Europe. This is compared with the recent success of identifying a chromosomal locus for schizophrenia in Finland, despite genotyping a relatively small number of individuals (Hovatta et al. 1997; Peltonen, 1998, personal communication). Our group has initiated a study focusing on relatively rural regions in Northern Finland that were founded by small groups within the last four centuries. This study is currently in its early phases, but preliminary studies of the known dylsexia locus on chromosome 6 have not supported a role for this locus in the Finnish sample.

THE STUDY OF PATIENTS WITH KLINEFELTER'S SYNDROME—A RATIONALE

A complementary, and potentially powerful approach involves the identification of an even more homogeneous population, such as persons with a common genetic syndrome, who manifest signs of anomalous dominance and specific reading disability, in this case patients with Klinefelter's syndrome (XXY). Klinefelter's syndrome occurs at a rate of approximately one out of eight hundred male births and is manifested in adulthood by tall stature, hypogonadism, infertility, behavioral problems, and learning disabilities (Mandoki et al. 1991; Ratcliffe et al. 1994). A number of longitudinal studies in small numbers of XXY patients (Bender, Linden, and Robinson 1993; Netley and Rovet 1982a; Robinson et al. 1986; Robinson et al. 1990; Rovet et al. 1996) demonstrate that children with Klinefelter's syndrome (XXY) have verbal learning disabilities. Approximately 80% of KS boys and adolescents studied longitudinally demonstrate difficulties with verbal learning that are similar to non-aneuploidic dyslexics. Rovet

(Rovet et al. 1996) reviewed 27 studies on academic and intellectual functioning in boys with KS and other sex chromosome aneuploidies in addition to their own sample of 41 patients. By age 7 or 8, these children demonstrate reading and spelling difficulties. To extend these observations, a multidisciplinary study of adult and adolescent patients with KS that includes linguistic, neuropsychological and genetic components has been initiated to identify chromosomal regions that contribute to the alterations in cerebral dominance and developmental dyslexia in this population (Geschwind et al. 1998). Although X chromosome gene(s) can represent only a portion of the genetic risk for dyslexia, the identification of such genes would be an important step toward understanding the neurobiology of this complex condition.

NEUROPSYCHOLOGICAL PROFILE OF XXY MALES

A four-hour battery of comprehensive neuropsychological testing was administered in 30 adults with KS (Geschwind et al. 1998)—a subgroup of those tested for handedness with the Octave Illusion described below. Patients were recruited by advertisement through Klinefelter's Syndrome and Associates (a national patient advocacy organization) and the Endocrinology Clinic at Harbor-UCLA Medical Center. The majority of these patients (> 90%) are referred or diagnosed because of infertility or other disturbance of androgen functioning such as hypogonadism, rather than behavioral or cognitive dysfunction. An attempt to recruit patients without a history of known verbal learning disabilities was initiated to increase the likelihood of identifying normal readers among patients with KS for future genotype-phenotype correlations. Subjects had no history of neurologic illness, substance abuse, or head injury. Twenty-five patients were on testosterone replacement therapy. Reading disability was defined in two ways (Geschwind et al. 1998): (1) Discrepancy between IQ and verbal performance (performance one level below IQ on at least two of Boston Naming, RAVLT, or WRAT-R), or (2) performance below a standard criterion (performance below low-average [the 24th percentile] on two from among the three tests: Boston Naming, RAVLT, and WRAT-R). About 70% of subjects with KS demonstrated verbal learning disability using both the criteria of discrepancy between IQ and poor performance on reading and naming tasks, and absolute performance below the low-average range on these tasks. The number of those classified as disabled was the same whether the discrepancy criteria (one level below IQ) or absolute criteria (below 24%) was used (Geschwind et al. 1998). Previous work has suggested that studies of naming are one of the more sensitive measures for identifying adult dyslexics (Denckla 1993; Denckla et al. 1981). In this context, it is interesting that the subjects with KS performed on average at the 5th percentile on the Boston Naming Test. Other areas of impaired language-related performance included spelling (21st percentile), reading (19th percentile), and verbal memory (14th percentile). This is in contrast to nonverbal visual memory (59th percentile), Block Design, and Picture Completion (both at the 50th percentile).

Possible Compensatory Mechanisms and Classic Right Hemisphere Functions

Longitudinal studies of children and adolescents with KS have demonstrated a decrease in verbal IQ relative to performance IQ in many cases—although this has not been universal. However, study of adolescent and adult patients with KS suggests that this discrepancy may be somewhat compensated in the adult (Geschwind et al. 1998). Males with KS (age range 16 to 61) in this sample performed at the 40th percentile on performance IQ testing and at the 50th percentile on verbal IQ. It is possible that these results may have been biased relative to previous longitudinal studies by the recruitment methods, which may have favored subjects with higher IQs. However, the significant deficits in specific tests of naming, verbal memory, reading and spelling achievement observed in these same subjects with KS and normal verbal IQ demonstrate that the verbal learning disabilities persist, but that the subjects have learned to compensate, probably by adopting alternative strategies for problem-solving. The neural substrate of this compensation is unknown, but represents an interesting avenue for future research.

In conjunction with the simplified concept that verbal abilities are predominantly left-hemisphere attributes and many spatial talents reside in the right hemisphere, it is interesting that many of those KS patients with the poorest verbal performance demonstrate normal or above normal spatial performance. In many subjects with KS, there was an inverse correlation between what are considered typical right- or left-hemisphere abilities. The 11 subjects scoring at least 10 percentile points higher on Block Design than on Boston Naming Test performed at the 9th percentile on the WRAT-R, whereas those showing the same quantitative discrepancy favoring Boston Naming over Block Design, performed at the 64th percentile on the WRAT-R. It is interesting to note that the patient with the largest discrepancy between IQ (77th percentile) and reading (3rd percentile), was left-handed. These results are consistent with a trade-off between verbal and spatial abilities that has been suggested previously in patients with sex chromosome aneuploidies (Crow 1989, 1994; Rovet and Netley 1980). This apparent trade-off also alludes to the notion that KS patients with reading disability may have highly developed skills in certain arenas—an area for future studies that is relatively unexplored.

Skill-Preference Dissociation in Handedness

To further investigate the notion that dominance may be altered in males with KS, testing for handedness skill, handedness preference, and functional dominance using the Octave Illusion (Deutsch 1983) was carried out. A modified version of the Edinburgh handedness battery (Oldfield 1971; Schachter 1993; Urion 1988), which has been widely used and normed, was used to test handedness preference in 96 patients between age 10 and 61. Those with scores of 70 or greater (70 to 100) were considered right-handers, and those with scores less than 0 (0 to 100) were considered left-handers (Oldfield 1971; Schachter 1993). An analysis of handedness based solely on writing hand was also done, because this information is easily extractable from the questionnaire. Fine motor testing was used to determine handedness skill in a subset of 24 patients (Denckla 1985). Whether handedness was categorized by writing hand or by the Edinburgh handedness battery, there was a slight, but not statistically significant increase in left-handedness among males with KS (14%) (Geschwind et al. 1998). However, testing of fine motor skill revealed increased left-handedness among subjects with KS (29%) versus normal controls (11%), showing a dissociation between handedness skill and preference that was not observed in control male subjects. This dissociation between handedness preference and skill is unusual, as in most populations tested, the two are highly correlated as long as tests of distal fine motor skills are used (McManus 1991). Likewise, motor overflow and mirror movements were observed in over one-third of subjects with KS over age 10 (n = 24). Typically, these movements are developmental phenomena that normally do not persist past age 6 (Denckla 1985). In some developmental disorders such as dyslexia, and other acquired conditions involving poor inter-hemispheric sensorimotor integration, poor bimanual coordination and mirror movements may persist past childhood or occur de-novo (Geschwind et al. 1995; Wolff et al 1990). In this regard, it is important that bimanual coordination was poor in a subset of patients with KS, as has been observed in non-aneuploidic subjects with developmental dyslexia (Wolff et al. 1990), indicating another feature that patients with KS and non-aneuploidic dyslexics share in common. The high incidence of mirror movements and motor overflow further supports the notion that typical inter-hemispheric sensorimotor interactions are somehow interrupted in patients with KS.

In this context, it is important to consider the work of McManus, who has reported a dissociation between hand preference and skill in autistic children, a population with widespread developmental abnormalities which include severely impaired left-hemisphere language capabilities (Cornish and McManus 1996). Based on these observations, McManus has reasoned that handedness preference is likely to antedate skill during development. Similar dissociations have not been observed in mentally retarded children, so this dissociation is not a general marker for brain damage. Left-handedness does not imply reversal of normal symmetry patterns but, rather, a loss of bias in favor of left-hemisphere asymmetry (Geschwind and Galaburda 1985; Klar 1996). Thus, cerebral lateralization in patients with KS is not reversed, but likely randomized, as is observed in some models of visceral asymmetry (Lowe et al. 1996). This randomization would predispose to, but not insure, disruption of the usual left-hemisphere asymmetry on which language functioning and motor dominance develop.

Further evidence for a randomization of typical left-hemisphere dominance patterns comes from testing with the Octave Illusion (Deutsch 1974). Patients with KS demonstrated anomalous dominance by performing differently from non-aneuploidic controls and indistinguishably from left-handed subjects in the general population (Craig 1979; Deutsch 1983). Typically, a high tone is heard in the right ear, alternating with a low tone in the left ear. Similar to left-handers, only 48% of the subjects with KS heard this illusory percept. The neurobiological substrate of this illusion is currently unknown. However, the frequency where the illusion is most salient in distinguishing left-from right-handers (400–800 Hz) represents that of spoken vowels (Craig 1979). Additionally, the octave illusion not only varies as a function of handedness, but as a function of family history of handedness (Deutsch 1983), suggesting that it is associated with some of the same genetic factors as handedness itself. It is thus remarkable that subjects with KS demonstrate an increase in left-handedness (skill) relative to the population frequency, mirror movements, and overflow, as well as the left-hander's perception of the octave illusion.

Additional evidence that patients with KS have anomalous cerebral dominance comes from a smaller study of handedness in those patients. Netley and Rovet (1982b) found a 24% incidence of non-right-handedness in 33 subjects with KS, an increase compared with controls. The definition for anomalous hand dominance was narrower in the study by Geschwind et al. (1998), resulting in a 14% incidence of left-handedness. When the same criteria used by Netley and Rovet were applied to this population, 25% of patients with KS were non-right-handed. However, 25% non-right-handedness was no different from the control or population prevalence (Geschwind et al. 1998;

Schachter 1993). Dichotic listening studies in small groups of subjects with KS have also demonstrated a significant shift away from right-ear dominance, indicating an alteration in language dominance on several dichotic listening tasks involving verbal material (Netley and Rovet 1984). This pattern is parallel with that observed in this study using the octave illusion. Additionally, the KS subjects' poor performance in tests of verbal memory, reading, and naming, with normal IQ, is indicative of a developmental language disability and consistent with altered left-hemisphere functioning (Denckla 1993; Galaburda 1993; Netley and Rovet 1984). Preserved spatial functions, including memory and constructional abilities along with impaired fine motor dexterity, are also typical of non-aneuploidic patients with developmental dyslexia as mentioned above (Denckla 1993). Thus, patients with KS appear to provide a genetic model for the study of cerebral lateralization and developmental dyslexia (Bender, Linden, and Robinson 1993; Rovet et al. 1996; Geschwind et al. 1988). Preliminary analysis of structural brain magnetic resonance imaging in a small group of XXY subjects appears to show reversed asymmetry or symmetry in typically asymmetric language regions (Bender, personal communication 1998), as would be predicted from the neuropsychological data presented above. Structural brain imaging studies are ongoing to determine the anatomical correlates of the observed anomalous dominance patterns in a large group of patients with KS who have undergone extensive neuropsychological evaluation.

Frontal-Attentional Dysfunction

Because frontal lobe deficits had not been previously described in patients with KS, an unexpected finding was poor performance on a variety of tests that tap measures of frontal-executive function. A variety of tasks of attention, executive problem-solving skills, verbal fluency, planning, and the ability to inhibit improper responses revealed widespread difficulties among many patients with KS. Interestingly, frontal-executive dysfunction was most pronounced in the left hemisphere, as performance on design fluency was average, whereas verbal fluency was impaired (Geschwind et al. 1998; K. Boone, unpublished data). These frontal-attentional deficits parallel what can be described as the core of the adult residua of ADD (Denckla 1993). Thus, subjects with KS appear to be at increased risk, not only for reading disability, but also for frontal-attentional deficits that one would expect to observe in adults with a history of ADD. Given this co-morbidity and poor verbal fluency, an important issue to address was whether verbal and frontal-attentional difficulties were caused by the same underlying neural or genetic substrate. Ironically, the title of the present volume acknowledges a large literature describing the co-morbidity of ADD and reading disability. To determine whether measures of language and reading correlated with frontal-attentional measures, correlations were calculated to assess the relationship between these variables. Individually and as a group, frontal-executive deficits were not directly related to verbal deficits, as there was no correlation between the level of frontal-executive dysfunction and performance on any language-related tasks. In contrast, there were significant correlations between reading scores and all language tests, (K. Boone, unpublished results; Geschwind et al, 1998).

In summary, it appears that adults with KS exhibit a learning disability with associated language abnormalities (word-retrieval, word generation, rapid language processing), but also a dissociated cluster of cognitive abnormalities characterized by frontal-executive impairment and slowed motor and mental speed. The presence of dysexecutive syndrome could help account for the behavioral abnormalities, including poor judgement, impulsivity, failure to consider consequences of one's behavior, and deficits in social skills that are frequently anecdotally reported in this population. Further studies are ongoing to examine the relationship between frontal functioning and measures of social functioning. In the future, extending the testing paradigms from standard clinical batteries to more specific tests used in cognitive neuroscience will help to delineate a precise localization of cognitive dysfunction in this population.

A POSSIBLE GENE DOSAGE EFFECT

The cognitive and behavioral phenotypes of XXY, XYY, and XXX subjects differ considerably in many domains (Bender, Linden, and Robinson 1993; Robinson et al. 1986; Robinson, Bender, and Linden 1990). However, it is interesting that most studies of children and adolescents with sex chromosome trisomies have demonstrated that verbal learning disabilities are an area of cognitive intersection in subjects with all three genotypes (Netley and Rovet 1982c; Robinson, Bender, and Linden 1990; Stewart et al. 1982). This suggests that somehow an extra copy of the sex chromosomes is the major contributing factor (Corballis et al. 1996). Further support for a dosage effect comes from the study of Turner's syndrome subjects, who have only one X chromosome and have relative preservation of linguistic capabilities, with poor spatial performance (the inverse of the KS phenotype) (Crow 1989, 1994). The overlapping reading and verbal learning phenotype in XXY, XXX, and XYY subjects suggests that a region or regions common to the sex chromosomes may contribute to dyslexia by a gene dosage effect. Since typically the extra X chromosome is inactivated, this implicates either (1) faulty inactivation of a normally inactivated gene or region, or more likely, (2) gene(s) from regions that are normally not inactivated—the pseudoautosomal regions (PAR) present on both the X and Y chromosomes (Geschwind et al. 1998; Rappold 1993).

Alternative theories linking gonadal steroids to language dominance and hence verbal learning disabilities have been proposed (Geschwind and Behan 1982; Geschwind and Galaburda 1985), but several facts argue against sex hormones, such as testosterone, having a major influence on the phenotype of dyslexia in XXY, XXX, or XYY subjects. First, these patients have diverse and opposing gonadal hormone profiles, yet overlap in terms of dyslexia (e.g., Robinson et al. 1986; Robinson, Bender, and Linden 1990). Secondly, abnormal levels of testosterone are not found in utero in either XXY or XYY males (Ratcliffe et al. 1994). Third, men who are congenitally hypogonadal for other reasons, do not report similar difficulties in school, nor do they do poorly on language tests (Porter et al. 1988). Finally, the males with KS have cognitive deficits that are more "male" than "female," opposite from what one would predict based on gonadal function.

These data, coupled with the reasoning above, strongly implicate a direct genetic effect from a non-inactivated region or gene on the extra sex chromosome. In patients with three copies of the PARs (XXY) left-hemisphere functions such as verbal memory, naming, and reading are impaired, whereas right-hemisphere functions such as spatial reasoning and non-verbal memory are preserved or even enhanced. This trade-off is entirely consistent with the finding that KS patients with the best spatial skills demonstrate the worst verbal or reading performance (Geschwind et al. 1998; Rovet et al. 1996). Further, Turner's syndrome patients with the greatest left-hemisphere advantage, exhibit the worst spatial skills (Netley and Rovet 1982c; Netley and Rovet 1984; Rovet et al. 1996).

Although other genetic mechanisms or loci may be causal, one likely and testable locus (or loci) lies in one of the PARs of the X chromosome. Genes in the PAR are normally not inactivated and thus are expressed in three copies in patients with sex chromosome trisomies, two copies in those with a normal sex chromosome complement and in one copy in patients with Turner's Syndrome. Thus, PAR genes are well suited for contributing to alterations in gene dosage in those with variable numbers of sex chromosomes (Rappold 1993). This is especially intriguing in light of genetic models of human handedness that suggest a handedness locus on the PAR, or regions of high X-Y homology on the X chromosome (Crow 1989; 1994; Corballis et al. 1996). Because there are two PARs, one on Xp and the other on Xq, either region could be involved. Because Turner's syndrome patients with three Xq PARs do not show verbal learning difficulties, the most likely sex chromosome locus lies on the short arm of the X or Y chromosomes.

A GENETIC APPROACH USING DNA MICROARRAYS

If three copies of all PAR genes are present in most patients with KS (those with dyslexia) and two copies of the hypothesized reading-critical region on the PAR are present in some of the subset of KS patients who read normally, we simply need to compare gene dosage over this region in dyslexic and non-dyslexic KS subjects. Standard techniques such as Southern hybridization and Fluorescent In Situ Hybridization onto Metaphase Chromosomes (FISH), are either not well suited to detect the difference between 3:2 and 2:2 dosage, or too expensive to perform a high density screen of a 3 Mb region, such as the Xp PAR. To circumvent these problems, a high density DNA microarray that will allow a high resolution screen of the sex chromosome PARs has been developed in order to test the gene dosage hypothesis discussed above (Geschwind et al. 1998).

The DNA microarrays are simple in concept. They consist of mapped, ordered genomic clones, gridded down at high density onto a glass microscope slide. Since thousands of individual clones can be arrayed onto a small region of a slide, the microarray theoretically allows for the simultaneous monitoring of gene dosage at thousands of points along any region of the genome and thus offers an efficient method for this analysis. The first-generation microarray was constructed using inter-*Alu* amplified clones derived from mapped cosmids. This array covers the Xp PAR with 80kB gaps on average and contains an almost complete contig covering the Xq PAR. Thus, the resolution is an order of magnitude or more greater than current Comparative Genomic Hybridization (CGH) techniques (Piper et al. 1995). To control for variations in hybridization or probe labeling, clones from an autosome, such as chromosome 17, are also included on the array.

To compare gene copy number (dosage) in two subjects, each subject's DNA is amplified by polymerase chain reaction (PCR) and labeled with a different color fluor. The two samples are co-hybridized onto the array and the signal intensity at each clone (spot) is compared. These arrays can be used to assay chromosome dosage in the 3:2 ratio necessary to detect deletions in patients with KS who read normally (Geschwind et al. 1998). The resolution of the array is being increased by adding clones to an average density of 50kB throughout the Xp PAR, and determining what is the minimum size deletion that the array can detect. At the same time, several patients with KS without any verbal learning difficulties have been identified and the microarray can be used to assay PAR gene dosage in these non-dyslexic subjects compared with subjects with KS who are dyslexic.

A POSSIBLE PARENT OF ORIGIN EFFECT

Another potential mechanism contributing to the variability in cognitive or behavioral phenotypes observed in KS or other sex chromosome aneuploidies is a genetic imprinting effect. In this case, a particular phenotype would be more or less severe depending upon whether the (extra) X chromosome comes from mother or father. For example, an imprinted locus for social behavior has been suggested by the study of the parent of origin of the X chromosome in patients with Turner's syndrome (Skuse et. al. 1997). Two studies of the origin of the extra X chromosome in patients with KS indicate that the supernumerary chromosome originates from parents of each sex about equally (Lorda-Sanchez et al. 1992; Harvey et al. 1990). Because more than 80% of patients with KS have dyslexia, it is unlikely that an imprinting effect could fully explain verbal learning disability in patients with KS. Studies of small numbers of subjects followed longitudinally also confirm the lack of association between language dysfunction and parental chromosome of origin. However, because testing for parent of origin is relatively simple, the correlation of both frontal executive and language performance with parent of origin is worthwhile to pursue. It is possible that several X chromosome loci are involved and that an imprinted locus contributes partially to the phenotype of reading disability.

FUTURE DIRECTIONS

This chapter raises more questions than it answers. There are many future directions that need to be explored, including the anatomical and functional imaging correlates of the KS neuropsychological profile. For example, do KS patients have altered patterns of structural brain asymmetry, or do they exhibit alterations in functional brain activation that are observed in other dyslexic children (Woods this volume; Shaywitz this volume)? What is the nature of the linguistic deficits associated with the verbal learning difficulties? The study of frontal-attentional systems needs to be extended from the realm of clinical neuropsychology using experimental paradigms derived from cognitive neuroscience in order to make more precise structure-function correlation. Additionally, do the deficits in frontal functioning underlie the psychiatric and social difficulties that have been reported by patients with KS? Whether these frontal-executive deficits respond to androgen replacement needs to be addressed in controlled studies. Although this chapter has focused on defining the areas of relative deficits in patients with KS, we have noticed that many patients have significant strengths. The study of cognitive talent is another frontier area that could be very fruitful for future genotype-phenotype correlation in patients with KS, as it may be in non-aneuploidic dyslexics.

ACKNOWLEDGMENTS

The authors gratefully acknowledge the contributions of their collaborators: Ronald Swerdloff, M.D., who has spearheaded the Harbor-UCLA KS project, Bruce Miller, M.D. who introduced us to this population, Stanley Nelson, M.D. who has developed the DNA microarray system at UCLA, Jeff Gregg, M.D., Julianna Karrim, Ph.D., and Mr. Vinh Ho who worked to fabricate the microarrays, and Gudren A. Rappold, Ph.D. and Michael D'Urso, Ph.D. for providing the mapped X chromosome cosmid clones. This work was partially suported by a grant (#95–36) from the James S. McDonnell Foundation. We also thank the KS subjects and Klinefelter Syndrome and Associates for their participation. The authors thank Ms. Bonita Porch for editorial and secretarial assistance, as well as Roger Woods, M.D. for many stimulating discussions.

EDITOR'S COMMENTS

Dr. Daniel Geschwind is a cousin of the late Norman Geschwind and it is a pleasure to have another generation of the Geschwind family involved in dyslexia research. Daniel Geschwind and Kyle Boone point out the likely complexity of the dyslexic problem, both genetically and neurophysiologically. To narrow the focus and reduce some of the variables, they employ two strategies. First, they find an isolated in-bred genetic group with dyslexia, (in this instance a small group in Finland) and study their neuropsychology, neurophysiology, and genetic locus. Next, they find subjects with a genetic variant (here Klinefelter syndrome with a duplicate X chromosome, XXY), with dyslexia and intensely study their neurophysiology, neuropsychology, and neuromotor status, as well as their genetic make up. Further, they study effects of the dose of the X gene on reading, motor skills, and degree of handedness which, as it happens, is similar to non-XXY dyslexics.

These clever strategies may clarify some of the factors that lead to the dyslexic state.

—DDD

REFERENCES

Alexander, M. P., and Annett, M. 1996. Crossed aphasia and related anomalies of cerebral organization: Case reports and a genetic hypothesis. *Brain and Language* 55(2):213–39.

Annett, M. 1985. *Left- Right, Hand and Brain: The Right Shift Theory.* London: Lawrence Erlbaum Associates.

Bender, B. G., Linden, M. G., and Robinson, A. 1993. Neuropsychological impairment in 42 adolescents with sex chromosome abnormalities. *American Journal of Medical Genetics* 48(3):169–73.

Bogen, J. E. 1993. The callosal syndromes. In *Clinical Neuropsychology,* eds. K. M. Heilman and E. Valenstein. New York: Oxford University Press.

Cardon, L. R., Smith, S. D., Fulker, D. W., Kimberling, W. J., Pennington, B. W., and DeFries, J. C. 1994. Quantitative trait locus for reading disability on chromosome 6. *Science* 266:276–79.

Chi, J. G., Dooling, E. C., and Gilles, F. H. 1976. Gyral development of the human brain. *Annals of Neurology* 1(1):86–93.

Corballis, M. C. 1997. The genetics and evolution of handedness. *Psychological Review* 104(4):714–27.

Corballis, M. C., Lee, K., McManus, I. C., and Crow, T. J. 1996. Location of the handedness gene on the X and Y chromosomes. *American Journal of Medical Genetics* 67(1):50–2.

Cornish, K. M., McManus, I. C. 1996. Hand preference and hand skill in children with autism. *Journal of Autism and Developmental Disorders* 26(12): 597–609.

Craig, J. D. 1979. The effect of musical training and cerebral asymmetries on perception of an auditory illusion. *Cortex* 15:671–77.

Crow, T. J. 1989. Pseudoautosomal locus for the cerebral dominance gene [letter]. *Lancet* 2(8658):339–40.

Crow, T .J. 1994. The case for an X-Y homologous determinant of cerebral asymmetry. *Cytogenetics and Cell Genetics* 67: 393–94.

Denckla, M. B. 1985. Revised Neurological Examination for Subtle Signs. *Psychopharmacology Bulletin* 21(4):773–800.

Denckla, M. B. 1993. The child with developmental disabilities grown up: Adult residua of childhood disorders. *Journal of Neuropsychiatry and Clinical Neuroscience* 5(2):195–9.

Denckla, M. B., Rudel, R. G., and Broman, M. 1981. Tests that discriminate between dyslexic and other learning-disabled boys. *Brain and Language* 13(1): 118–29.

Denckla, M. B., Rudel, R. G., Chapman, C., and Krieger, J. 1985. Motor proficiency in dyslexic children with and without attentional disorders. *Archives of Neurology* 42(3):228–31.

Deutsch, D. 1974. An auditory illusion. *Nature* 251:307–09.

Deutsch, D. 1983. The octave illusion in relation to handedness and familial handedness background. *Neuropsychologia* 21(3):289–93.

Duara, R., Kushch, A., Gross-Glenn, K., Barker, W. W., Jallad, B., Pascal, S., Lowenstein, P.A., Sheldon, M., Rabin., M., Levin, B., and Lubs, H. 1991.

Neuroanatomic differences between dyslexic and normal readers on magnetic resonance imaging scans. *Archives of Neurology* 48:410–416.

Field, L. L., Kaplan, B.J. 1998. Absence of linkage of phonological coding dyslexia to chromosome 6p23-p21.3 in a large family data set. *American Journal of Human Genetics* 63(5):1448–56.

Foundas, A. L., Leonard, C.M., and Heilman, K .M. 1995. Morphologic cerebral asymmetries and handedness. The pars triangularis and planum temporale. *Archives of Neurology* 52(5):501–8.

Galaburda, A. M. 1993. Neurology of developmental dyslexia. *Optometry and Vision Science* 70(5):343–7.

Galaburda, A. M., LeMay, M., Kemper, T.L. and Geschwind, N. 1978. Right-left asymmetries in the brain. *Science* 199(4331):852–6.

Geschwind, D. H., Iacoboni, M., Mega, M. S., Zaidel, D. W., Cloughesy, T., and Zaidel E. 1995. Alien hand syndrome: Interhemispheric motor disconnection due to a lesion in the midbody of the corpus callosum. *Neurology* 45(4):802–8.

Geschwind, D. H., Gregg, J., Boone, K., Karrim, J., Pawlikowska-Haddal, A., Rao, E., Ellison, J., Ciccodicola, A., D'Urso, M., Woods, R., Rappold, G. A., Swerdloff, R., and Nelson, S. F. 1998. Klinefelter's syndrome as a model of anomalous cerebral laterality: Testing gene dosage in the X chromosome pseudoautosomal region using a DNA microarray. *Developmental Genetics* 23(3):215–29.

Geschwind, N. 1978. Anatomical asymmetry as the basis for cerebral dominance. *Federation Proceedings* 37(9):2263–6.

Geschwind, N., and Behan, P. 1982. Left handedness: Association with immune disease, migraine, and developmental learning disability. *Proceedings of the National Academy of Science* USA 79:5097–100.

Geschwind, N., and Galaburda, A. 1985. Cerebral lateralization: Biological mechanisms, associations, and pathology. *Archives of Neurology* 42:428-58; 521–52.

Geschwind, N., and Levitsky, W. 1968. Human brain: Left-right asymmetries in temporal speech region. *Science* 161(837):186–7.

Grigorenko, E. L., Wood, F. B., Meyer, M. S., Hart, L. A., Speed, W. C., Shuster A., Pauls, D. L. 1997. Susceptibility loci for distinct components of developmental dyslexia on chromosomes 6 and 15. *American Journal of Human Genetics* 60(1):27–39.

Habib, M., Demonet, J. F., and Frackowiak, R. 1996. [Cognitive neuroanatomy of language: Contribution of functional cerebral imaging.] *Revue Neurologique* (Paris) 152(4):249–60.

Harvey, J., Jacobs, P. A., Hassold, T., and Pettay, D. 1990. The parental origin of 47,XXX males. *Birth Defects (Original Article Series)* 26(4):289–96.

Hastbacka, J., de la Chapelle, A., Kaitila, I., Sistonen, P., Weaver, A., and Lander, E. 1992. Linkage disequilibrium mapping in isolated founder populations: Diastrophic dysplasia in Finland. *Nature Genetics* 2(3):204–11.

Hécaen, H., and Consoli, S. 1973. Analyse des troubles de language au cours des lesions de l'aire de Broca. *Neuropsychologia* 11:377–88.

Hinke, R. M., Hu, X., Stillman, A. E., Kim, S. G., Merkle, H., Salmi, R., and Ugurbil, K. 1993. Functional magnetic resonance imaging of Broca's area during internal speech. *Neuroreport* 4(6):675–8.

Hovatta, I., Terwilliger, J. D., Lichtermann, D., Makikyro, T., Suvisaari, J., Peltonen, L., and Lonnqvist, J. 1997. Schizophrenia in the genetic isolate of Finland. *American Journal of Medical Genetics* 74(4):353–60.

Klar, A . J. 1996. A single locus, RGHT, specifies preference for hand utilization in humans. *Cold Spring Harbor Symposia on Quantitative Biology* 61:59–65.

Klein, D., Milner, B, Zatorre, R. J., Meyer, E., and Evans, A. C. 1995. The neural substrates underlying word generation: A bilingual functional-imaging study. *Proceedings of the National Academy of Science* USA 92(7):2899–903.

Kushch, A., Gross-Glenn, K., Jallad, B., Lubs, H., Rabin, M., Feldman, E., and Duara, R. 1993. Temporal lobe surface area measurements on MRI in normal and dyslexic readers. *Neuropsychologia* 31(8):811–21.

Lander, E., and Kruglyak, L. 1995. Genetic dissection of complex traits: Guidelines for interpreting and reporting linkage results [see comments]. *Nature Genetics* 11(3):241–7.

Lander, E. S., and Schork, N. J. 1994. Genetic dissection of complex traits. *Science* 265(5181):2037–48

Larsen, J. P., Hoien, T., Lundberg, I., and Odegaard, H. 1990. MRI evaluation of the size and symmetry of the planum temporale in adolescents with developmental dyslexia. *Brain and Language* 39:289–301.

Lorda-Sanchez, I., Binkert, F., Maechler, M., Robinson, W. P., Schinzel, A. A. 1992. Reduced recombination and paternal age effect in Klinefelter syndrome. *Human Genetics* 89(5):524–30.

Lowe, L. A., Supp, D. M., Sampath, K., Yokoyama, T., Wright, C. V., Potter, S. S., Overbeek, P., Kuehn, M. R. 1996. Conserved left-right asymmetry of nodal expression and alterations in murine situs inversus [see comments]. *Nature* 381(6578):158–61.

Mandoki, M. W., Sumner, G. S., Hoffman, R. P., and Riconda, D. L. 1991. A review of Klinefelter's syndrome in children and adolescents [published erratum appears in *Journal of the American Academy of Child and Adolescent Psychiatry* 1991 May; 30(3):516]. *Journal of the American Academy of Child and Adolescent Psychiatry* 30(2):167–72.

McManus, I. C. 1991. The inheritance of left-handedness. *Ciba Foundation Symposium* 162(251):251–67; discussion 267–81.

Netley, C., and Rovet, J. 1982a. Verbal deficits in children with 47,XXY and 47,XXX karyotypes: A descriptive and experimental study. *Brain and Language* 17(1):58–72.

Netley, C., and Rovet, J. 1982b. Handedness in 47,XXY males [letter]. *Lancet* 2(8292):267.

Netley, C., and Rovet, J. 1982c. Atypical hemispheric lateralization in Turner syndrome subjects. *Cortex* 18(3):377–84.

Netley, C., and Rovet, J. 1984. Hemispheric lateralization in 47,XXY Klinefelter's syndrome boys. *Brain and Cognition* 3(1):10–8.

Oldfield, R. C. 1971. The assessment and analysis of handedness: The Edinburgh Inventory. *Neuropsychologia* 9(1):97–113.

Pennington, B. F. 1990. The genetics of dyslexia. *American Journal of Medical Genetics* 35(1):28–35.

Pennington, B. F., Gilger, J. W., Pauls, D., Smith, S. A., Smith, S. D., and DeFries, J. C. 1992. Evidence for major gene transmission of developmental dyslexia. *Optometry and Vision Science* 69(2):148–51.

Piper, J., Rutovitz, D., Sudar, D., Kallioniemi, A., Kallioniemi, O. P., Waldman, F. M., Gray, J. W., and Pinkel, D. 1995. Computer image analysis of comparative genomic hybridization. *Cytometry* 19(1):10–26.

Porter, M. E., Gardner, H. A., DeFeudis, P., and Endler, N. S. 1988. Verbal deficits in Klinefelter (XXY) adults living in the community. *Clinical Genetics* 33:246–53.

Rappold, G. A. 1993. The pseudoautosomal regions of the human sex chromosomes. *Human Genetics* 92(4):315–24.

Ratcliffe, S. G., Read, G., Pan, H., Fear, C., Lindenbaum, R., and Crossley, J. 1994. Prenatal testosterone levels in XXY and XYY males. *Hormone Research* 42(3):106–9.

Risch, N. 1990. Linkage strategies for genetically complex traits. II. The power of affected relative pairs [see comments]. *American Journal of Human Genetics* 46(2):229–41.

Risch, N., and G. Pringle. 1985. Segregation analysis of human hand preference. *Behavioral Genetics* 15(4):385–400.

Robinson, A., Bender, B. G., Borelli, J. B., Puck, M. H., Salbenblatt, J. A., and Winter, J.S. 1986. Sex chromosomal aneuploidy: Prospective and longitudinal studies. *Birth Defects* 22(3):23–71.

Robinson, A., Bender, B. G., and Linden, M. G. 1990. Summary of clinical findings in children and young adults with sex chromosome anomalies. *Birth Defects (Original Article Series)* 26(4):225–8.

Robinson, A., Bender, B. G., Linden, M. G., and Salbenblatt, J. A. 1990. Sex chromosome aneuploidy: The Denver Prospective Study. *Birth Defects (Original Article Series)* 26(4):59–115.

Rovet, J., and Netley, C. 1980. The mental rotation task performance of Turner syndrome subjects. *Behavioral Genetics* 10(5):437–43.

Rovet, J., Netley, C., Keenan, M., Bailey, J., and Stewart, D. 1996. The psychoeducational profile of boys with Klinefelter syndrome. *Journal of Learning Disabilities* 29(2):180–96.

Schachter, S. 1993. Neurobiological aspects of extra-ordinary brains. In *Dyslexia and Development: Neurobiological Aspects of Extra-Ordinary Brains*, ed. A. Galaburda. London: Harvard University Press.

Skuse, D. H., James, R. S., Bishop, D. V., Coppin, B., Dalton, P., Aamodt-Leeper, G., Bacarese-Hamilton, M, Creswell, C., McGurk, R., and Jacobs, P.A. 1997. Evidence from Turner's syndrome of an imprinted X-linked locus affecting cognitive function. *Nature* 387(6634):705–8.

Stewart, D. A., Bailey, J. D., Netley, C. T., Rovet, J., Park, E., Cripps, M., and Curtis, J. A. 1982. Growth and development of children with X and Y chromosome aneuploidy from infancy to pubertal age: The Toronto study. *Birth Defects* 18(4):99–154.

Tonnessen, F. E., Lokken, A., Hoien, T., and Lundberg, I. 1993. Dyslexia, left-handedness, and immune disorders. *Archives of Neurology* 50:411–416.

Urion, D. K. 1988. Nondextrality and Autoimmune disorders among the relatives of language-disabled boys. *Annals of Neurology* 24:267–269.

Warburton, E., Wise, R. J., Price, C. J., Weiller, C., Hadar, U., Ramsay, S., and Frackowiak, R. S. 1996. Noun and verb retrieval by normal subjects. Studies with PET. *Brain* 119(Pt 1):159–79.

Witelson, S. F., and Pallie, W. 1973. Left hemisphere specialization for language in the newborn. Neuranatomical evidence of asymmetry. *Brain* 96:641–46.

Wolff, P. H., Michel, G. F., Ovrut, M., Drake, C. 1990. Rate and timing precision of motor coordination in developmental dyslexia. *Developmental Psychology* 26(3):349–59.

Chapter • 5

The Magnocellular/Parietal System and Visual Symptoms in Dyslexia

Margaret S. Livingstone

Prevailing opinions on the etiology of dyslexia have seesawed between visual and phonological. The earliest clinical descriptions of dyslexia assumed it was a visual problem and called it "congenital word blindness," essentially a kind of agnosia (Morgan 1896). Later studies, however, determined that individuals with dyslexia have phonological decoding problems (Orton 1937; Vellutino et al. 1977). Still later, more specific visual tests found that individuals with dyslexia can be shown to exhibit selective visual symptoms (Stein and Walsh 1997). In particular, several studies on low-level visual processing have found that people with dyslexia show visual abnormalities that implicate a defect in the transient (magnocellular) subdivision of the visual pathway. Moreover, other studies testing higher-level tasks implicate the dorsal visual stream—a subdivision of the visual pathway that begins at lower levels as the magnocellular subdivision of the subcortical visual pathway. In this article, I describe the anatomy and functions of the magnocellular pathway in primates, I review the evidence that dyslexia involves the magnocellular/dorsal subdivision of the visual pathway, and I try to reconcile the many kinds of observations that have been reported about this fascinating condition.

ANATOMICAL EVIDENCE FOR PARALLEL CHANNELS

In primates, the part of the visual pathway that is involved in conscious perception, the pathway from the retina to the lateral geniculate nucleus to the primary visual cortex, is subdivided into two, possibly three, major subdivisions that remain largely segregated and independent throughout the visual system, possibly even up through higher cortical association areas. This subdivision is most apparent in, and was first discovered in, the lateral geniculate nucleus where cells in the ventral, or magnocellular, layers are larger than cells in the dorsal, or parvocellular, sets of layers. Though it is most obvious in the geniculate, the subdivision of the primate visual system begins in the retina and is perpetuated into the primary visual cortex. The large Type A retinal ganglion cells project to the magnocellular geniculate layers, which in turn project to layer $4C\alpha$ of V-1; smaller type B ganglion cells project to the parvocellular layers, which project to layers $4C\beta$ and 4A of V1 (Livingstone and Hubel 1987). Magno-recipient layer $4C\alpha$ projects to layer 4B which in turn projects to Visual Area 2 and to MT, and the parvo-recipient layer $4C\beta$ projects to layers 2 and 3 and from there to Visual Area 2. There is some evidence that there is a third subdivision, specifically concerned with color in follow up, which may originate in the W-cells of the retina (Casagrande et al. 1990). Though the magnocellular and parvocellular inputs to the cortex seem to remain separate in layer 4C, the separation at subsequent stages may not be as complete.

Functional Differences Between the Channels

Anatomical, physiological, and perceptual studies indicate that the magnocellular and parvocellular subdivisions of the primate visual system are largely independent and are responsible for different aspects of visual perception: The magno system is fast, has high contrast sensitivity, is color blind, and has slightly lower acuity than the parvo division, which is slower, responsive to color contrast, and much lower in contrast sensitivity (Livingstone and Hubel 1987).

The response properties of cells at stages beyond Visual Area 2 suggest that the segregation of functions begun at the earliest stages is perpetuated at the highest levels studied so far. Indeed, the segregation seems to become more and more pronounced at each successive level so that subdivisions that are interdigited in Visual Areas 1 and 2 become segregated into entirely separate areas at still higher levels. Physiological studies at higher levels indicate that the magno system carries information about motion and stereopsis; and perceptual studies suggest that it may be responsible for spatial localization, depth perception from many kinds of depth cues, figure/ground segregation, and hyperacuity. The parvo system seems to be concerned with color perception and object recognition.

Different aspects of human visual perception, such as motion detection, stereopsis, and other forms of depth perception, color discrimination, and high-resolution form discrimination, differ markedly in the same four characteristics that distinguish the geniculate subdivisions, suggesting that at even higher levels the magno and parvo systems maintain their segregation, functionally as well as anatomically.

The idea that different aspects of vision are processed separately in humans as well, is supported by clinical observations that people with strokes can suffer surprisingly specific visual losses—for example, loss of color discrimination without impairment of form or motion perception, loss of motor perception without loss of color or form perception, or the selective loss of face recognition (Bodamer 1947; Damasio et al. 1980; Zihl, Von Cramon, and Mai 1983). Though the degree to which the subdivisions remain separate is a subject of some controversy in the fields of both human psychophysics and primate physiology and anatomy, it is nevertheless clear that parallel processing must be a fundamental strategy of the primate visual system.

Despite many gaps, the picture beginning to emerge from the anatomy and electrophysiology just outlined is that the segregation apparent at very early stages of the visual system gives rise to separate and independent parallel pathways. At early stages, where there are two major subdivisions, the cells in these two subdivisions exhibit at least four very basic differences; color selectivity, speed, acuity, and contrast sensitivity. At higher stages, the continuations of these pathways are selective for quite different aspects of vision—form, color, movement, and stereopsis—thus generating the counter intuitive prediction that different kinds of visual tasks should differ in their color, temporal acuity, and contrast characteristics. Indeed, for several decades psychologists have accumulated evidence for two channels in human vision, one chromatic and the other achromatic, by showing that different tasks can have very different sensitivities to color and brightness contrast.

HUMAN PERCEPTUAL CORRELATES

Temporal differences in color and brightness discrimination

From the fact that the magno system is color blind and is faster than the parvo system, we can predict that discrimination of color and discrimination of brightness should have different temporal properties. This is indeed so. Ives (1923) showed that brightness alternations can be followed at much faster rates than can pure color alternations.

Movement perception

The high incidence of movement and direction selectivity in MT suggests that this area may be particularly concerned with movement perception. Because, anatomically, MT receives its major inputs from layer 4B of the primary visual cortex and from the thick stripes of Visual Area 2, both part of the magno pathway, one would predict that human movement perception should somehow reflect magno characteristics; color blindness, quickness, high contrast sensitivity, and low acuity. Perceptual experiments indicate that movement perception does indeed have these characteristics. First, it is impaired for patterns made up of equiluminant colors (Cavanagh, Boeglin, and Favreau 1985); second, movement perception is impaired at high spatial frequencies, consistent with the lower acuity of the magno system (Campbell and Maffei 1981). What is most surprising about the perception of both the equiluminant stripes and the very fine stripes is that even though the sensation of movement is entirely, or almost entirely lost, the stripes themselves are still clearly visible—they are clear enough that changes in their position can be seen, even though they do not seem to be *moving*. Lastly, movement can be vividly perceived with very rapidly alternating or very low contrast images (Livingstone and Hubel 1987). Thus, the properties of human movement perception are remarkably consistent with the properties of the magno system.

Stereopsis

Finding retinal-disparity-tuned cells in the thick stripes of Visual Area 2 and in MT suggests that the magno system is also involved in stereoscopic depth perception. Consistent with this, subjects cannot see depth in equiluminant, color-contrast, random-dot stereograms, even though the dots making up the stereogram remain perfectly clear. This finding has been disputed, but we found that differences in results can arise from variations in an individual's equiluminance point with eccentricity, which make it difficult to achieve equiluminance across the visual field. Like movement perception, stereopsis falls for stereograms containing only high, but resolvable, spatial frequencies, but it is not diminished for rapidly alternating or very low contrast stereograms (Livingstone and Hubel 1987).

DEDUCTION OF FURTHER MAGNO OR PARVO FUNCTIONS FROM PERCEPTUAL TESTS

Depth from motion

Because both motion perception and stereoscopic depth perception are lost at equiluminance, David Hubel and I (1987) suspected that the ability to use relative motion as a depth cue might be lost also. We found that depth from motion, both from the viewer parallax and from object motion, seems also to depend on luminance contrast and could well be a function of the magno system. Consistent with this idea, we could see depth from motion at very low levels of luminance contrast.

Depth from shading

The retinal image is of course two-dimensional; and to capture the three-dimensional relationships of objects, the visual system uses many kinds of cues beside stereopsis and relative motion—perspective, gradients of texture, shading, occlusion, and relative position in the image. We wondered whether sensation of depth from any of these other cues might also exhibit magno characteristics. Cavanagh and Leclerc (1985) found that the perception of three-dimensional shape from shading, indeed, does depend solely on luminance contrast. That is, in order to produce a sensation of depth and three dimensionality, shadows can be any hue as long as they are darker than unshaded regions of the same surface. Many artists seem to be aware of this—for example, in some self-portraits of Van Gogh and Matisse, the shadows on their faces are green or blue, but they still convey a normally shaped face. Black-and-white photographs of these paintings (using film that has approximately the same spectral sensitivity as humans) confirm that the shadows are actually darker than the unshaded parts.

Depth from Perspective

Perspective was well known to artists by the time of the Renaissance and is a powerful indicator of depth. Converging lines or gradients of texture are automatically interpreted by the visual system as indicating increasing distance from the observer. We found that when images with strong perspective are rendered in equiluminant colors instead of black and white, the depth sensation is lost or greatly diminished, as are illusions of perspective.

WHY SHOULD THE VISUAL SYSTEM BE SUBDIVIDED?

Electrophysiological studies suggest that the magno system is responsible for carrying information about movement and depth. We extended our ideas about the possible functions of the magno system with perceptual studies and concluded that the magno system may have a more global function of interpreting spatial organization. Magno functions may include deciding which visual elements such as edges and discontinuities, belong to and define individual objects in the scene, as well as determining the overall three-dimensional organization of the scene and the positions of objects in space and movements of objects.

If the magno system covers such a broad range of functions, then what is the function of the tenfold more massive parvo system? The color selectivity of the parvo system should enable us to see borders using color information alone and, thus, borders that might be camouflaged to the color-blind magno system. But defeating camouflage may be only a small part of what the parvo system is specialized for. Experiments with fading of low contrast images indicate that the magno system is not capable of sustained scrutiny since images that can be seen by only the magno system disappear after a few seconds of voluntary fixation (Livingstone and Hubel 1987). Thus, while the magno system is sensitive primarily to moving objects and carries information about overall organization of the visual world, the parvo system seems to be important for analyzing the scene in much greater and more leisurely detail. These postulated functions would be consistent with the evolutionary relationship of the two systems: The magno system seems to be more primitive than the parvo system and is possibly homologous to the entire visual system of non-primate mammals (Guillery 1979; Sherman 1985). If so, it should not be surprising that the magno system is capable of what seem to be the essential functions of vision for an animal that uses vision to navigate in its environment, catch prey, and avoid predators. The parvo system, which is well developed only in primates, seems to have added the ability to scrutinize in much more detail the shape, color, and surface properties of objects, creating the possibility of assigning multiple visual attributes to a single object and correlating its parts. Indeed, if the magno system needs to use the various visual attributes of an object in order to link its parts, this could preclude its being able to analyze the attributes independently. It thus seems reasonable to us that the parvo-temporal-lobe system is especially suited for visual identification and association.

Is the existence of separate pathways an accident of evolution or a useful design principle? Segregating the processing of different types of information into separate pathways might facilitate the interactions between cells carrying the same type of information. It is also much more efficient to carry information about the identity of an object separately from information about its position or motion; otherwise, many more cells are needed to identify specific particular object attributes at every position and/or trajectory.

EVIDENCE THAT THE MAGNO SYSTEM IS DEFECTIVE IN INDIVIDUALS WITH DYSLEXIA

It has been suggested that subjects with dyslexia differ from controls in fast, or phasic, visual information processing (Stein and Walsh

1997). In the primate, fast, transient visual information is carried by the magno subdivision of the visual pathway. The observations that subjects with dyslexia often have poor stereoacuity, visual instability and problems in visual localization, and poor double flash order discrimination are all consistent with a selective deficit in the magnocellular pathway. I hypothesize that at least a subset of people with dyslexia, in particular those with visual disturbances, will show defects in visual functions carried by the magnocellular pathway.

Other sensory and motor systems are also functionally subdivided (Mountcastle 1957; Abeles and Goldstein 1970; Woolsey and Van der Loos 1970), and it is likely that the columnar architecture in these areas, like the visual system, is segregated into fast and slow subdivisions. This is particularly likely in light of the observations of McGuire, Hockfield, and Goldman-Rakic (1989). They found that an antibody, CAT 301, selectively stains the magnocellular subdivision of the visual pathway, from the geniculate through primary and secondary visual cortices up to higher parietal visual areas. They also found that this same antibody stains many other cortical areas, including some somatosensory areas (but not others), a subset of the motor areas, and many other less well-defined areas. Most of these areas differ from areas that do not stain with CAT 301 in that they are heavily myelinated. This suggests that these areas all process information rapidly. Therefore, the neuronal subdivisions involved in the fastest information processing in each modality may share some particular molecular entities.

Dyslexia has been thought to be a very high level, even cognitive, defect because subjects with dyslexia have been shown to do poorly in some auditory, somatosensory, visual, and motor tasks. But Tallal, Stark, and Mellits (1985) found that individuals with dyslexia failed in each of these modalities only in tasks that required very rapid processing of information. It is therefore possible that people with dyslexia have a specific defect in the rapid subdivisions, the magnocellular homologues, of all neuronal systems.

THE PARIETAL LOBE

Because the visual subdivision of the parietal lobe receives its information almost exclusively from the magnocellular pathway (Felleman and Van Essen 1991), its functions are relevant to a discussion of the symptomatology of dyslexia, if dyslexia indeed involves a magnocellular defect. Most of our knowledge on the parietal visual pathway comes from neurological studies of symptoms in people who have suffered damage to the parietal lobe. One of the best descriptions of the results of parietal damage is written by a patient himself, Zasetsky, a Russian soldier in World War II, who had suffered a bullet wound to his left temporo-parieto-occipital area (Luria 1972). Zasetsky describes his vision as being severely disorganized and fractured spatially, though his recognition of individual objects was unimpaired. That is, his spatial visual function was damaged, but his object recognition was not. He had trouble grasping objects that he could plainly see because they would turn out to be to one side or the other of where they appeared to be. He had trouble seeing entire objects or scenes, and could only see one small part at a time. He could not distinguish right from left. Such spatial visual problems are characteristic of patients with parietal lobe damage. Milder spatial problems are common in dyslexia as many people with dyslexia do have problems with left/right reversals. Some individuals with developmental dyslexia have been observed to show left neglect (Stein and Walsh 1997), which is also characteristic of parietal damage (Critchley 1953).

The original idea that dyslexia is a kind of agnosia (Morgan 1896) may be valid to the extent that it represents not a specific agnosia, agnosias being symptomatic of ventral visual system damage (Ungerleider and Mishkin 1982), but rather a kind of simultagnosia in which patients lose the ability to recognize several items at once or to recognize an object based on its being composed of several parts. This inability to recognize objects made up of parts is characteristic of parietal lobe damage (Benito-Leon et al. 1997).

If the parietal system is responsible for motion perception and spatial perception, it is easy to imagine that damage to this system would result in erroneous motion perception and spatial displacements. Zasetsky says the world would "glimmer fitfully and become displaced, making everything appear as if it were in a state of flux." Similarly, individuals with dyslexia commonly complain that words on the printed page jump around, swirl, or flow.

Like many patients with dorsal system damage, Zasetsky could not read, though he could speak and write. He could not even read words he had just written. Thus, a quite specific acquired reading difficulty, alexia with agraphia, can be associated with dorsal-system damage (Benito-Leon et al. 1997) and is consistent with the idea that dyslexia might be a dorsal-system problem.

HOW DO THE VARIOUS VISUAL SYMPTOMS OF DYSLEXIA RELATE TO MAGNO/PARIETAL FUNCTION?

Several papers have suggested explanations for how a magnocellular defect could produce the visual symptomatology of dyslexia.

Breitmeyer (1984) and Williams and LeCluyse (1990) proposed that defective visual masking underlies the visual problems of people with dyslexia. Specifically, they suggest that after each saccade the image from the previous fixation must be erased by backward masking by the magnocellular system; otherwise, the images from each successive fixation pile up, resulting in double images. Stein has suggested that spatial disorganization, as well as failure to erase the image from the previous fixation, is the reason for the double image (Stein and Walsh 1997). The idea that the image from the previous fixation must be erased by backward masking is based on the theory that backward masking results from inhibition of sustained-channel activity by transient-channel activity. However, Macknik and I (1998) have shown that backward masking cannot be explained by transient-on-sustained inhibition, but can more simply be explained by lateral inhibition of transient on-and-off responses. Moreover, parvocellular-channel activity does not, at the level of the geniculate or primary visual cortex, dribble on after stimulus cessation (Livingstone and Hubel 1984), and therefore does not require active inhibition by transient-system activity.

I propose instead that the jumping of text during reading arises from another well-known function of the parietal lobe: The remapping of visual information from retinocentric coordinates to body-centric or real-world-based coordinates. As you move your eyes, the images on your retinas shift correspondingly, yet your perception is that the world is stable. Thus, your retinal images must be remapped, almost instantaneously, as you move your eyes around. There is good evidence that this remapping is likely to be a parietal-lobe function (Andersen and Zipser 1988). To separate the functions of object identification from object position is very efficient informationally because information about object identity, carried by the ventral pathway, can be position invariant, while the positional information can be object invariant. I specifically propose that the symptom of words jumping around on the page during reading occurs because the identification of words is carried by the ventral pathway, but the spatial remapping that must occur with each saccade is done by the dorsal pathway, which is not fast enough to remap the image as fast as the eyes move during reading.

How do the visual problems, which I hope I have provided an explanation for, relate to the phonological problems also known to occur in dyslexia? One explanation is that both the visual system and the auditory system are subdivided into fast and slow subdivisions and that it is the fast subdivision of both modalities (and perhaps the other modalities as well) that are affected in dyslexia. A global fast-system defect might arise from effects on common proteins or damage during common developmental stages. However, it is known that severe otitis media during early childhood can lead to language problems and then to dyslexia (Merzenich and Jenkins 1995). It is not known, however, whether visual symptoms are experienced by people who are dyslexic due to otitis media during childhood. It would be interesting to know, because if those particular individuals do experience visual problems during reading, it would suggest that sufficient competent reading experience is necessary to train the visual system for reading. If individuals with dyslexia who have had otitis media do not experience visual problems, it would suggest that in others with dyslexia who do experience both visual symptoms and phonological problems, those symptoms must arise from a common developmental insult.

Some of the "different abilities" of people with dyslexia may arise from the proposed differences in temporal processing. For example, slightly diminished spatial processing may contribute to artistic abilities by making it easier to render a 3-dimensional world into 2 dimensions. Most of us have great trouble drawing a chair because our perception of its 3-D shape interferes with our ability to draw it in two dimensions. People who already see the characteristic somewhat flatted might have less trouble. Similarly, music involves slower auditory transitions than speech; so people with dyslexia might be particularly perceptive of musical elements. Lastly, one of the slowest elements of speech is prosody, which carries emotional content. It would, therefore, not be surprising if individuals with dyslexia might be particularly talented in fields like drama in which the emotional content of speech is critical.

EDITOR'S COMMENTS

From the initial visual sensation, the visual system divides signals into two categories. Large cells are involved in motion, depth, high contrast and night "perception," while the small cells react to color and low contrast images along pathways that are physiologically slower. This parcelization of function exists throughout the visual system from the retina, through the geniculate nucleus, to the parietal cortex.

Dr. Livingstone has implicated a reduced efficiency of the older magnocellular (large cell) system in at least one form of dyslexia involving difficulty with script detection. This script detection disadvantage may, however, provide advantages for other skills, as she suggests, in the visual and performing arts. In the decades ahead, it will be interesting to see whether all forms of dyslexic syndrome share this same property of magnocellular inefficiency and underdevelopment. The question of what other traits separate affected individuals will also be of interest.

—DDD

REFERENCES

Abeles, M., and Goldstein, M. H., Jr. 1970. Functional architecture in cat primary auditory cortex: Columnar organization and organization according to depth. *Journal of Neuro Physiology* 33:172–87.

Andersen, R. A., and Zipser, D. 1988. The role of the posterior parietal cortex in coordinate transformations for visual-motor integration. *Canadian Journal of Physiological Pharmacology* 66:488–501.

Benito-Leon, J., Sanchez-Suarez, C., Diaz-Guzman, J., and Martinez-Salio, A. 1997. Pure alexia could not be a disconnection syndrome. *Neurology* 49:305–6.

Bodamer, J. 1947. Die prosop-agnosie. *Archiv. Fur Psychiatr. Nervenkr.* 179:6–53.

Breitmeyer, B. 1984. *Visual Masking: An Integrative Approach.* Oxford: Clarendon Press.

Campbell, F. W., and Maffei, L. 1981. The influence of spatial frequency and contrast on the perception of moving patterns. *Vision Research* 21:713–21.

Casagrande, V. A., Beck, P. D., Condo, G. J., Lachica, E. A. 1990. *Invest. Ophthal. and Visual Science* 31:1945–? .

Cavanagh, P., Boeglin, J., and Favreau, O. E. 1985. Perception of motion and equiluminous kinematograms. *Perception* 14:151–62.

Cavanagh, P., and Leclerc, Y. 1985. *Invest. Ophthal. and Visual and Supplement* (Supplement) 26:282–??.

Crichtley, M. 1953. *The Parietal Lobes.* London: Arnold.

Damasio, A., Yamada, T., Damasio, H., Corbett, J., and McKee, J. 1980. Central achromatopsia: Behavioral, anatomic, and physiologic aspects. *Neurology* 30:1064–71.

Felleman, D. J., and Van Essen, D. C. 1991. Distributed hierarchical processing in the primate cerebral cortex. *Cerebral Cortex* 1:1–47.

Guillery, R. W. 1979. *Development and Chemical Specificity of Neurons (Progess in Brain Research)*, Vol.51, eds. M. Cuenod, G. W. Kreutzberg, and F. E. Bloom. Amsterdam: Elsevier/North-Holland Biomedical Press.

Ives, H. E. 1923. A chart of the flicker photometer. *Journal of the Optical Society of America, Rev. Sci. Instr* 7:363–75.

Livingstone, M. S., and Hubel, D. H. 1984. Anatomy and physiology of a color system in the primate visual cortex. *Journal of Neuroscience* 4:309–56.

Livingstone, M. S., and Hubel, D. H. 1987. Psychophysical evidence for separate channels for the perception of form, color, movement, and depth. *Journal of Neuroscience* 7:3416–68.

Luria, A. R. 1972. *The Man With a Shattered World.* New York: Basic Books.

Macknik, S., and Livingstone, M. 1998. Neuronal correlates of visibility and invisibility in the primate visual system. *Nature Neuroscience* 1:144–9.

McGuire, P. K., Hockfield, S., and Goldman-Rakic, P. S. 1989. Distribution of cat-301 immunoreactivity in the frontal and parietal lobes of the macaque monkey. *Journal of Comparative Neurology* 288:280–96.

Merzenich, M. M. and Jenkins, W. M. 1995. *Maturational Windows and Adult Plasticity*, eds. B. Julesz and I. Kovacs. New York: Addison-Wesley.

Morgan, W. P. 1896. A Case of Congenital Word Blindness. *British Medical Journal* 2:1378.

Mountcastle, V. B. 1957. Modality and topographic properties of neurons of cat's somatic sensory cortex. *Journal of Neurophysiology* 20:408–34.

Orton, S. T. 1937. *Reading, Writing, and Speech Problems in Children.* New York: Norton.

Sherman, S. M. 1985. In *Progress in Psychobiology and Physiological Psychology Vol. II.*, eds. J. M. Sprague and A. N. Epstein. New York: Academic Press.

Stein, J. and Walsh, V. 1997. To see but not to read: The magnocellular theory of dyslexia. *Trends in Neurosciences* 20:147–52.

Tallal, P., Stark, R. E., and Mellits, E. D. 1985. Identification of language-impaired children on the basis of rapid perception and production skills. *Brain and Language* 25:314–22.

Ungerleider, L. G., and Mishkin, M. 1982. In *Analysis of Visual Behavior*, eds. D. G. Ingle, M. A. Goodale, and R. J. Q. Mansfield. Cambridge, MA: MIT Press.

Vellutino, F. R., Steger, B. M., Moyer, S. C., Harding, C. J., and Niles, J. A. 1977. Has the perceptual deficit hypothesis led us astray? *Journal of Learning Disabilities* 10:375–85.

Williams, M. C., and LeCluyse, K. 1990. Perceptual consequences of a temporal processing deficit in reading disabled children. *Journal of the American Optometrical Society Association* 61:111–21.

Wolpert, I. 1924. Die Simultanagnosie-Storung Der Gesamtaussassung. *Z. Gest. Neurol. Psychiat.* 93:397–425.

Woolsey, T. A. and Van der Loos, H. 1970. The structural organization of layer IV in the somatosensory region (SI) of mouse cerebral cortex. The description of a cortical field composed of discreet cytoarchitectonic units. *Brain Research* 17:205–42.

Zihl, J., Von Cramon, D., and Mai, N. 1983. Selective disturbance of movement vision after bilateral brain damage. *Brain* 106:313–40.

Chapter • 6

Moving Research from the Laboratory to Clinics and Classrooms

Paula Tallal, Michael Merzenich,
William M. Jenkins, and Steve L. Miller

The role that central auditory processing plays in the development of phonological systems has been a topic of increased research concentration. It has been increasingly documented that phonological systems are developed through exposure to the native language (Kuhl et al. 1997). As infants are exposed to a continuous speech stream from the environment, they must parse the incoming acoustic signal into consistent, replicable chunks that will come to represent the phonemes of their language(s). Clearly infants do not know which language or languages they will be exposed to. Rather, neural firing patterns that recur most frequently in the incoming speech stream will come to be represented as the building blocks— phonemes—of the native language.

Neurophysiologists have mapped the features of the sensory world at the single cell level. This work has shown that, within each sensory modality, the features that represent the physical world come to be mapped neuronally in a highly organized fashion. For example, in the auditory modality, there is a tonotopic representation of frequency in which the single cells that fire to a specific frequency reside physically next to the cells that fire to the next higher frequency, in a continuous manner throughout the frequency range (Clopton,

Winfield, and Flammino 1974; Pantev et al. 1993). That sensory maps must be learned from environmental exposure is evidenced by neurophysiological research showing the effects of sensory deprivation (Neville 1985). Although it was previously thought that environmental exposure had to occur during critical periods of development, and that once established, these maps were immutable, more recent research has challenged that perspective. The detailed neuronal connections to and between cortical neurons are being continually remodeled by our experiences. The phenomenological nature of those changes have been documented by numerous experiments in which the cortex has been engaged to change by the induction of new experiences or by the training of new perceptual, cognitive or motor skills. For example, Jenkins, Merzenich, and colleagues have recently conducted a series of studies in adult monkeys and have shown that the sensory map for the fingers was significantly altered through training (Jenkins et al. 1990). Recanzone, Schreiner, and Merzenich (1993) showed a similar result in primary auditory cortex. These physiological changes in the neuronal sensory map are the physical instantiation of sensory learning in the brain.

What aspects of learning are necessary to drive these physiological changes? Behavioral training studies coupled with physiological recording at the level of a single cell show that there are several components of the learning process that are critical. First, the animal must attend closely to features of a sensory task. Second, in order for attention to be maintained, the animal must be able to perform the task at a high level of accuracy. If the task is too difficult, learning cannot be achieved and changes in the sensory map do not occur. Behavior must be reinforced in a highly consistent and rewarding manner to maintain motivation and drive learning through corrective feedback. Highly consistent, repetitive input must be given over an intense period of time so that consistent patterns of neuronal activation occur repetitively, building specific stimulation patterns to "represent" this input from the environment in the brain. Finally, having established a behavior that can be responded to accurately and consistently, learning can be driven most effectively by systematically increasing the difficulty of the task as performance improves. Merzenich and colleagues have referred to these features of the learning process as "scientific learning principles" and have demonstrated that neuroplasticity at the neuronal level accompanies behavioral learning (Merzenich and Jenkins, 1998).

As speech, at its essence, is a complex sensory signal, these neurophysiological sensory mapping studies tell us a great deal about how the brain may come to represent speech. Think about the processes that occur in the brains of infants as they experience the ongoing acoustic waveform of speech. Most theories of language development begin with the assumption that language is innate, with no need to train it explicitly. However, each language has its own set of phonemes. Because infants have no way of knowing which native language they will be born into, the phonemes of their native language must be learned from environmental exposure and represented as distinct firing patterns in the auditory cortex. But how does this representation occur? As is the case in all other sensory modalities, the complex acoustic information within phonemes is broken down into its distinct physical features, each of which is represented in detail in the auditory system (Kraus et al. 1995).

Hebbian neuroplasticity (Hebb 1949) proposes a mechanism by which learning-induced "selection" of behaviorally important inputs that excite neurons nearly simultaneously "bind" together to form perceptually relevant representations. When a complex signal occurs, all of the neurons that are activated by this complex series of features, *per unit time*, fire simultaneously. According to Hebb (1949), repeated exposure to consistent sensory input will result in that input being neurally represented. The likelihood that a particular pattern will come to be represented increases with each additional exposure and firing pattern ensemble.

It would be a simple matter to understand how the individual phonemes come to be represented in this way if they occurred one at a time, in an invariant acoustic pattern, with distinct boundaries separating the end of one from the beginning of another. Unfortunately, none of this is the case. Rather, speech occurs in an ongoing acoustic stream (waveform) without distinct boundaries. The acoustic patterns produced by the articulators differ from utterance to utterance, especially within different phoneme contexts (Liberman et al. 1967). Further, in ongoing speech there is no distinct boundary that tells the brain where one phoneme ends and the next one begins. In learning to represent the acoustic world of speech, the brain must segment an ongoing speech stream in chunks of time, and then seek consistencies in the neural firing patterns that result from these segmented chunks. Consistencies can be derived from chunking in both smaller and larger units. Smaller unit chunking (in tens of milliseconds) will result in representations consistent with individual phonemes within a language. Chunking within a larger time period (hundreds of milliseconds) will equally result in consistent firing patterns, but in this case the firing patterns will be consistent with syllable level representations rather than phoneme representations. Thus, speech may be represented in fine grain phonemic precision and/or more course grain syllabic precision, based on temporal parameters of segmentation applied to the ongoing speech stream.

There is now substantial evidence that many individuals with language learning impairments chunk information only at the longer (hundreds of milliseconds) time period across the life span. Table I lists studies demonstrating this finding when non-verbal stimuli are used and table II lists studies using verbal stimuli. Numerous studies have shown that individuals with established oral and subsequent written language learning problems have been shown to require hundreds of milliseconds between non-verbal rapidly successive sensory inputs to discriminate or sequence them (see table 1). Figure 1 shows that normally developing 6- to 8- year-old children required only ten milliseconds between two 75 millisecond tones to respond at 80% correct or better. Children with language learning problems required hundreds of milliseconds to respond at the same level of accuracy (Tallal and Piercy 1973a,b). Subsequent studies indicated that this difference in processing rate occurs across sensory modalities (auditory, visual, somatosensory) (Tallal and Piercy 1974; see Farmer and Klein 1995 for review), and also occurs in the processing and production of speech (Stark and Tallal 1979; Tallal and Stark, 1981; see Tallal, Miller, and Fitch 1993 for review). For example, as seen in figure 2, syllables incorporating acoustic changes that differed one from the other across hundreds of milliseconds, such as the vowels /a/ and /ae/ were easily discriminated by children with language learning problems. However, syllables like /ba/ versus /da/, that can only be discriminated based on more fine grain, brief acoustic distinctions, that change rapidly in succession within the tens of millisecond time period, are less discriminable (Tallal and Piercy 1974; Tallal and Stark1981). Furthermore, extending the duration of brief, rapidly changing acoustic *intrasyllabic* cues, has proven highly effective in improving speech discrimination in these children (Tallal and Piercy 1975).

Table I.   Studies that Demonstrate that Individuals with Language Learning Impairment have Deficits In processing Brief, Rapidly Successive Acoustic Cues in Non-Verbal Stimuli

Lowe and Campbell 1965	Tallal 1980	Hari and Kiesla 1996
Stark 1967	McCrosky and Kidder 1980	Benasich and Tallal 1996
Aten and Davis 1968	Tallal et al 1981	McAnnally and Stein 1997
Griffith 1972	Thal and Barone 1983	Wright et al 1997
Tallal and Piercy 1973a	Robin et al 1989	Protopappas et al 1997
Tallal and Piercy 1973b	Stefanatos et al 1989	Llinas et al 1998
Kracke 1975	Lincoln et al 1992	Nagarajan et al 1998
Lea 1975	Tomblin et al 1992	Witton et al 1998
Tallal et al 1976	Neville et al 1993	Ribary et al 1999
Haggerty and Stamm 1978		

Table II.   Studies that Demonstrate that Individuals with Language Learning Impairment have Deficits In processing Brief, Rapidly Successive Acoustic Cues in Verbal Stimuli

McReynolds 1966	Tallal et al 1980a, b	Reed 1989
Rosenthal 1972	Tallal and Stark 1981	Sussman 1993
Tallal and Piercy 1974	Godfrey et al 1981	Kraus et al 1995
Tallal and Piercy 1975	Alexander and Frost 1982	Kraus et al 1996
Henderson 1978	Werker and Teas 1987	Stark and Heinz 1996
Thibodeau and Sussman 1979	Elliott and Hammer 1988	
Frumkin and Rapin 1980	Elliott et al 1989	

A recent series of studies has demonstrated that segmentation rates in infancy correlate very highly and significantly with subsequent language development (Benasich and Tallal 1996; Spitz, Tallal, and Benasich 1997). For these studies, the auditory temporal integration threshold of infants born into families with a family history of language learning problems was assessed at 6 months and compared to that of infants born into families with no history of language or learning problems. Figure 3 shows the significant difference in sensory integration threshold obtained in a family history positive child as compared to a family history negative child.

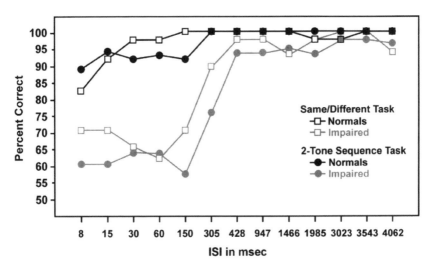

Figure 1.   Controls and impaired children performed same/different and 2-tone sequence tasks. Percent correct is plotted as a function of ISI. Duration of complex tones = 75 ms (tone 1 fundamental = 100 Hz, tone 2 fundamental = 305 Hz). (Tallal and Piercy 1973a)

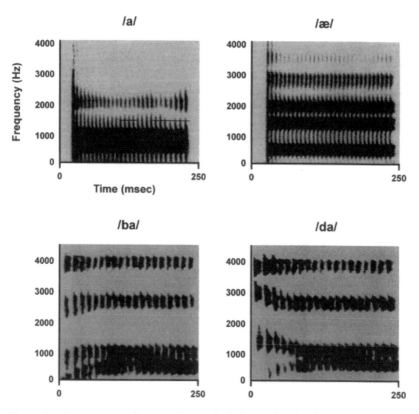

Figure 2.   Spectrogram for vowel stimuli /a/ and /ae/ and consonant-vowel (CV) syllables /ba/ and /da/.

The familial nature of language learning problems has been estab-lished in a number of studies (Tallal, Ross, and Curtis 1989; Gilger et al. 1994; Spitz et al. 1997). An autosomal dominant mode of genetic transmission appears to be most consistent with these data. As such, every infant born into a family history positive family will have a 50% chance of also having a language learning problem. Benasich and Tallal (1996; 1998), found that, at 6 months of age approximately half of the infants in the family history positive group had temporal inte-gration thresholds in the hundreds of millisecond time period, whereas the other half had integration thresholds in the tens of mil-lisecond time period, similar to the thresholds found in the family his-tory negative infants. These infants are being followed prospectively and their language development is being assessed longitudinally using the MacArthur Child Development Inventory (Fenson et al. 1993). Importantly, the auditory temporal integration thresholds es-tablished at 6 months of age have proven to be highly predictive of

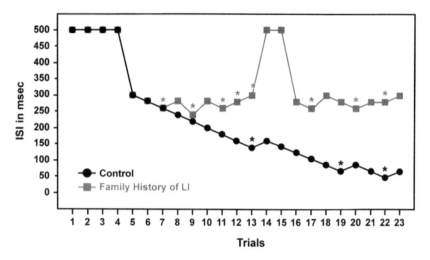

Figure 3. This task is an adaptive two-alternate forced choice task using head turn responses. Plots of two infants (control and family history of language impairment) show ISI for different trials. Following a series of correct responses at 500 ms, ISI is decreased to 300 ms. Inter-stimulus intervals are decreased for correct responses and increased for incorrect responses (*) in 20 ms steps while ISI remains the same for no response. Probe trials are delivered at 500 ms if there are three consecutive incorrect responses. The probes verify the child is still performing the task.

subsequent receptive and expressive language development. That is, those infants with slow temporal integration rates are developing language more slowly than those with more rapid integration rates (Benasich and Tallal, 1998). A similar finding has been reported by Trehub and Henderson (1996) with normally developing children, using a measure of gap detection thresholds.

It is hypothesized that children who can segment speech only in larger time chunks will have considerable difficulty being able to learn to break words into the finer grain phonetic units important for developing phonological awareness skills for establishing letter sound correspondence (phonics) rules. To investigate this hypothesis, the processing rate of individuals with dyslexia has been studied. Tallal (1980) was the first to show a striking correlation between rates of acoustic processing of tones presented rapidly in succession and error rates for reading nonsense words in children with dyslexia. More recently, Whitton et al (1998) reported a similar finding using acoustic modulating tones as well as visual transient stimuli in adults with a history of developmental language learning problems. Similar findings have also been reported for adults with dyslexia on several psychoacoustic measures (Protopapas, Ahissar, and Merzenich 1997).

These deficits in responding to rapidly successive stimuli also have been demonstrated physiologically in recent studies using magnetoencephalography (MEG) (Nagarajan et al. 1998). In this study the neurophysiological MEG response to two brief tone pips presented with differing inter-stimulus intervals (ISIs) was recorded. Results for normal adults showed that two distinct neural responses occur for each of two distinct, successive acoustic tone pips with only a 50 msec ISI. However, the brain's response to the same stimuli is distinctly different for dyslexic subjects. Although the neural response to the first tone pip is initiated normally, this response is prolonged well into the period in which the second response should have, but does not, occur. These results demonstrate that when brief, rapidly successive sensory information converge in the nervous system within tens of milliseconds, these signals are not processed normally by most subjects with dyslexia.

These results, taken in aggregate, demonstrate that certain individuals begin life as slow sensory processors and this information processing rate constraint continues throughout the lifespan. In addition to slow processing rates, these same individuals are generally characterized by both oral and written language deficits.

Leonard (1998) recently published a comprehensive review of the literature on specific language impairment (SLI). He concluded his book by proposing an integrating theory that best seems to account for the acoustic, perceptual, conceptual, neuroscientific and linguistic data in this field. He concludes that the majority of data, regardless of scientific approach used, are parsimonious, with a general information processing constraint that specifically affects the *rate* of information processing across sensory modalities, and affects both verbal and non-verbal information processing.

If infants destined to be slow language learners are characterized early in life by a basic processing constraint in the rate at which incoming sensory information is segmented and represented, this should have important implications for remediation strategies. Recently, Tallal et al (1996) and Merzenich et al (1996) hypothesized that the "scientific learning principles," which had been shown in studies with monkeys to drive neuroplasticity, might be adapted to ameliorate the rate processing constraints of children with language learning problems. Specifically, a hierarchy of computer-based training exercises (now called Fast ForWord™) were developed to (1) attempt to drive neural processing of rapidly successive acoustic stimuli to faster and faster rates and (2) to improve speech perception and language comprehension by providing training exercises utilizing speech stimuli that had been acoustically modified to extend temporally and to amplitude-enhance brief, rapidly successive (phonetically non-salient) intrasyllabic cues. Seven training exercises were developed in the form of computer games. The exercises were programmed to be individually adaptive. The goal was to find, for each child, a level of acoustic and linguistic functioning he or she could respond to correctly at a high rate of accuracy, through the use of acoustically modified speech. Once established, the exercises were programmed to change adaptively trial by trial, based on each individual child's responses. That is, trials got more difficult (moving toward more rapid, natural speech) following correct responses or more simplified (slower and more acoustically modified) following incorrect responses. The goal was to move the individual child from a reliance on the acoustically modified speech toward the ability to process more and more complex linguistic information with rapidly successive, *natural* speech. Similarly, adaptive training was also undertaken to effect temporal integration thresholds directly for rapidly successive acoustic sweep tones. The goal was to drive each child into the normal processing rate of tens of milliseconds through adaptive training.

Initial laboratory studies demonstrated dramatic success with a prototype of this training method. (Merzenich et al. 1996; Tallal et al. 1996). The results seen in figure 4 showed that intensive daily training (approximately two hours a day, five days a week, for four weeks) resulted in highly significant improvements in temporal integration rates (which were improved fourfold), speech discrimination, language processing, and grammatical understanding (which improved on average by 1.5 to 2 years). This controlled laboratory study demonstrated the specificity of this training method. A control group, who received essentially identical linguistic training that used natural, unmodified speech and who played visual computer games that were not temporally adaptive, showed significantly poorer outcomes.

Based on these initial promising results from controlled laboratory studies, two large scale field trials have been conducted to assess the efficacy of the Fast ForWord™ training program in clinical and educational settings. The purpose of the first trial was to determine whether the dramatic efficacy that was demonstrated in the laboratory could be replicated in clinics and classrooms under the supervision of clinicians and teachers (rather than trained researchers). This is a very important essential first step in the process of moving research from the laboratory into clinics and classrooms. In order to assure consistency in program delivery, data collection and analysis, and quality control across multiple sites and long distances, the adaptive training programs were created in the form of a CD-ROM that is activated and monitored through data exchange over the Internet. A second randomized control trial is currently underway in public schools.

The first field trial included over 500 children identified by 60 professionals at 35 clinical or educational sites. Clinicians were instructed to use standardized speech and language tests to include children

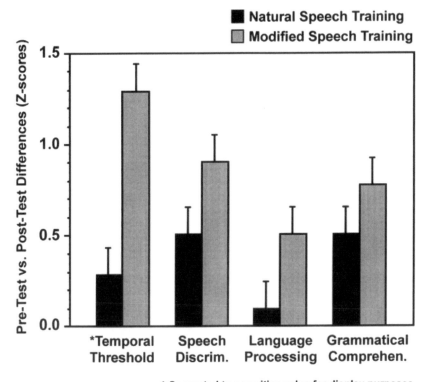

* Converted to a positive value for display purposes

Figure 4. Difference z scores (post-training minus pre-training are shown for subjects with language learning impairment (LLI) in study 2 who received speech and language training with either acoustically modified or natural speech. Difference z scores are presented for measures of temporal threshold, speech discrimination (GFW), language processing (Token Test), and grammatical comprehension (CYCLE-R). To facilitate group comparisons across each of the measures, we converted raw scores to z scores on the basis of the pre-training performance of all subjects on each individual test. Mean and standard error values for each measure demonstrate that significantly larger improvements were achieved by the LLI children receiving the acoustically modified speech training (black bars) as compared with the performance improvements recorded for the subjects receiving natural speech training (white bars). The temporal threshold values were converted to positive values for display purposes. (Adapted from Tallal et al. 1996)

who were at least one or more standard deviations below the mean in central auditory processing, speech discrimination, and/or language comprehension. Clinicians were encouraged to select a battery of standardized speech, language and central auditory processing tests that they used most commonly in their practice. Case history records indicated that children who met these study criteria had one or more of the following diagnostic classifications: specific language impairment, attention deficit disorder (ADHD), pervasive developmental disability (PDD), autism, central auditory processing disorder (CAPD), or dyslexia.

The goals of the first clinical trial were to determine (1) whether or not the results obtained in the laboratory could be replicated by the clinicians who most often treat children with language/learning problems, (2) whether the result obtained in the laboratory with SLI subjects, would generalize to a broader population of children with a variety of speech, oral and written language, and/or central auditory processing disorders, and (3) whether efficacy could be obtained using the wide variety of standardized speech, language and central auditory processing tests that are most commonly used clinically. Results are reported in detail in Tallal and Merzenich (1997) as well as in Merzenich et al (in press).

A summary of results are shown in figures 5, 6, and 7, comparing pre-Fast ForWord training standardized test scores to post-test scores for each child. Figures 5 and 6 demonstrate that the laboratory results

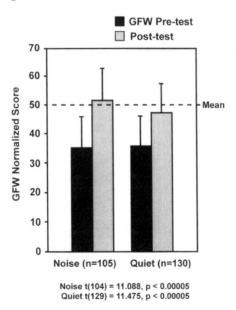

Figure 5.   Shows pre- vs. post-Fast ForWord training for the Goldman Fristoe Woodcock (GFW) test of auditory discrimination. the test is normed for presentation either in quiet or noise. The group of children in this study, assessed with the GFW, demonstrated mean test scores approximately 1.5 *SD*s below the mean at pre-test. Post-test scores demonstrated a significant improvement in both the quiet and noise conditions *p* < 0.00005) after training, with average scores approaching or exceeding the mean.

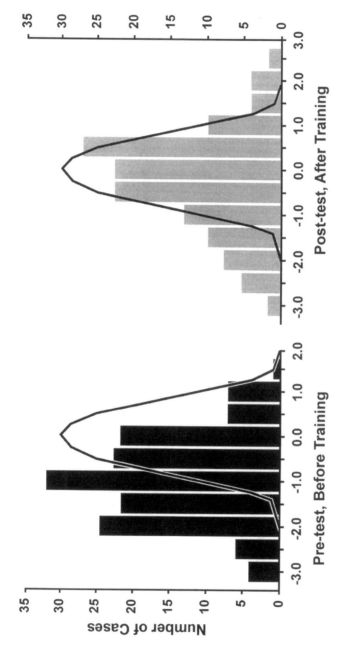

Figure 6.   Shows pe- and post-Fast ForWord training for the TOLD I:1 and P:2 combined in terms of z scores The normal distribution for the TOLD is shown as a black bell-shaped curve. The number of individual cases scoring in each z score bin are plotted before and after training. Before training, 70 children (54%) scored 1 or more SD below the mean and 19 scored at or above the mean on this test. After training, only 33 children (26%) scored 1 or more SD below the mean while 54 children (42%) scored at or above the mean. Before training group (mean = 84.89, SD = 13.37) and the after training group (mean = 95.35, SD = 14.96) differed significantly (t(128) = 15.938. p = .00005). (Adapted from Tallal and Merzenich 1997)

were replicated in clinics and classrooms. That is, significant change from pre- to post-testing performance was obtained in the target skill areas of central auditory processing, speech discrimination, and language comprehension. Furthermore, results showed that efficacy may be extended to include improved expressive language abilities as well. Overall, the results of this field trial demonstrated that approximately 90% of children who complied with the study protocol showed significantly improved performance (at least one standardized deviation change from pre-test to post-test) on one or more standardized speech, language and/or auditory processing measure, regardless of the precise clinical measure selected by each professional.

There was considerable variability among children as to the degree and pattern of improvements they made across domains, as would be expected, based on the variety of symptomatology and clinical classifications of this large heterogeneous group of children with language learning problems. Figure 7 shows, however, that significant efficacy was obtained for a much broader group of children than had been included in the initial laboratory studies. Furthermore, neither the number of children showing significant improvement or the degree of improvement from pre- to post-test was found to be based on the child's clinical diagnostic classification(s) (autism, PDD, ADHD, CAPD, SLI, dyslexia), age, gender, or degree of impairment. On average, the language skills of children who completed the protocol improved by a year and a half following six weeks of training.

Clearly both the controlled laboratory and field study results indicate the immediate efficacy of this new training approach. However, it is also important to determine the longer term effectiveness of this brief, but intensive training. Figure 8 shows follow-up results for the SLI subjects who participated in the original controlled laboratory study (Bedi et al. 1999). This graph shows that training results were sustained at follow up at both 6 weeks and 6 months, without additional training. Children who received training in the controlled laboratory studies not only maintained their advances as compared to their matched controls, but continued to improve at an accelerated rate during the three months following the conclusion of the program. These significant improvements and group difference were maintained to 6 months. Longer term follow up is currently in progress.

This report outlines the steps we have taken, thus far, to integrate physiological and cognitive neuroscience studies and to develop new diagnostic and treatment approaches for individuals with language learning problems. Although these studies raise many new questions, it is our hope that this line of research will lead to improved diagnostic, clinical and educational programs for individuals affected with developmental language learning problems.

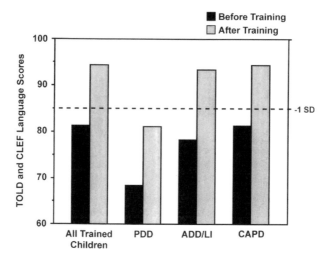

Figure 7. Shows TOLD and CELF Language Quotients for all children assessed with these test batteries at pre-test as well as post-Fast ForWord training. Scores are shown for all children with language impairments (LI) combined; as well as for LI children diagnosed as having pervasive developmental disorder (PDD), or with co-morbid diagnoses of attention deficit disorder (ADD), or central auditory processing disorder (CAPD). Although the degree of language deficit differed at pre-test among these groups of children (with children diagnosed as PDD having the most severe language disorder and CAPD having the least severe), there were no significant differences in the magnitude of improvement across groups achieved with training. All groups were 1 or more *SD* below the mean at pre-test and showed significant improvement (*p* < .0001) from pre- to post-testing. Although the PDD group improved significantly following training, they still remained more than 1 *SD* below the mean following training, based on these test batteries. The children with language impairments co-morbid for ADD or CAPD entered the study with pre-test scores more than 1 *SD* below the mean, while their average post-test scores approached the normal median. (Adapted from Tallal and Merzenich 1997)

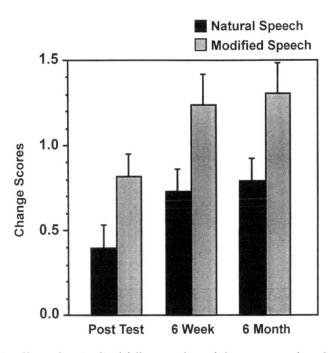

Figure 8.   Shows longitudinal follow-up data of change scores from baseline: immediately after 4 weeks of training (post-test); 6 weeks after training was completed and 6 months after training. Change scores are shown for children receiving language training using *modified speech* and adaptive computer games compared to a matched control group of children who received the same language training, but with *natural speech* and non-adaptive computer games. The results immediately following the training (post-test) have been published previously in *Science* (Tallal et al 1996). The modified speech group showed significantly greater improvement than the natural speech group ($p < .015$). Follow-up testing 6 weeks and 6 months after training shows that both groups continue to improve, with the difference between the groups continuing to be significant. These results address one of the most frequently asked questions about this new training procedure—do the gains last? These results demonstrate that not only do they last, but children receiving training continue to improve even after training is completed. Furthermore, the additional significant benefit of providing the training using the modified speech and adaptive temporal training is maintained over 6 months following training. Other frequently asked questions pertaining to the effects of both test-retest reliability over short periods, as well as the effects of regression toward the mean, on the interpretation of these data can also be addressed by these longitudinal follow-up data. As groups were initially matched on degree of receptive language deficit, performance IQ, and age, and both groups received the same longitudinal testing schedule, significant group differences in change scores at three different testing points demonstrate that these results cannot be attributed to these other factors. (Adapted from Bedi 1999)

EDITOR'S COMMENTS

Dr. Tallal and her colleagues emphasize the, perhaps, cardinal impor-tance of slow processing rate as a key deficit in language and reading disorders observed several times since her initial report in the mid 1970s. As Livingstone has shown elsewhere in this book, slow visual processing accompanies the slowed auditory processing deficit ob-served by Tallal et al. Both of these observations, as well as those on motor execution mentioned by Voeller elsewhere in this book, in-volved non-verbal processing. The effects on both verbal and nonver-bal function may explain why the intervention conceived by Tallal and Merzenich additionally might benefit non-verbal developmental disorders, a thesis still to be proved. The rigor of the Fast ForWord™ program and the Merzenich persistent plasticity hypothesis should re-inforce all teachers and clinicians to persist in their treatment, as re-programming of brain function may be possible when the parameters are consistently reinforced and scientifically defined.

—DDD

REFERENCES

Alexander, D. W., and Frost, B. P. 1982. Decelerated synthesized speech as a means of shaping speed of auditory processing of children with delayed language. *Perceptual and Motor Skills* 55:783–92.

Aten, J., and Davis, J. 1968. Disturbance in the perception of auditory se-quence in children with minimal cerebral dysfunction. *Journal of Speech and Hearing Research* 11:236–45.

Bedi, G., Tallal, P., Miller, S., and Byma, G. 1999. Efficacy of neuroscience-based training for receptive language and auditory discrimination deficits in language-learning impaired children: A follow up study. Paper pre-sented at Society for Cognitive Neuroscience, Washington, DC.

Benasich, A. A., and Tallal, P. 1996. Auditory temporal processing thresholds, habituation, and recognition memory over the first year. *Infant Behavior and Development* 19:339–57.

Benasich, A. A., and Tallal, P. 1998. Infant processing of auditory temporal in-formation: Links to family history and later language outcome. *Society for Neuroscience Abstracts*, Los Angeles, CA.

Clopton, B. M., Winfield, J. A., and Flammino, F. J. 1974. Tonotopic organiza-tion: Review and analysis. *Brain Research* 76:1–20.

Elliott, L., and Hammer, M. 1988. Longitudinal changes in auditory discrimi-nation in normal children and children with language-learning problems. *Journal of Speech and Hearing Disorders* 53:467–74.

Elliott, L. L., Hammer, M. A., and Scholl, M. E. 1989. Fine-Grained Auditory Discrimination in Normal Children and Children with Language-Learning Problems. *Journal of Speech and Hearing Research* 32:112–19.

Farmer, M., and Klein, R. M. 1995. The evidence for temporal processing deficit linked to dyslexia: A review. *Psychonomic Bulletin and Review* 2(4): 460–93.

Fenson, L., Dale, P. S., Reznick, J. S., Thal, D., Bates, E., Hartung, J. P., Pethick, S., and Reilly, J. S. 1993. *Technical Manual for the MacArthur Communicative Development Inventory*. San Diego: Singular Publishing Group.

Frumkin, B., and Rapin, I. 1980. Perception of vowels and consonant-vowels of varying duration in language impaired children. *Neuropsychologia* 18:443–54.

Gilger, J. W., Borecki, I. B., DeFries, J. C., and Pennington, B. F. 1994. Commingling and segregation analysis of reading performance in families of normal reading probands. *Behavior Genetics* 24(4):345–55.

Godfrey, J. J., Syrdal-Lasky, A. K., Millay, K. K., and Knox, J. 1981. Performance of dyslexic children on speech perception tests. *Journal of Experimental Child Psychology* 32(3):401–24.

Griffith, D. 1972. *Developmental Aphasia: An Introduction*. London: Invalid Children Aid Association.

Haggerty, R., and Stamm, J. 1978. Dichotic auditory fusion levels in children with learning disabilities. *Neuropsychologia* 16:349–60.

Hari, R., and Kiesila, P. 1996. Deficit of temporal auditory processing in dyslexic adults. *Neuroscience Letters* 205:138–40.

Hebb, D. O. 1949. *The Organization of Behavior: A Neuropsychological Theory*. New York: Wiley.

Henderson, B. 1978. Older language impaired children's processing of rapidly changing acoustic signals. Paper presented at the American Speech-Language-Hearing Association, San Francisco: CA. November.

Jenkins, W. M., Merzenich, M. M., Ochs, M. T., Allard, T., and Guic, R. E. 1990. Functional reorganization of primary somatosensory cortex in adult owl monkeys after behaviorally controlled tactile stimulation. *Journal of Neurophysiology* 63:82–104.

Kracke, I. 1975. Perception of rhythmic sequences by receptive aphasic and deaf children. *British Journal of Disorders of Communication* 10:43–51.

Kraus, N., McGee, T., Carrell, T. D., and Sharma, A. 1995. Neurophysiologic bases of speech discrimination. *Ear and Hearing* USA:

Kraus, N., McGee, T. J., Carrell, T. D., Zecker, S. G., Nicol, T. G., and Koch, D. B. 1996. Auditory neurophysiologic responses and discrimination deficits in children with learning problems. *Science* 273:971–73.

Kuhl, P. K., Andruski, J. E., Chistovich, I. A., Chistovich, L. A., Kozhevnikova, E. V., Ryskina, V. L., Stolyarova, E. I., Sundberg, U., and Francisco, L. 1997. Cross-language analysis of phonetic units in language addressed to infants. *Science* 277:684–86.

Lea, J. 1975 An investigation into the association between rhythmic ability and language ability in a group of children with severe speech and language disorders. Unpublished Master's Thesis, University of London.

Leonard, L. B. 1998. *Children with Specific Language Impairment*. Cambridge: MIT Press.

Liberman, A. M., Cooper, F. S., Shankweiler, D. P.,and Studdert-Kennedy, M. 1967. Perception of the speech code. *Psychological Review* 74(6):431–61.

Lincoln, A., Dickstein, P., Courchesne, E. R. E., and Tallal, P. 1992. Auditory processing abilities in non-retarded adolescents and young adults with developmental receptive language disorder and autism. *Brain and Language* 43:613–22.

Llinas, R., Ribary, U., and Tallal, P. 1998. Dyschronic language-based learning disability. In *Basic Mechanisms in Cognition and Language*, ed. C. von Euler. Stockholm: Wenner-Gren International.

Lowe, A., and Campbell, R. 1965. Temporal discrimination in aphasic and normal children. *Journal of Speech and Hearing Research* 8:313–14.

McAnally, K. I., and Stein, J. F. 1997. Scalp potentials evoked by amplitude-modulated tones in dyslexia. *Journal of Speech, Language and Hearing Research* 40:939–45.

McCrosky, R., and Kidder, H. 1980. Auditory fusion among learning disabled, reading disabled, and normal children. *Journal of Learning Disabilities* 13:69–76.

McReynolds, L.V. 1996. Operant conditioning for investigating speech sound discrimination in aphasic children. *Journal of Speech and Hearing Research* 9:519–28.

Merzenich, M. M., Jenkins, W. M., Johnston, P., Schreiner, C., Miller, S. L., and Tallal, P. 1996. Temporal processing deficits of language-learning impaired children ameliorated by training. *Science* 271(5245):77–81.

Merzenich, M. M., and Jenkins, W. M. 1998. Cortical plasticity, learning, and learning dysfunction. In *Maturational Windows and Adult Cortical Plasticity*, eds. B. Julesz and I. Kovacs. New York: Addison-Wesley Pub. Co.

Merzenich, M. M., Miller, S., Jenkins, W. M., Protopapas, A., Saunders, G., Peterson, B., Ahissar, M., and Tallal, P. In Press. A novel training strategy for amelioration of language learning impairments: Initial results of a large field trial. *Journal of Learning Disabilities*.

Nagarajan, S. S., Blake, D. T., Wright, B. A., Byl, N., and Merzenich, M. M. 1998. Practice-related improvements in somatosensory interval discrimination are temporally specific but generalize across skin location, hemisphere, and modality. *Journal of Neuroscience* 18(4):1559–1570.

Neville, H. J. 1985. Effects of early sensory and language experience on the development of the human brain. In *Neonate Cognition: Beyond the Blooming Buzzing Confusion*, eds. J. Mehler and R. Fox Hillsdale, NJ: Lawrence Erlbaum Associates.

Neville, H., Coffey, S., Holcomb, P., and Tallal, P. 1993. The neurobiology of sensory and language processing in language-impaired children. *Journal of Cognitive Neuroscience* 5:235–53.

Pantev, C., Hoke, M., Lutkenhoner, B., and Lehnertz, K. 1989. Tonotopic organization of the auditory cortex: pitch versus frequency representation. *Science* 246:486–88.

Protopapas, A., Ahissar, M., and Merzenich, M. M. 1997. Auditory processing deficits in adults with a history of reading difficulties. *Society for Neuroscience* 23:491.

Recanzone, G. H., Schreiner, C. E., and Merzenich, M. M. 1993. Plasticity in the frequency representation of primary auditory cortex following discrimination training in adult owl monkeys. *The Journal of Neuroscience* 13(1):87–103.

Reed, M. A. 1989. Speech perception and the discrimination of brief auditory cues in reading disabled children. *Journal of Experimental Child Psychology* 48:270–92.

Ribary, U., Joliot, M., Miller, S.L., Kronberg, E., Cappell, J., Tallal, P. and Llinas R. 1998. Cognitive temporal binding and its relation to 40Hz activity in Humans: Alteration during dyslexia. In: *Biomag '96 Advances in Biomagnetism Research*, Wood, Okada, Aine, (eds.), Springer Verlag.

Rice, M. L., and Wexler, K. 1996. Tense as a clinical marker of specific language impairment in English-speaking children. *Journal of Speech and Hearing Research* 39(6):1239–57.

Robin, D., Tomblin, J. B., Kearney, A., and Hug, L. 1989. Auditory temporal pattern learning in children with severe speech and language impairment. *Brain and Language* 36:604–13.

Rosenthal, W. 1972. Auditory and linguistic interaction in developmental aphasia: Evidence from two studies of auditory processing. *Papers and Reports on Child Language Development* 4:19–34.

Spitz, R. V., Tallal, P., and Benasich, A. A. 1997. Look who's talking: A prospective study of familial transmission of language impairments. *Journal of Speech, Language and Hearing Research* 40(5);990–1001.

Stark, J. 1967. A comparison of the performance of aphasic children on three sequencing tests. *Journal of Communication Disorders* 1:31–34.

Stark, R. E., and Tallal, P. 1979. Analysis of stop consonant production errors in developmentally dysphasic children. *Journal of the Acoustical Society of America* 66(6):1703–12.

Stark, R. E., and Heinz, J. M. 1996. Perception of stop consonants in children with expressive and receptive-expressive language impairments. *Journal of Speech and Hearing Research* 39(4):676–86.

Stefanatos, G. A., Green, G. G. R., and Ratcliff, G. G. 1989. Neurophysiological Evidence of Auditory Channel Anomalies in Developmental Dysphasia. *Archives of Neurology* 46:871–75.

Sussman, J. 1993. Perception of formant transition cues to place of articulation in children with language impairments. *Journal of Speech and Hearing Research* 36:1286–99.

Tallal, P., and Piercy, M. 1973a. Defects of non-verbal auditory perception in children with developmental aphasia. *Nature* 241:468–69.

Tallal, P., and Piercy, M. 1973b. Developmental aphasia: Impaired rate of non-verbal processing as a function of sensory modality. *Neuropsychologia* 11:389–98.

Tallal, P., and Piercy, M. 1974. Developmental aphasia: Rate of auditory processing and selective impairment of consonant perception. *Neuropsychologia* 12(1):83–93.

Tallal, P., and Piercy, M. 1975. Developmental aphasia: The perception of brief vowels and extended stop consonants. *Neuropsychologia* 13(1):69–74.

Tallal, P., Stark, R. E., and Curtiss, B. 1976. Relation between speech perception and speech production impairment in children with developmental dysphasia. *Brain and Language* 3:305–17.

Tallal, P. 1980. Auditory temporal perception, phonics, and reading disabilities in children. *Brain and Language* 9(2):182–98.

Tallal, P., Stark, R., Kallman, C., and Mellits, D. 1980a. Perceptual constancy for phonemic categories: A developmental study with normal and language impaired children. *Applied Psycholinguistics* 1:49–64.

Tallal, P., Stark, R., Kallman, C., and Mellits, D. 1980b. Developmental aphasia: The relation between acoustic processing deficits and verbal processing. *Neuropsychologia* 18:273–84.

Tallal, P., Stark, R., Kallman, C., and Mellits, D. 1981. A reexamination of some nonverbal perceptual abilities of language-impaired and normal children as a function of age and sensory modality. *Journal of Speech and Hearing Research* 24:351–57.

Tallal, P., and Stark, R. 1981. Speech acoustic cue discrimination abilities of normally developing and language impaired children. *Journal of the Acoustical Society of America* 69:568–74.

Tallal, P., Ross, R., and Curtiss, S. 1989. Familial aggregation in specific language impairment. *Journal of Speech and Hearing Disorders* 54:167–73.

Tallal, P., Miller, S., and Fitch, R. H. 1993. Neurobiological basis of speech: A case for the preeminence of temporal processing. *Annals of the New York Academy of Sciences* 682:27–47.

Tallal, P., Miller, S. L., Bedi, G., Byma, G., Wang, X., Nagarajan, S. S., Schreiner, C., Jenkins, W. M., and Merzenich, M. M. 1996. Language comprehension in language-learning impaired children improved with acoustically modified speech. *Science* 271(5245):81–84.

Tallal, P., and Merzenich, M. 1997. Fast ForWord training for children with language-learning problems: Results from a national field study by 35 independent facilities. Paper presented at the annual meeting of American Speech-Language-Hearing Association, Boston, MA. November.

Thal, D. J., and Barone, P. 1983. Auditory Processing and Language Impairment in Children: Stimulus considerations for intervention. *Journal of Speech and Hearing Disorders* 48:18–24.

Thibodeau, L., and Sussman, H. 1979. Performance on a test of categorical perception of speech in normal and communicatively disordered children. *Journal of Phonetics* 7:375–91.

Tomblin, J. B., Freese, P., and Records, N. 1992. Diagnosing specific language impairment in adults for the purpose of pedigree analysis. *Journal of Speech and Hearing Research* 35:832–43.

Trehub, S. E. and Henderson, J. L. 1996 Temporal resolution in infancy and subsequent language development. *Journal of Speech and Hearing Research* 39:1315–20.

Werker, J. F., and Tees, R. C. 1987. Speech perception in severely disabled and average reading children. *Canadian Journal of Psychology* 41(1):48–61.

Witton, C., Talcott, J. B., Hansen, P.C., Richardson, A. J., Griffiths, T.D., Rees, A., Stein, J. F., Green, G. G. R. 1998. Sensitivity to dynamic auditory and visual stimuli predicts nonword reading ability in both dyslexic and normal readers. *Current Biology* 8(14):791–97.

Wright, B. A., Lombardino, L. J., King, W. M., Puranik, C. S., Leonard, C. M., and Merzenich, M. M. 1997. Deficits in auditory temporal and spectral resolution in language-impaired children. *Nature* 387:176–78.

Chapter • 7

Dyslexia: From Epidemiology to Neurobiology

Sally E. Shaywitz
Bennett A. Shaywitz

Developmental dyslexia is characterized by an un-expected difficulty in reading in children and adults who otherwise possess the intelligence, motivation, and schooling considered necessary for accurate and fluent reading. Dyslexia (or specific reading disability) is the most common and most carefully studied of the learning disabilities, affecting 80% of all individuals identified as learning disabled (Lerner 1989). Although in the past, the diagnosis and implications of dyslexia were often uncertain, recent advances in our knowledge of the cognitive influences, the epidemiology, and the neurobiology of the disorder now allow dyslexia to be approached within a rational framework. In this chapter we review some of these issues and their implications for the approach to individuals with dyslexia.

COGNITIVE INFLUENCES

Reading, the process of extracting meaning from print, involves both visual-perceptual and linguistic processes and theories of dyslexia based on the visual system (Stein 1993), on the language system

---

1. Portions of this chapter appeared in Shaywitz, S. E., 1998. Dyslexia. Current Concepts. New England Journal of Medicine. 338, January 29, 1998, with permission; Shaywitz, S. E. et al., Functional disruption in the organization of the brain for reading in dyslexia. Proceedings of the National Academy of Science 95:2636–41; and in Swaiman, Pediatric Neurology, In Press.

(Shankweiler et al. 1979), and on other factors such as temporal processing of stimuli within these systems (Stein and Walsh 1997; Tallal and Stark 1982) each have been proposed. Whatever the contributions of other systems and processes, there is now a strong consensus among investigators that the core difficulty in dyslexia reflects a deficiency within a specific component of the language system—the phonologic module—engaged in processing the sounds of speech (Fletcher et al. 1999; Share and Stanovich 1995). According to the phonologic deficit hypothesis, dyslexics have difficulty developing an awareness that words, both written and spoken, can be broken into smaller units of sound and that, in fact, the letters constituting printed words represent the sounds heard in spoken words.

The phonologic deficit hypothesis

Within a modular framework, the language system is conceptualized as a hierarchical series of components: at higher levels are neural systems engaged in processing, for example, semantics, syntax, and discourse; at the lowest level is the phonologic module dedicated to processing the distinctive sound elements that constitute language. The functional unit of the phonologic module is the phoneme, defined as the smallest discernible segment of speech; for example, the word "bat" consists of three phonemes: /b/ /ae/ /t/ (buh, aah, tuh). To speak a word, the speaker retrieves the word's phonemic constituents from the lexicon, assembles the phonemes, and then utters the word. Conversely, to read a word, the reader must first segment that word into its underlying phonologic elements. Abundant evidence relates a deficit in phonologic analysis to difficulties in learning to read: phonologic measures predict later reading achievement (Bradley and Bryant 1983; Stanovich, Cunningham, and Cramer 1984; Torgesen, Wagner, and Rashotte 1994) deficits in phonologic awareness (i.e. awareness that words can be broken into smaller segments of sound) consistently separate dyslexic and nondisabled children (Fletcher et al. 1994; Stanovich and Siegel 1994); phonologic deficits persist into adulthood (Felton, Naylor, and Wood 1990; Bruck 1992); and instruction in phonologic awareness promotes the acquisition of reading skills (Ball and Blachman 1991; Bradley and Bryant 1983; Foorman et al.1997; Stanovich and Siegel 1994; Torgesen, Morgan, and Davis 1992). Additional findings of strong heritability for phonologic awareness suggest that it may be the main proximal cause of most genetically based deficits in word recognition, and thus it may be the most appropriate focus for diagnosis and remediation (Olson, Fosberg, and Wise 1994.

EPIDEMIOLOGY

Recent epidemiologic data indicate that like hypertension and obesity, dyslexia fits a dimensional model. In other words, within the population, reading and reading disability occur along a continuum, with reading disability representing the lower tail of a normal distribution of reading ability (Shaywitz et al. 1992; Gilger et al. 1996). Dyslexia is perhaps the most common neurobehavioral disorder affecting children, with prevalence rates varying from 5% to 10% (Interagency Committee on Learning Disabilities 1987) to 17.5% (Shaywitz, Fletcher, and Shaywitz 1994). Previously, it was believed that dyslexia affected primarily males (Finucci and Childs 1981), however, more recent data (Flynn and Rahbar 1994; Shaywitz et al. 1990; Wadsworth et al. 1992;) indicate comparable numbers of affected males and females. Data derived from the Connecticut Longitudinal Study (Shaywitz et al. 1990) provided evidence that the presumed increase in prevalence in males found in some studies may reflect sampling bias. This study, based on a sample survey of Connecticut schoolchildren followed from kindergarten to third grade, is unique in that all 445 children in the sample received complete ability and reading achievement tests. In this population-based study comparable numbers of reading-disabled males (8.7%) and females (6.9%) were found. Sampling bias inherent in school identification procedures may result in reports of an increased prevalence of reading disability in males in school-identified samples. In contrast, when results are based on test scores in studies in which all children in a population are individually tested, no significant differences in prevalence rates between males and females are observed.

The Matthew effect, which posits that the gap between good and poor readers widens over time, is now increasingly invoked both to explain and predict change in reading ability over time. This hypothesis has been widely accepted as a model describing the developmental course of reading ability. Intuitively appealing, the Matthew effect has rarely been empirically documented in longitudinal studies of reading. Data from the Connecticut Longitudinal Study were examined to test for the Matthew effect (Shaywitz, Holford et al. 1995). When reading achievement scores based on the reading slope—reading mean relationship are plotted by grade—the hypothesized fan-spread effect was not found (figure 1), indicating no significant relationship between reading achievement scores in early grades and the rate of change in reading. A Matthew effect for reading was not observed, suggesting that investigators should use the term Matthew effect with more care and precision.

In contrast, there is a great deal of evidence to support the belief that children who are reading at the lowest levels in early grades

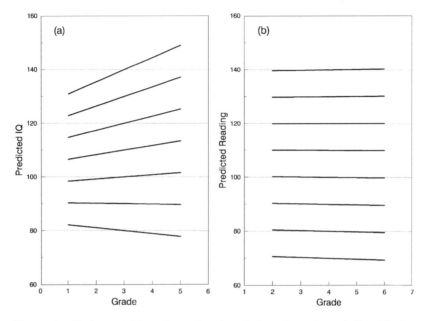

Figure 1.   Estimated IQ and reading trends based on the relationship between slopes and mean scores derived from regression models in Shaywitz et
al., 1995.
a) Predicted IQ scores from the IQ slope - IQ mean model.
b) Predicted reading scores from the reading slope - reading mean model.
A Matthew effect is evident in Figure 1a but no Matthew effect is evident in
Figure 1b.

continue to read at lower levels in later grades (and those reading at
average or above average levels in early grades tend to continue to
read well over time). Such studies do not truly address the question of
a Matthew effect for reading. Rather, these studies indicate only that
children tend to remain close to their original age cohort ranks in
reading levels over time (Clay 1979; Juel 1988; Lundberg 1984). Such
data meshes with that from longitudinal studies, both prospective
(Shaywitz, Holford et al.1995; Francis et al. 1996) and retrospective
(Bruck 1992; Felton, Naylor, and Wood 1990; Scarborough 1984),
which indicate that dyslexia is a persistent, chronic condition; it does
not represent a transient developmental lag. Over time, poor readers
and good readers tend to maintain their relative positions along the
reading spectrum (Shaywitz, Holford et al.1995) (figure 2).

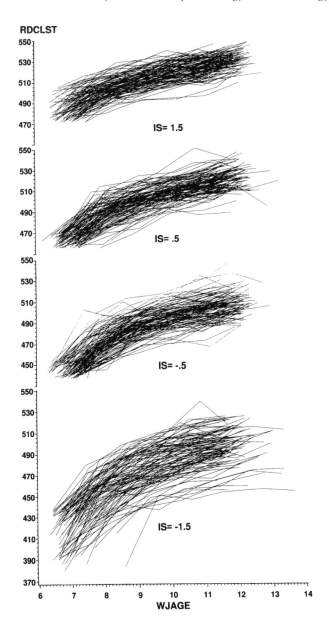

Figure 2. Growth in Woodcock-Johnson Reading Cluster Scores (Rasch scale; RDCLST) by Age (WJ Age) and Initial Status (IS) of Reading Ability. The Children are Divided into Quartiles of Grade 1 Reading Ability. Readers in the Lower Quartiles (IS = -.5, -1.5) Show More Change with Increasing Age than Readers in the Higher Quartiles (IS = .5, 1.5). (From Shaywitz et al, 1995).

NEUROBIOLOGICAL INFLUENCES

The Localization of the Neural Systems Influencing Dyslexia

Neuroanatomic and Morphometric Studies in Dyslexia. Historically, the earliest studies attempting to determine the cerebral localization of a particular cognitive function exploit the postmortem examination of the brain in individuals with, for example, a history of dyslexia. Based on findings in the brains of four young men with histories of reading problems as children, Galaburda and his associates reported structural abnormalities in the perisylvian region of the left temporal lobe, which included large numbers of heterotopias as well as abnormalities of size of the superior surface of the temporal lobe, the planum temporale. They reported finding symmetry of the planum temporale rather than the usual pattern of a larger planum temporale on the left (Galaburda et al. 1985). Such findings were consonant with a hypothesis proposed by Geschwind (Geschwind 1985) that dyslexia results from damage or maldevelopment of language regions in fetal life. Thus, when the language area on the left side of the brain is damaged during fetal life, the corresponding area on the right side of the brain "sends many connections to regions to which the damaged area would have normally projected . . ." so that ". . . damage in the developing speech region on the left side may lead to an increase in right-hemispheric functions while left-hemispheric functions are permanently diminished." (Geschwind 1985 p. 206).

Not only is it very rare that the brains of individuals with dyslexia are available for study, but in addition, significant methodologic limitations (e.g., the often inadequate documentation of a difficulty in reading in the subjects in question) (Hynd and Semrud-Clikeman 1989) are imposed on such post-mortem studies. The development of structural neuroimaging procedures, first CT and for the last two decades, MRI, provided new methods with which to examine neuroanatomic correlates of dyslexia. Based on the anatomic studies by Galaburda and his associates described above, investigators used CT and MRI to compare brain images in dyslexic individuals and controls. Given that current MRI methods are still not sensitive enough to detect the presence of small heterotopias, the focus of most studies was on comparisons of structures that could be easily identified, for example, the determination of brain symmetry in cerebral hemispheres (particularly temporal lobe regions) and the size of the corpus callosum. The rationale for studying the size of particular regions of the corpus callosum was that posterior regions of the corpus callosum (splenium and perhaps isthmus) reflect pathways influencing verbal performance, although those more anterior portions of the structure contain fibers influencing visuospatial performance (Hines et al.1992). Neuroimaging studies carried out prior to 1987 have been critically reviewed by Hynd and Semrud-Clikeman (1989) and more recent studies reviewed by Filipek (1996). Although early CT studies seemed to confirm a reversed asymmetry or lack of normal asymmetry in dyslexic individuals (Hier et al.1978; LeMay 1981; Leisman and Ashkenazi 1980; Rosenberger and Hier 1980), later reports failed to confirm any differences (Denckla , LeMay, and Chapman 1985; Haslam et al. 1981; Parkins et al. 1987; Rumsey et al. 1986) and more recent MRI reports have not clarified the controversy (Duara et al. 1991; Hynd et al. 1990; Jernigan et al. 1991; Larsen et al. 1990; Leonard et al. 1992. We (Schultz et al. 1994) used morphometric MRI techniques to compare the planum in a sample of right-handed children with dyslexia and non-impaired children of comparable age, IQ, handedness, and sex. Findings indicated that sex, age, and overall brain size significantly influence specific morphometric measures of brain, especially the surface area of the planum temporale. Filipek et al. (this volume) examined 30 twin pairs with dyslexia and found significant differences compared to controls in the perisylvan language region, white matter, basal ganglia, thalamus, and parietal association areas.

The lack of consistent results among studies might be explained by differences in subject characteristics (e.g., wide variations in subjects' age, sex, handedness, and diagnostic criteria used to define dyslexia), as well as methodologic variations in measurement of anatomic regions of interest, such as the planum temporale. In fact, difficulties in reliably and accurately measuring the planum, led Jernigan et al. (1991) specifically to omit examining the structure ". . . owing to the difficulty of reliably determining its boundaries" (p. 545).

Electrophysiologic studies. Much has been learned from studies of cerebral localization of cognitive function based on studies of individuals with brain damage and such studies continue to provide important information, particularly with the emergence of modern imaging methods that allow very fine-grained anatomical resolution (Damasio and Damasio 1989). However, studies localizing cerebral function using morphometric measures provide a static picture of brain anatomy, rather than a dynamic view of brain function while individuals are performing a cognitive task. What is necessary is to be able to identify the functional units of the working nervous system, the neural networks that are engaged by specific cognitive functions. One approach uses electrophysiological methods, including event related potentials. Older studies were detailed by Hughes (1977) and more recent ones are reviewed by Dool, Steimack, and Rourke (1993). Methodological reviews of progress and newer electrographic technologies are provided in reviews elsewhere (Swick, Kutas, and Neville 1994; Thatcher 1996; Wood et al. 1996). One of the most recent studies of this kind (Salmelin et al. 1996) used magnetoencephalography (MEG) and found that in contrast to normals, dyslexics failed to activate the left inferior temporo-occipital region (including Wernicke's area) while reading real words. However, while MEG is useful for determining the time course of cognitive processes, it is not nearly as precise as the imaging modalities for localizing where in the brain these processes occur.

Functional Brain Imaging. Functional imaging, the ability to measure brain function during performance of a cognitive task, meets such a requirement and became possible in the early 1980s. For the first time, rather than being limited to examining the brain in an autopsy specimen, or measuring the size of brain regions using static morphometric indices based on CT or MRI, investigators were able to envision studying brain metabolism while individuals were performing specific cognitive tasks. When an individual is asked to perform a discrete cognitive task, that task places processing demands on particular neural systems in the brain. Meeting those demands requires activation of neural systems in particular brain regions, and those changes in neural activity are, in turn, reflected by changes in brain metabolic activity (e.g., changes in cerebral blood flow or changes in cerebral utilization of metabolic substrates such as glucose); it is possible to measure those changes in metabolic activity in specific brain regions while subjects are engaged in cognitive tasks.

A number of studies have used a variety of functional imaging methods to examine brain activation patterns in dyslexic subjects. These efforts have been inconclusive largely because the experimental tasks used to activate a brain tapped the several aspects of the reading process in somewhat unsystematic ways. As noted above (see Cognitive Influences) there is now overwhelming evidence that phonologic awareness is characteristically lacking (or deficient) in dyslexic readers who, therefore, have difficulty mapping the alphabetic characters onto the spoken word. To find the location and extent of the functional disruption in neural systems that underlies this impairment, we (Shaywitz et al. 1998) used functional magnetic resonance imaging to compare brain activation patterns in dyslexic and non-impaired subjects as they performed tasks that made progressively greater demands on phonologic analysis. In performing the tasks, subjects viewed two simultaneously presented stimulus displays, one above the other, and were asked to make a same/different judgment by pressing a response button if the displays matched on a given cognitive dimension: line orientation judgment; letter case judgment; single letter rhyme; nonword rhyme and category judgment. The five tasks were ordered hierarchically; at the lowest level, the Line orientation (L) judgment task (e.g., Do [\\\/] and [\\\/] match?) taps visual-spatial processing, but makes no orthographic demands. Next, the Letter Case C judgment task (e.g., Do [bbBb] and [bbBb] match in the pattern of upper and lower case letters?) adds an orthographic processing demand, but makes no phonologic demands, since the stimulus items, which consist entirely of consonant strings are, therefore, phonotactically impermissible. The third task, Single Letter Rhyme (SLR) (e.g., Do the letters [T] and [V] rhyme?), while orthographically more simple than C, adds a phonologic processing demand, requiring the transcoding of the letters (orthography) into phonologic structures and then, a phonologic analysis of those structures sufficient to determine that they do or do not rhyme; the fourth task, Nonword Rhyme (NWR) (e.g., Do [leat] and [jete] rhyme?), requires analysis of more complex structures. The final task, Semantic Category (SC) judgment (e.g., Are [corn] and [rice] in the same category?), also makes substantial demands on transcoding from print to phonology (Van Orden, Pennington, and Stone 1990; Lukatela 1994), but requires, in addition, that the printed stimulus items activate particular word representations in the reader's lexicon to arrive at the word's meaning. Reading performance in the DYS subjects was significantly impaired: the mean standard score on a measure of nonword reading (Woodcock 1987) was 81 ± 1.9 (mean ± SEM) in DYS readers compared to 114 ± 1.5 in NI readers, with no overlap between groups. Similarly, error patterns on the fMRI tasks revealed that DYS differed from NI most strikingly on the NWR task.

Brain activation patterns differed significantly between the groups with dyslexic readers showing relative underactivation in posterior regions (Wernicke's area, the angular gyrus, and striate cortex) and relative overactivation in an anterior region (inferior frontal gyrus). This is illustrated in figure 3. What is particularly interesting is that the findings from this most recent functional imaging study of dyslexia now help reconcile the seemingly contradictory findings of previous imaging studies of dyslexia, some of which involved anomalous findings in the visual system (Eden et al. 1996) while others indicated abnormal activation within components of the language system (Flowers, Wood, and Naylor 1991; Gross-Glenn et al. 1991; Paulesu et al. 1996; Rumsey 1992; Rumsey et al. 1997; Salmelin et al. 1996). These data indicate that dyslexic readers demonstrate a functional disruption in an extensive system in posterior cortex encompassing both traditional visual and traditional language regions, as well as a portion of association cortex. Involvement of this latter region centered about the angular gyrus is of particular interest, because this portion of association cortex is considered pivotal in carrying out those cross-modal

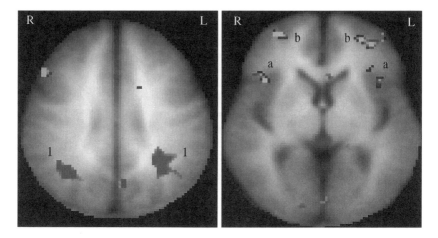

Figure 3. Composite activation maps in dyslexic and nonimpaired readers during phonologic processing. These maps were generated from a general linear model based on a randomization of statistical parametric maps and show activations at p = .01. During phonologic processing, dyslexic readers demonstrated more activation than nonimpaired readers anteriorly in the inferior frontal gyrus bilaterally (a) and the middle frontal gyrus (b). In contrast, nonimpaired but not dyslexic readers activated a large area in the posterior region, the angular gyrus (1). (Figure is property of Sally Shaywitz and may be reproduced only with permission).

integrations necessary for reading, i.e., mapping the visual percept of the print onto the phonologic structures of the language (Benson 1994; Black and Behrmann 1994; Geschwind 1965). Consistent with this study of developmental dyslexia, a large literature on acquired inability to read (alexia) describes neuroanatomic lesions most prominently centered about the angular gyrus (Dejerine 1891; Damasio and Damasio 1983; Friedman, Ween, and Albert 1993). It should not be surprising that both the acquired and the developmental disorders affecting reading have in common a disruption within the neural systems serving to link the visual representations of the letters to the phonologic structures they represent. While reading difficulty is the primary symptom in both acquired alexia and developmental dyslexia, associated symptoms and findings in the two disorders would be expected to differ somewhat, reflecting the differences between an acquired and a developmental disorder. In acquired alexia, a structural lesion resulting from an insult (e.g. stroke, tumor) disrupts a component of an already functioning neural system and the lesion may extend to involve other brain regions and systems. In developmental dyslexia, as a result of a constitutionally based functional disruption, the system never develops normally so that the symptoms reflect the emanative effects of an early disruption to the phonologic system. In either case, the disruption is within the same neuroanatomic system.

These findings, too, support the speculation by Geschwind of hemispheric differences between dyslexic and nonimpaired individuals. Hemispheric differences are observed in the angular gyrus and area 37, a region of the middle temporal gyrus contiguous with the angular gyrus.

For dyslexic readers, these brain activation patterns provide evidence of an imperfectly functioning system for segmenting words into their phonologic constituents; accordingly, this disruption is evident when dyslexic readers are asked to respond to increasing demands on phonologic analysis. These findings now add neurobiologic support for previous cognitive/behavioral data pointing to the critical role of phonologic analysis, and its impairment, in dyslexia. The pattern of relative underactivation in posterior brain regions contrasted with relative overactivation in anterior regions may provide a neural signature for the phonologic difficulties characterizing dyslexia.

ACKNOWLEDGMENT

The authors are supported by grants from the National Institute of Child Health and Human Development (PO1 HD-21888 and P50 HD-25802).

EDITOR'S COMMENTS

The Doctors Shaywitz have given us an excellent contemporary update on several aspects of disorders of reading. They have shown that males slightly exceed females in population studies of reading disability, the difference about 9% versus 7%. Furthermore, when readers are identified as having reading problems in childhood, they continue to have reading problems throughout adulthood, consistent with longitudinal population surveys in Europe and clinical experience. The anatomic correlates in the living person are much more difficult to verify, one study from the next, because of the limitations of the investigative techniques, as well as the heterogeneity of the populations studied. These same limitations likely affect those studies attempting to characterize the electrophysiology of developmental reading disorders. Bringing together the prior disparate observations on correlates of reading disorders—visual, auditory, and linguistic, is their own work, utilizing functional imaging by PET demonstrating more than dysfunction in the visual system, rather disconnection between the visual, association and language system as Norman Geschwind had speculated three decades ago.

—DDD

REFERENCES

Ball, E. W., and Blachman, B. A. 1991. Does phoneme awareness training in kindergarten make a difference in early word recognition and developmental spelling? *Reading Research Quarterly* 26(1):49–66.

Benson, D. F. 1994. *The Neurology of Thinking.* New York: Oxford University Press.

Black, S. E., and Behrmann, M. 1994. Localization in alexia. In *Localization and Neuroimaging in Neuropsychology*, edited by Andrew Kertesz. New York: Academic Press.

Bradley, L., and Bryant, P. E. 1983. Categorizing sounds and learning to read—A causal connection. *Nature* 301:419–21.

Brown, J. I., Fishco, V. V., and Hanna, G. S. 1993. *Nelson-Denny Reading Test, Forms G and H.* Itasca, IL: Riverside Publishing Co.

Bruck, M. 1992. Persistence of dyslexics' phonological awareness deficits. *Developmental Psychology* 28(5):874–86.

Clay, M. M. 1979. *Reading: The Patterning of Complex Behavior.* Auckland, New Zealand: Heinemann.

Damasio, A. R., and Damasio, H. 1983. The anatomic basis of pure alexia. *Neurology* 33:1573–83.

Damasio, H., and Damasio A. 1989. *Lesion Analysis in Neuropsychology.* New York: Oxford University Press.

Denckla, M. B., LeMay, M., and Chapman, C. A. 1985. Few CT scan abnormalities found even in neurologically impaired learning disabled children. *Journal of Learning Disabilities* 18:132–35.

Dool, C. B., Steimack, R. M., and Rourke, B. P. 1993. Event-related potentials in children with learning disabilities. *Journal of Clinical Child Psychology* 22(3):387–98.

Duara, R., Kushch, A., Gross-Glenn, K., Barker, W., Jallad, B., Pascal, S., Loewenstein, C. A., Sheldon, J., Rabin, M., Levin, B., and Lubs, H. 1991. Neuroanatomic differences between dyslexic and normal readers on magnetic resonance imaging scans. *Archives of Neurology* 48(4):410–16.

Eden, G. F., VanMeter, J. W., Rumsey, J. M., Maisog, J. M., Woods, R. P., and Zeffiro, T. A. 1996. Abnormal processing of visual motion in dyslexia revealed by functional brain imaging. *Nature* 382:66–69.

Felton, R. H., Naylor, C. E., and Wood, F. B. 1990. Neuropsychological profile of adult dyslexics. *Brain and Language* 39:485–97.

Filipek, P. A. 1996. Structural variations in measures in the developmental disorders. In *Developmental Neuroimaging: Mapping the Development of Brain and Behavior*, edited by R. W. Thatcher, G. R. Lyon, J. Rumsey, and N. Krasnegor. Orlando, FL: Academic Press.

Finucci, J. M., and Childs, B. 1981. Are there really more dyslexic boys than girls? In *Sex Differences in Dyslexia*, edited by A. Ansara, N. Geschwind, M. Albert, and N. Gartrell. Towson, MD: The Orton Dyslexia Society.

Fletcher, J. M., Foorman, B. R., Shaywitz, S. E., and Shaywitz, B. A. 1999. Conceptual and methodological issues in dyslexia research: A lesson for developmental disorders. In *Neurodevelopmental Disorders*, edited by H. Tager-Flusberg. Cambridge, MA: MIT Press.

Fletcher, J. M., Francis, D. J., Shaywitz B. A., Foorman, B. R., and Shaywitz, S. E. In press. Diagnostic utility of intelligence testing and the discrepancy model for children with learning disabilities: Historical perspective and current research. In *IQ Testing and Decision Making*, edited by National Research Council. Washington, DC: National Academy of Sciences.

Fletcher, J. M., Shaywitz, S. E., Shankweiler, D. P., Katz, L., Liberman, I. Y., Stuebing, K. K., Francis, D. J., Fowler, A. E., and Shaywitz, B. A. 1994. Cognitive profiles of reading disability: Comparisons of discrepancy and low achievement definitions. *Journal of Educational Psychology* 86(1):6–23.

Flowers, D. L., Wood, F. B., and Naylor, C. E. 1991. Regional cerebral blood flow correlates of language processes in reading disability. *Archives of Neurology* 48:637–43.

Flynn, J. M., and Rahbar, M. H. 1994. Prevalence of reading failure in boys compared with girls. *Psychology in the Schools* 31:66–71.

Foorman, B. R., Francis, D. J., Beeler, T., Winikates, D., and Fletcher, J. M. 1997. Early interventions for children with reading problems: Study designs and preliminary findings. *Learning Disabilities: A Multidisciplinary Journal* 8(1):63–71.

Francis, D. J., Shaywitz, S. E., Stuebing, K. K., Shaywitz, B. A., and Fletcher, J. M. 1996. Developmental lag versus deficit models of reading disability: A longitudinal, individual growth curves analysis. *Journal of Educational Psychology* 88(1):3–17.

Friedman, R. F., Ween, J. E., and Albert, M. L. 1993. Alexia. In *Clinical Neuropsychology*, edited by Kenneth M. Heilman and Edward Valenstein. New York: Oxford University Press.

Galaburda, A. M., Sherman, G. F., Rosen, G. D., Aboitiz, F., and Geschwind, N. 1985. Developmental dyslexia: Four consecutive patients with cortical anomalies. *Annals of Neurology* 18(2):222–33.

Geschwind, N. 1985. Biological foundations of reading. In *Dyslexia: A Neuroscientific Approach to Clinical Evaluation*, edited by F. H. Duffy and N. Geschwind. Boston, MA: Little, Brown and Company.

Geschwind, N. 1965. Disconnexion syndromes in animals and man. *Brain* 88:237-94.

Gilger, J. W., Borecki I. B., Smith, S. D., DeFries J. C., and Pennington, B. F. The etiology of extreme scores for complex phenotypes: An illustration using reading performance. In *Developmental Dyslexia: Neural, Cognitive, and Genetic Mechanisms*, edited by C. H. Chase, G. D. Rosen and G. F. Sherman. Baltimore, MD: York Press, 1996.

Gross-Glenn, K., Duara, R., Barker, W. W., Loewenstein, D., Chang, J.-Y., Yoshii, F., Apicella, A. M., Pascal, S., Boothe, T., Sevush, S., Jallad, B.J., Novoa, L., and Lubs, H. A. 1991. Positron emission tomographic studies during serial word-reading by normal and dyslexic adults. *Journal of Clinical and Experimental Neuropsychology* 13(4):531–44.

Haslam, R. H. A., Dalby, J. T., Johns, R. D., and Rademaker, A. W. 1981. Cerebral asymmetry in developmental dyslexia. *Archives of Neurology* 38:679–82.

Hier, D. B., LeMay, M., Rosenberger, B. P., and Perlo, V. P. 1978. Developmental dyslexia: Evidence for a subgroup with a reversal of cerebral asymmetry. *Archives of Neurology* 35:90 –92.

Hines, M., Chiu, L., McAdams, L. A., Bentler, P. M., and Lipcamon, J. 1992. Cognition and the corpus callosum: Verbal fluency, visuospatial ability, and language lateralization related to midsagital surface areas of callosal subregions. *Behavioral Neuroscience* 106:1,3–14.

Hughes, J. R. 1977. Electroencephalographic and neurophysiological studies in dyslexia. In *Dyslexia: An Appraisal of Current Knowledge*, edited by A. L. Benton and D. Pearl. New York: Oxford University Press.

Hynd, G. W., and Semrud-Clikeman, M. 1989. Dyslexia and brain morphology. *Psychological Bulletin* 106(3):447–82.

Hynd, G. W., Semrud-Clikeman, M., Lorys, A. R., Novey, E. S., and Eliopulos, D. 1990. Brain morphology in developmental dyslexia and attention deficit disorder/hyperactivity. *Archives of Neurology* 47:919–26.

Interagency Committee on Learning Disabilities. 1987. Learning disabilities: A report to the U.S. Congress. Washington, DC: U.S. Government Printing Office.

Jernigan, T. L., Hesselink, H. E., Sowell, E., and Tallal, P. A. 1991. Cerebral structure on magnetic resonance imaging in language- and learning-impaired children. *Archives of Neurology* 48:539–45.

Juel, C. 1988. Learning to read and write: A longitudinal study of 54 children from first through fourth grades. *Journal of Educational Psychology* 80(4): 437–47.

Larsen, J. P., Hoien, T., Lundberg, I., and Odegaard, H. 1990. MRI evaluation of the size and symmetry of the planum temporale in adolescents with developmental dyslexia. *Brain and Language* 39(2):289–301.

Leisman, G., and Ashkenazi, M. 1980. Aetiological factors in dyslexia: IV. Cerebral hemispheres are functionally equivalent. *Neuroscience and Biobehavioral Review* 11:157–64.

LeMay, M. 1981. Are there radiological changes in the brains of individuals with dyslexia? *Bulletin of The Orton Society* 31:135–41.

Leonard, C.M., Voeller, K.K.S., Lombardino, L.I., et al. 1992. Anomalous cerebral structure in dyslexia revealed with magnetic resonance imaging. *Archives of Neurology* 30:73–87.

Lerner, Janet W. 1989. Educational interventions in learning disabilities. *Journal of the American Academy of Child and Adolescent Psychiatry* 28(3): 326–31.

Lukatela, G., and Turvey, M. T. 1994. Visual lexical access is initially phonological: 2. Evidence from phonological priming by homophones and pseudohomophones. *Journal of Experimental Psychology: General* 123:331–53.

Lundberg, I. *Learning to read.* 1984. Sweden: School Research Newsletter, National Board of Education.

Olson, R. K., Forsberg, H. and Wise, B. 1994. Genes, environment, and the development of orthographic skills. In *The Varieties of Orthographic Knowledge I: Theoretical and Developmental Issues*, ed. V. W. Berninger. Dordrecht, The Netherlands: Kluwer Academic Publishers.

Parkins, R., Roberts, R. J. Reinarz, S. J., and Varney, N. R. January 1987. CT asymmetries in adult developmental dyslexics. Paper presented at the Annual convention of the International Neuropsychological Society, Washington, DC.

Paulesu, E., Frith, U., Snowling, M., Gallagher, A., Morton, J., Frackowiak, R. S. J., and Frith, C. D. 1996. Is developmental dyslexia a disconnection syndrome? Evidence from PET scanning. *Brain* 119:143–57.

Rosenberger, P., and Hier, D. 1980. Cerebral asymmetry and verbal intellectual deficits. *Annals of Neurology* 8:300–4.

Rumsey, J. M. 1992. The biology of developmental dyslexia. *Journal of the American Medical Association* 268(7):912–15.

Rumsey, J. M., Dorwart, R., Vermess, M., Denckla, M. B. Kruesi, M. J. P., and Rapoport, L. J. 1986. Magnetic resonance imaging of brain anatomy in severe developmental dyslexia. *Archives of Neurology* 43:1045–46.

Rumsey, J. M., Nace, K., Donohue, B., Wise, D., Maisog, J. M., and Andreason, P. 1997. A positron emission tomographic study of impaired word recognition and phonological processing in dyslexic men. *Archives of Neurology* 54:562–73.

Salmelin, R., Service, E., Kiesila, P., Uutela, K., and Salonen, O. 1996. Impaired visual word processing in dyslexia revealed with magnetoencephalography. *Annals of Neurology* 40:157–62.

Scarborough, H. S. 1984. Continuity between childhood dyslexia and adult reading. *British Journal of Psychology* 75:329–48.

Schultz, R. T., Cho, N. K., Staib, L. H., Kier, L. E., Fletcher, J. M., Shaywitz, S. E., Shankweiler, D. P., Katz, L., Gore, J. C., Duncan, J. S., and Shaywitz, B. A. 1994. Brain morphology in normal and dyslexic children: The influence of sex and age. *Annals of Neurology* 35(6):732–43.

Shankweiler, D., Liberman, I. Y., Mark, L. S., Fowler, C. A., and Fischer, F. W. 1979. The speech code and learning to read. *Journal of Experimental Psychology: Human Learning and Memory* 5(6):531–45.

Share, D. L., and Stanovich, K. E. 1995. Cognitive processes in early reading development: Accommodating individual differences into a model of acquisition. *Issues in Education: Contributions from Educational Psychology* 1(1):1–57.

Shaywitz, B. A., Fletcher, J. M., Holahan, J. M., and Shaywitz, S. E. 1992. Discrepancy compared to low achievement definitions of reading disability: Results from the Connecticut Longitudinal Study. *Journal of Learning Disabilities* 25(10):639–48.

Shaywitz, B. A., Fletcher, J. M., Holahan, J. M., Shneider, A. E., Marchione, K. E., Stuebing, K. K., Francis, D. J., Shankweiler, D. P., Katz, L., Liberman, I. Y., and Shaywitz, S. E. 1995. Interrelationships between reading disability and attention-deficit/hyperactivity disorder. *Child Neuropsychology* 1(3): 170–86.

Shaywitz, B. A., Holford, T. R., Holahan, J. M., Fletcher, J. M., Stuebing, K. K., Francis, D. J., and Shaywitz, S. E. 1995. A Matthew effect for IQ but not for reading: Results from a longitudinal study. *Reading Research Quarterly* 30(4):894–906.

Shaywitz, S. E., Shaywitz, B. A., Pugh, K. R., Fulbright, R. K., Constable, R. T., Mencl, W. E., Shankweiler, D. P., Liberman, A. M., Skudlarski, P., Fletcher, J. M., Katz, L., Marchione, K. E., Lacadie, C., Gatenby, C., and Gore, J. C. 1998. Functional disruption in the organization of the brain for reading in dyslexia. *Proceedings of the National Academy of Science USA* 95:2636–41.

Shaywitz, S. E. 1996. Dyslexia. *Scientific American* 275(5):98–104.

Shaywitz, S. E., Escobar, M. D., Shaywitz, B. A., Fletcher, J. M., and Makuch, R. 1992. Evidence that dyslexia may represent the lower tail of a normal distribution of reading ability. New England Journal of Medicine 326(3): 145–50.

Shaywitz, S. E., Fletcher, J. M., and Shaywitz, B. A. 1994. Issues in the definition and classification of attention deficit disorder. *Topics in Language Disorders* 14(4):1–25.

Shaywitz, S. E., Shaywitz, B. A., Fletcher, J. M., and Escobar, M. D. 1990. Prevalence of reading disability in boys and girls: Results of the Connecticut Longitudinal Study. *Journal of the American Medical Association* 264(8): 998–1002.

Stanovich, K. E., Cunningham, A. E., and Cramer, B. B. 1984. Assessing phonological awareness in kindergarten children: Issues of task comparability. *Journal of Experimental Child Psychology* 38:175–90.

Stanovich, K. E., and Siegel, L. S. 1994. Phenotypic performance profile of children with reading disabilities: A regression-based test of the phonological-core variable-difference model. *Journal of Educational Psychology* 86(1):24–53.

Stein, J., and Walsh, V. 1997. To see but not to read; the magnocellular theory of dyslexia. *Trends in Neurosciences* 20(4):147–52.

Stein, J. F. 1993. Visuospatial perception in disabled readers. In *Visual Processes in Reading and Reading Disabilities*, edited by D. M. Willows, R. S. Kruk, and E. Corcos. Hillsdale, NJ: Lawrence Erlbaum Associates.

Swick, D., Kutas, M., and Neville, H. V. 1994. Localizing the neural genetics of event-related brain potentials. In *Localization and Neuroimaging in Neuropsychology*, edited by A. Kertesz. New York: Academic Press.

Tallal, P., and Stark, R. E. 1982. Perceptual/motor profiles of reading impaired children with or without concomitant oral language deficits. *Annals of Dyslexia* 32:163–76.

Thatcher, R. W. 1996. Neuroimaging of cyclic cortical reorganization during human development. In *Developmental neuroimaging: Mapping the Development of Brain and Behavior*, edited by R. W. Thatcher, G. R. Lyon, J. Rumsey, and N. Krasnegor. New York: Academic Press.

Torgesen, J. K., Morgan, S. T., and Davis, C. 1992. Effects of two types of phonological awareness training on word learning in kindergarten children. *Journal of Educational Psychology* 84(3):364–70.

Torgesen, J. K., Wagner, R. K., and Rashotte, C. A. 1994. Longitudinal studies of phonological processing and reading. *Journal of Learning Disabilities* 27(5):276–86.

Van Orden, G. C., Pennington, B. F., and Stone, G. O. 1990. Word identification in reading and the promise of subsymbolic psycholinguistics. *Psychological Review* 97(4):488–522.

Wadsworth, S. J., DeFries, J. C., Stevenson, J., Gilger, J. W., and Pennington, B. F. 1992. Gender ratios among reading-disabled children and their siblings as a function of parental impairment. *Journal of Child Psychology and Psychiatry* 33(7):1229–39.

Wood, F. B., Garrett, A. S., Hart, L. A., Flowers, D. L., and Absher, J. R. 1996. Event related potential correlates of glucose metabolism in normal adults during a cognitive activation task. In *Developmental Neuroimaging: Mapping the Development of Brain and Behavior*, edited by R. W. Thatcher, G. R. Lyon, J. Rumsey and N. Krasnegor. New York: Academic Press.

Woodcock, R. W. 1987. *Woodcock Reading Mastery Tests - Revised*. Circle Pines, MI: American Guidance Service.

Chapter • 8

Functional Neuroanatomy of Dyslexic Subtypes: A Survey of 43 Candidate Regions with a Factor Analytic Validation Across 100 Cases

Frank B. Wood and D. Lynn Flowers

During the last century, when dyslexia was behaviorally studied, there were numerous speculations about the neuroanatomical substrates of the syndrome. It is fair to say that almost no region of the brain has been spared from these speculations, but definitive tools for in vivo neuroimaging of this functional neuroanatomy have only recently become available for wide use. A series of edited volumes published in the 1990s have addressed this issue from several perspectives: see *The Reading Brain* (Duane 1991), *Developmental Neuroimaging* (Thatcher et al. 1996), and *Functional Neuroimaging in Child Psychiatry* (Ernst and Rumsey 1999). Numerous reviews have also provided perspectives on the question.

Supported by Public Health Service National Institutes of Health Grant: PO1 HD21887

Here we report one result from the past decade of our work involving positron emission tomography (PET) in adults with childhood histories of reading problems. It takes a fundamentally empirical, hypothesis-generating approach to the brain regions involved, seeking separate common factors of regional activation in a sample that maximizes reading-related variance. That strategy detects patterns of covariation that "stand alone," apart from any behavioral considerations. Once detected, however, the patterns are subject to behavioral validation. In this hypothesis-generating study, we concentrate on defining the regions, not only because of their intrinsic interest, but also in a manner that permits replication, identifies behavioral correlates, and leaves the interesting results mostly open to future hypothesis-testing and interpretation.

REGIONS OF INTEREST (ROIs)

The regions to be examined were chosen because preliminary data indicate that increases or decreases in glucose utilization could be expected in these regions, either due to phenotypic reading skill differences, attentional features, task performance, or subject variables not related to the hypotheses (e.g., gender, state anxiety, etc.). In the following descriptions, sulcal and gyral topography percentages are from Ono, Kubik, and Abernathey 1990. In addition to specific references for individual ROIs, the following sources are used as standard references: Carpenter 1991; Guyton 1991; FitzGerald 1996; Haines 1997. Referenced activation studies are PET regional cerebral blood flow findings unless otherwise noted. Procedures for manual placement of spheres of interest, representing these regions, are described in the appendix. Table I presents the Talairach coordinates of the average of these manual placements across 20 randomly selected brains. It should be noted that a mathematically stable estimate of the local maximum within each sphere is taken as the PET dependent measure of interest (Fahey et al. 1998). These spheres of interest, accordingly, permit some variation within them as to the exact location of the source of maximal activation. The spherical ROIs could thus be considered to define a neighborhood, not the exact house, in which the relevant activity is measured.

Thalamus

The thalamus is an egg-shaped collection of independent nuclei found between the interventricular foramen and the posterior commissure just lateral to the third ventricle. The bilateral thalami are fused at the massa intermedia in about 80% of individuals. Although a large and

Table I.   Summary of Regions of Interest:

Region	Average Talaraich Coordinates	Sphere Diameter: Location Description	Neurobehavioral and Dyslexic Relevance
Thalamus	L: –13,–22,1 R: 12,–20,3	2.5 cm: Encompasses the thalamus while avoiding nearby striatal structures	related to single word reading skill in dyslexia
Calcarine (Area 17)	L: –8,–90,–1 R: 12,–89,1	2.0 cm: In the calcarine fissure at the most medial aspect of the occipital lobe	bilateral activation during visual tasks
Parietal Occipital Sulcus	L: –10,–65,9 R: 9,–59,9	2.0 cm: At the junction of the parietal occipital sulcus and calcarine fissure on the medial aspect of the occipital lobe	activation during learning, recall, and recognition of complex geometric patterns
Anterior Lingual/ Fusiform Gyri: 1	L: –27,–49,–9 R: 26,–49,–9	2.0 cm: Within the collateral sulcus, posterior and superior to the hippocampal ROI and separate from it	greater activation in dyslexics during pronouncing or identifying phonologically regular nonwords
Posterior Lingual/ Fusiform Gyri: 2	L: –23,–68,–9 R: 21,–70,–9	2.0 cm: Posterior and tangent to above	as above
Hippocampus	L: –28,–20,–17 R: 28,–20,–19	1.5 cm: Posterior to and independent of the amygdala on the medial aspect of the temporal lobe	related to performance of a letter discrimination task in controls in our study; others report activation during novel visual lexical decision, learning of complex geometric patterns, and recognition of patterns
Posterior Inferior Temporal/ Area 37	L: –46,–68,–11 R: 48,–63,–12	2.5 cm: At the intersection of the occipitotemporal sulcus and the preoccipital incisura	active during visual naming, object recognition
Heschl's Gyrus	L: –45,–22,9 R: 44,–18,9	1.5 cm: Centered at the midway point of this gyrus as it transverses the temporal surface in an anterior posterior direction	lower activation in dyslexics during oral word reading; activated bilaterally in dyslexic and control subjects on letter discrimination tasks

continues

Table I. Summary of Regions of Interest, *continued*

Region	Average Talaraich Coordinates	Sphere Diameter: Location Description	Neurobehavioral and Dyslexic Relevance
Superior Temporal Sulcus	L: −58,−22,−9 R: 56,−18,−9	1.5 cm: Within the superior temporal sulcus, inferior and tangent to Heschl's gyrus ROI	active during numerous visual and auditory tasks, lower activation in dyslexics during nonword discrimination and oral reading
Inferior Temporal Sulcus	L: −62,−22,−24 R: 57,−20,−27	1.5 cm: Inferior and tangent to above	activation during visual object naming, silent reading and naming, picture meaning, passive viewing of nonwords
Angular Gyrus	L: −46,−58,41 R: 47,−53,42	2.0 cm: At the termination of the superior temporal sulcus within the inferior parietal lobule	active during numerous verbal tasks, less active in dyslexics during rhyme detection and more active in dyslexics during orthographic identification
Intraparietal Sulcus (Superior Posterior Parieto-Occipital)	L: −33,−56,47 R: 31,−58,47	2.0 cm: At the most posterior aspect of the sulcus dividing the superior and inferior parietal lobules	activation during location matching, perception and learning of visual patterns and recall of learned figures
Broca's Area	L: −38,20,−1 R: 40,20,−1	2.0 cm: At the stem of the Sylvan fissure in the frontal operculum, anterior to motor strip in posterior inferior frontal cortex	reduced activation in dyslexics during oral reading
Dorsolateral Prefrontal Cortex Inferior Sulcus	L: −41,33,29 R: 41,35,30	2.5 cm: Within the inferior frontal sulcus centered in a coronal plane tangent to the genu of the corpus callosum	activation during short term memory and naming tasks
Dorsolateral Prefrontal Cortex Superior Sulcus: 1	L: −23,37,39 R: 24,37,37	2.0 cm: Anterior-most sphere fitting wholly within the superior frontal gyrus	more motorically relevant than inferior sulcus, otherwise similar
Dorsolateral Prefrontal Cortex Superior Sulcus: 2	L: −26,20,51 R: 24,20,51	2.0 cm: Posterior to and tangent to the above; also wholly within gyrus	As above

continues

Table I.   Summary of Regions of Interest, *continued*

Region	Average Talaraich Coordinates	Sphere Diameter: Location Description	Neurobehavioral and Dyslexic Relevance
Orbital Frontal Cortex	L: –30,37,–13 R: 32,39,–13	2.0 cm: Superior to eye orbits, lateral to the rectal gyri	active in Stroop Test and face matching
Head of the Caudate Nucleus	L: –11,13,6 R: 11,15,3	2.0 cm: The most superior rostral position of the striatum measured at its "fullest" representation	lower activation reported in children with Attention Deficit Disorder
Dorsal Striatum	L: –12,15,9 R: 13,15,8	1.5 cm: Within the larger caudate measure reported above at its most superior aspect	not typically reported separately from head of the caudate
Ventral Striatum	L: –8,13,–6 R: 9,13,–6	1.5 cm: Ventral and tangent to the above encompassing the continuity between putamen and caudate head on the medial aspect of each hemisphere	involved in reward circuits and implicated in attentional disorders
Putamen	L: –23,11,3 R: 22,11,–3	1.5 cm: Lateral and posterior to the head of the caudate, avoiding its continuity with the caudate	activation during visual object naming, serial learning, and associated with attentional dysfunction
Anterior Cingulate	0,35,37	2.5 cm: Midline at the intersection of 2 planes tangent to the anterior edge and dorsal surface of the corpus callosum	activation to Stroop Test, visual lexical decision, visual object naming, and word retrieval

easily located subcortical structure, the thalamus has no clearly defined boundaries where it is adjacent to other neural tissue. Sensory
cortex projections, except olfactory, synapse in the thalamus preserv-
ing primary sensory organization, and efferents project diffusely to
the cerebral cortex. Usually there are reciprocal corticofugal fibers; for
example, granular prefrontal cortex and the frontal eye fields are reciprocal with regions of the medial dorsal nucleus. There are also integrative circuits important to motor output (for example, projections
from precentral gyrus, cerebellar nuclei, globus pallidus and substantia nigra converge in ventral nuclei). The thalamus has numerous

essential functions, including the gating of sensory input and the integration of information important for motor output, as well as limbic connections involved in cognition, judgment, and mood.

Rumsey et al. (1997) and Bookheimer et al. (1995) have reported thalamic activity during reading tasks. Price et al. (1994) found significant midline thalamic activity during the silent viewing of words.

Calcarine Fissure Area 17-18

This region in the primary visual cortex is topographically organized so that the foveal projection area occupies the posterior third of the calcarine fissure, which is continuous 92% of the time. This region is quite active in studies using visual stimuli; however, activity is often not revealed in subtraction studies using sensorimotor baselines.

Kiyosawa et al. (1996) reported bilateral primary visual cortex activity during a visual object naming task when compared to resting baseline and Howard et al. (1992) found bilateral striate and extrastriate activity during a visual control task wherein subjects viewed "false fonts." In an fMRI study, Schneider, Casey, and Noll (1993) found calcarine fissure activation during visual character search and reversing checkerboard stimuli, greater in the second condition. Also, Roland and Gulyas (1995) report perception and learning of complex visual geometric patterns activate area 17 (but recall of the patterns does not). In our visual task—letter/shape discrimination—primary occipital cortex is often the most metabolically active region in the brain.

Parietal Occipital Sulcus (POS)

The parietal occipital sulcus is a clearly defined sulcus visible from the medial aspect as the superior branch of a Y formation, the other branch of which is formed by the calcarine fissure. Visually, the POS is the demarcation of the occipital and parietal lobes from the medial aspect. It is uninterrupted 100% of the time.

Roland and Gulyas (1995) reported activation of parietal occipital sulcus and posterior precuneus during learning and recognition of complex geometric patterns.

Collateral Sulcus/Anterior and Posterior
Parahippocampal Lingual-Fusiform Gyri

The collateral sulcus is a deep sulcus, continuous 100% of the time, and clearly visualizable as a stream of gray matter positioned in an anterior-posterior direction and following the contour of the inferior aspect of the occipital lobe. In the anterior aspect the parahippocampal ramus divides the parahippocampal gyrus from the fusiform gyrus. Just posterior to that is the intralingual ramus, separating the lingual and fusiform gyri. Thus, several cytoarchitectual regions—30, 37, and 19—are traversed by the collateral gyrus.

Activation of the right parahippocampal region and adjacent areas has been reported by Sergent, Ohta, and MacDonald (1992) during performance of a face identity task. Fusiform activity is reported during visual object naming (Kiyosawa et al. 1996), face identity (Sergent, Ohta, and MacDonald 1992), attending visual stimuli (Heinze et al. 1994), auditory phoneme monitoring (Demonet et al. 1994b), attention to shape (Corbetta et al. 1991), and object identity (Moscovitch et al. 1995). In an FDG metabolism study, Gross-Glenn et al. (1991) found higher bilateral activity in subjects with dyslexia as compared to controls. Rumsey et al. (1997) reported higher left lingual gyrus activity in individuals with dyslexia during pronunciation or identification of phonologically regular non-words.

Left lingual gyrus activity is reported during viewing of non-words (Frith et al. 1995) and bilateral collateral sulcus activity (between the lingual and fusiform gyri) during a visual attention task (Caretta et al. 1991). Even in an auditory task, Diamagnet et al. (1994b) found that, as compared to monitoring pure tones, perceptually ambiguous auditory stimuli (monitoring phonemes) resulted in left fusiform activity, possibly in an attempt to visualize indecipherable word-like material. Using fMRI, fusiform-lingual activation was observed in response to visual character search (Schneider et al. 1993). Peterson et al. (1990) report left medial extrastriate visual cortex in response to viewing words or non-words. A reduction in right lingual gyrus activity was observed by Frith et al. (1995) under conditions of habituation to "incidental" processing of non-words.

Hippocampus

Like the thalamus, the hippocampus is easily visualized on the MRI, but its complex divisions are not distinguished. It is an area of s-shaped gray tissue within the medial temporal lobe lying along the floor of the lateral ventricle just caudal to the amygdala, but not clearly distinguishable from its posterior border. Major afferent projections are from the entorhinal cortex, septal nucleus, locus ceruleus, red nucleus, and VTA, and major efferents project back to entorhinal cortex and fornix. The hippocampus has well known memory functions, especially in the consolidation of newly acquired information. Ablation of the hippocampus prevents conscious recall of episodes of the recent or remote past. The hippocampus is reportedly altered in its activity in a number of demented and psychotic conditions.

Activation of the right hippocampus has been reported during a novel visual lexical decision task (FDG study, Halgren et al. 1994).

Anterior hippocampus was active during learning complex geometric patterns and posterior hippocampus showed enhanced activity during recognition of the patterns (Roland and Gulyas 1995).

Posterior Inferior Temporal (Area 37)

Also part of the ventral visual stream, area 37 receives input from extrastriate cortex (area 19) and outputs to inferior temporal cortex (areas 20 and 21) and to posterior Wernicke's area (area 39). The region is extensive, beginning laterally at the arbitrary demarcation between the temporal and occipital lobes approximately at the occipital incisura, and extending under the occipital lobe ventrally and then medially. Activation of left inferior temporal area 37 has been reported during visual naming of words and pictures and silent reading (Bookheimer et al. 1995), object recognition separate from facial recognition (Sergent, Ohta, and MacDonald 1992), and visual retrieval of object identity (Moscovitch et al. 1995). Bilateral activity has been obtained during presentation of non-words (Frith et al. 1995). This portion of the visual ventral "what" stream is inversely correlated with task performance in our large normal sample ($n = 60$).

Posterior Inferior Temporal Sulcus (Adjacent Anterior)

To extend the representation of the ventral ("what is it") stream, this additional and more anterior ROI was also included.

Heschl's Gyrus

Also known as the temporal transverse gyrus, Heschl's gyrus lies on the dorsomedial surface of the superior temporal gyrus and contains the primary auditory receptive cells (Brodmann's area 41) as well as auditory association cells (Brodmann's area 42). Heschl's is buried within the Sylvian fissure but is easily located on a 3D rendering of the MRI. Input from the medial geniculate nucleus of the thalamus is mainly to area 41 where tonotopic organization is maintained.

Lubs et al. (1988) reported lower peri-insular activation in individuals with dyslexia as measured by FDG PET during oral word reading. Paulesu et al. (1996) found that subjects with dyslexia did not activate the insular region during either a short-term memory or a rhyming task.

Superior Temporal Sulcus

The superior temporal sulcus is the enfolding between the superior and middle temporal gyri. It is frequently discontinuous (68% of the time) and quite variable in its posterior terminus, often branching before it ends (28% to 44% of the time on the right and left, respectively) and sometimes meeting the intraparietal sulcus in the right hemisphere (20% of the time).

The superior and middle temporal gyri are activated during numerous and diverse tasks presented in visual or auditory modalities: an auditory phoneme monitoring task (Diamagnet et al. 1994a), a visual phonological decision task (Sergent, Ohta, and MacDonald 1992), a visual word meaning task (Vandenberghe et al. 1996), single word repetition (FDG study, Karbe et al. 1995), visual word recognition (Small et al. 1996), listening to sound in the word production range as well as visual word repetition (Howard et al. 1992), attention to shape (Caretta et al. 1991), and reading silently and aloud (Price et al. 1994). Rumsey et al. (1997) reported lower activation in the posterior superior temporal region in a dyslexic group than in unaffected controls during a visual word-non-word discrimination task, and Ingvar et al. (1993) found less activation in Broca's area in individuals with dyslexia than in control subjects during an oral reading task.

Inferior Temporal Sulcus

The inferior temporal sulcus is the enfolding between the middle and inferior temporal gyri. Spanning the length of the inferior temporal lobe from the pole into the anterior inferior occipital lobe, it is discontinuous 100% of the time. The inferior temporal area includes Brodmann's areas 20, 21, and 37 known to be involved in processing of form and color and is part of the ventral visual stream important to the identification of objects. It has input from the visual lingual cortex and output to inferior prefrontal regions.

Activation of the inferior temporal region has been observed during visual object naming (Kiyosawa et al. 1996), silent reading and silent naming of words or pictures (Bookheimer et al. 1995), visual picture meaning (Vandenberghe et al. 1996), and visual presentation of non-words (Frith et al. 1995).

Angular Gyrus

Part of the inferior parietal lobule, the angular gyrus (area 39) is a bend of convex tissue formed at the posterior terminus of the superior temporal gyrus. It is cytoarchitecturally relatively granular, compared to the more pyramidal cytoarchitecture characterizing the cortex above this region (dorsal to the intraparietal sulcus). The angular gyrus receives projections from the lingual gyrus (inferior area 19) and projects to the temporal lobe (area 22). It is thus on one branch of the "what is it" ventral visual processing stream, and some have believed it to be the neural mediator of words and other meaningful symbols accessed through the visual system. Although rare, lesions exclusive to this area result in alexia without loss of auditory comprehension.

Activation of the left angular gyrus has been observed during auditory phoneme discrimination tasks (Zatorre et al. 1996; Diamagnet et al. 1994a), short-term memory for visually presented letters (Paulesu, Frith, and Frackowiak 1993), viewing words (Menard et al. 1996), and during a non-semantic word task (Vandenberghe et al. 1996). Rumsey et al. (1992) found less activity in the supramarginal/angular gyrus region in a dyslexic sample during rhyme detection while Flowers, Wood, and Naylor (1991) found greater activity in individuals with dyslexia as compared to controls in the same region during an orthographic identification task, while simultaneously, individuals with dyslexia activated left posterior superior temporal cortex less than did controls. Right angular gyrus activity is also observed during an auditory lexical semantic task (Diamagnet et al. 1994a) and speech from memory (Tamas et al. 1993) and related to anxiety during orthographic identification (Flowers, Wood, and Naylor 1991).

Intraparietal Sulcus (Superior Posterior Parieto-Occipital)

The intraparietal sulcus is an enfolding between the superior and inferior parietal lobules. It is interrupted into two segments 68% of the time on the right and 28% of the time on the left. Anteriorly it is adjacent to and frequently connects with postcentral somatosensory cortex (about 66% of the time). Posteriorly it always extends into the superior occipital lobe, often as a T-intersect with the transverse occipital sulcus (60% to 70% of the time). The superior lobule, Brodmann's area 7, receives projections from sensory and visual cortex and thus integrates information about body position in relation to its surroundings. Lesions here result in distorted body image and contralateral neglect. (Lesions to the parietal region just ventral to this in the inferior lobule—area 39—result in alexia.) Of particular importance to a functional study of brain response to a visual stimulus is that the parietal cortex is a part of the other, dorsal, visual stream believed to process the location of objects of importance. Projections from visual extrastriate area V5, concerned with motion and stereopsis, terminate in area 7. Other projections to area 7 are extrageniculate in nature, via the pulvinar, as well as from the anterior cingulate. Projection from the so-called parietal eye field in area 7 is to frontal eye fields and there are also projections from area 7 to the supramarginal gyrus (area 40).

One fMRI study has reported decreased function in individuals with dyslexia (Eden et al. 1996) in V5, a region that receives projections from the magnocellular region of the LGN of the thalamus and projects to the superior parietal area (Livingstone et al. 1991). Activation of the intraparietal sulcus has been observed bilaterally during a location matching task (Haxby et al. 1994). Bilateral posterior superior parietal has also been found to be activated during perception and learning of complex visual geometric patterns as well as during the recall (visualization) of those learned figures (Roland and Gulyas 1995).

Broca's Area

Broca's area, Brodmann's areas 44 and 45 (or pars triangularis), is a region at the stem of the Sylvian fissure in the frontal operculum, anterior to the motor strip in the posterior inferior frontal cortex. Broca's area connects to Wernicke's area in the posterior perisylvian region via the arcuate fasciculus. The region is known as the anterior speech cortex and is believed, based on lesion data and functional imaging studies, to be involved in verbal articulation and verbal working memory.

Broca's area activity has been observed during numerous tasks including viewing words (Menard et al. 1996), rhyme judgment for visually presented letters (Paulesu et al. 1996), auditory phoneme monitoring (Diamagnet et al. 1994a), and visually presented nonwords (Frith et al. 1995). Ingvar et al. (1993) found less activation in Broca's area in individuals with dyslexia than in control subjects in response to oral reading while the Paulesu group found a disconnection between Broca's area activation and posterior temporal regions in individuals with dyslexia during phonological tasks.

Dorsolateral Prefrontal—Inferior Sulcus

There are two principal sulci visible from a lateral view of the frontal lobe of the human cerebrum. The more ventral of these—the inferior sulcus, an enfolding between the inferior and middle frontal gyri—is identified by Brodmann's areas 45-46 and is frequently interrupted (52% of the time). There is significant reciprocal innervation between the medial dorsal nucleus of the thalamus and the prefrontal cortex, a circuit thought to be involved in affective behavior. Prefrontal cortex is also a projection area from posterior ventral extrastriate regions. The prefrontal cortex receives input as well via the long association fibers of the cortical fasciculi from multimodal association areas and is juxtaposed to the premotor region of the frontal lobe. Cytoarchitecturally, it is noteworthy that this region resembles the angular gyrus in its considerable granularity. It is also well supplied by projections from the angular gyrus, and may well be understandable both as an extension of angular gyrus sensory-perceptual processing (perhaps more in the "what is it" ventral visual processing stream) and as a source of motor planning or "executive" functions including working memory (Goldman-Rakic 1987). Its motor-related output is by way of the caudate-thalamic circuit. Lesions in the human prefrontal cortex characteristically result in hypokinesia and apathy.

Activation is reported in this region during performance of many tasks: visual attention to letter shapes (Liotti et al, 1995), maintenance of words and non-words in short term memory (Fiez et al. 1995), visual object naming (Kiyosawa et al. 1996), divided attention (Caretta et al. 1991), word meaning (Vandenberghe et al. 1996), face matching (Haxby et al. 1994), and lexical decisions (Price et al. 1994), for example.

Dorsolateral Prefrontal Superior Sulcus—1 (Anterior) and 2 (Posterior)

The superior sulcus, represented over its length by parts of Brodmann's areas 6, 8, and 9, is dorsal to the inferior sulcus and parallel to it. This sulcus is an enfolding between the middle and superior gyri and is usually discontinuous (64% of the time). In its dorsal aspect, especially, it is cytoarchitecturally more pyramidal, analogous to the superior parietal cortex. There are reciprocal connections between area 6 and several thalamic nuclei and between area 8 and the parietal lobe. There are also connections to parts of the temporal lobe by way of the arcuate fasciculus which travels through the insular cortex.

Superior frontal activation or deactivation have been reported during Wisconsin Card sorting (Van Horn, Berman, and Weinberger 1996), location matching (Haxby et al. 1994), and reading aloud (Ingvar et al. 1993). In the latter case, nonaffected controls deactivated prefrontal regions while subjects with dyslexic did not.

Orbital Frontal Cortex

The orbital frontal cortex lies over the eye orbits on the ventral aspect of the frontal lobe. It is connected to the anterior temporal lobe by the uncinate fasciculus. The orbital sulci, short and always multi branched, lie lateral to the rectal gyri (the most ventromedial, anterior-posterior going sulci of the frontal lobes). Lesions here may result in externally directed hyperkinesia.

Naming of color incongruent words (Stroop test) has been shown to activate the right orbital region (Bench et al. 1993) as has a face matching task (Haxby et al. 1994).

Head of the Caudate Nucleus

A subcortical gray mass of the basal ganglia, the caudate nucleus is c-shaped and divided into a head, body, and a tail that curves around the inferior horn of the lateral ventricle and terminates near the amygdala. Afferent fibers originate mostly in association areas of the cortex and the substantia nigra. Of the five circuits through the basal ganglia mediating motor functions (Alexander, DeLong, and Strick 1986), of particular interest is the so-called cognitive loop that includes the caudate nucleus. There are two circuits in this loop that terminate either in the dorsolateral prefrontal or the lateral orbitofrontal regions involved with forward planning (especially of integrated patterns of movement) by way of input from all neocortical association areas and output through the globus pallidus to the ventral anterior nucleus of the thalamus and then to frontal cortex terminals.

Note that the head of the caudate should be distinguished from the ventral caudate or nucleus accumbens, more prominently involved with projections from anterior cingulate, entorhinal cortex, and the temporal lobes. The ventral caudate has efferent projections reciprocally to the substantia nigra and also to the pallidum and magnocellular layer of the medial-dorsal nucleus of the thalamus. Nucleus accumbens is involved in the reward circuits of the brain and is believed to be particularly important in the abuse of addictive dopamine enhancing substances such as cocaine. Nucleus accumbens can arguably be isolated as a differential local maximum in PET, but was not isolated for purposes of this study.

The dorsal (head of) caudate circuits are of particular interest for their role in planning, timing, and gauging learned serial motor patterns, of which speech production is one. Underactivity has been reported in children with attention deficit disorder (Lou et al. 1989). Bookheimer et al. (1995) found left caudate activation in normal subjects during reading words but not during viewing words or objects or when naming objects and right caudate activation during viewing objects but not during language processing or naming objects. Rumsey et al. (1997) reported greater activation in controls than in dyslexic subjects in the right caudate during a lexical decision task, the local maximum of which was located on the medial aspect of the caudate head.

Putamen

Also part of the basal ganglia, the putamen is grouped either with the caudate nucleus (with which it is rostrally continuous) or with the globus pallidus to form the lentiform nucleus. The lentiform nucleus lies ventrolateral to the caudate nucleus and is surrounded medially by the limbs of the internal capsule and laterally by the external capsule and claustrum. The putamen is central to the striatal motor loop, involved in learned motor patterns and sequencing of serial order activities. Consequently, movement disorders, such as Parkinson's Disease, result from malfunction of putamen circuits. Damage can also result in loss of the ability to write the letters of the alphabet, cut with scissors, hammer nails, or perform other skilled movements while small lesions in the putamen result in choreas.

Activity in the putamen has been recorded during visual object naming (Kiyosawa et al. 1996), learning a serial reaction time response task (Hazeltine, Grafton, and Ivry 1997), complex sequential finger movements (Sadato et al. 1996), and in relation to attentional dysfunction (Lou et al. 1996). In normal subjects, Price et al. (1994) reported left and right posterior putamen activation during reading aloud and Bookheimer et al. (1995) found right putamen activation (the local maximum of which was in the superior posterior aspect) during verbal production (reading or naming objects) but not during viewing of words or objects. In a group of dyslexic subjects, Rumsey et al. (1997) found right putamen activation during pronunciation of regular nonwords. Left putamen activation is response to passive viewing of single words (Petersen et al. 1988, 1989).

Anterior Cingulate

The cingulate gyrus is visualized from the medial aspect of either hemisphere divided through the longitudinal fissure. It follows the dorsal contour of the corpus callosum and is part of a ring of limbic tissue that communicates between the prefrontal cortex and subcortical limbic structures, and it has a substantial efferent connection to area 7 in the posterior parietal lobule. It includes Brodmann's areas 32 and 24. The anterior portion responds to pain, subjective emotion, visceral response to emotional state, and anticipatory movement. Lesions result in release of septal function leading to rage reactions.

Activation of the anterior cingulate has been observed during Stroop test performance (Bench et al. 1993; Pardo et al. 1990), visual lexical decision (FDG study, Halgren et al. 1994), visual object naming (Kiyosawa et al. 1996), and verb and noun retrieval (Warburton et al. 1996).

PET TECHNIQUE

Our method assumes and requires registration of the MRI and PET image in Talairach space (Talairach and Tournoux 1988), which may be accomplished in several ways (Evans, Marrett, and Collins 1989; Woods, Cherry, and Mazziotta 1992, 1993; Hoehne and Hanson 1992). The registration then permits the above spherical volumes to be defined on the MRI so that subsequent measurements of glucose metabolic activity can be made on the corresponding PET image regions. For that purpose, we consider all gray matter voxels (defined on MRI) within the region of interest. The corresponding voxels within the PET image then constitute a population of voxels within the spherical ROI.

The 95th percentile of the PET gray matter voxels is then taken as the dependent measure of interest for that region, in a method previously validated in phantom studies to represent the overall best measure of activity in the volume (Fahey et. al. 1998).

A value for total cerebral activity is also determined and this is used to calculate relative (i.e., normalized) values, as quotients of individual regions over the total region. as well as absolute values. A sphere of approximately 19 cm diameter is centered in the brain, determined empirically to take in the entire cerebrum placed within Talairach space (the size of the sphere may be adjusted to the best visual fit). On average, the center of this sphere was determined in a normal sample to fall within the third ventricle 6 cm above the AC-PC line and 16 cm posterior to the vertical frontal plane. Consistent with its role as a reference value, the 50th percentile of the gray matter voxels was taken for the denominator of the quotients (in which individual regions of interest were the numerators).

The MRI measurements employed a T1 weighted image acquired on a 1.5 Tesla GE Signa MRI scanner (Signa, GE Medical Systems, Milwaukee, WI). One hundred twenty slices were acquired in the axial plane according the following protocol: 3D-SPGR pulse sequence; TR = 35 ms; TE = 5ms; flip angle = 35 degrees; matrix = 256 x 256; slice thickness = 2.0 mm; NEX = 2.

PET imaging was performed using the Siemens ECAT 951/31 Scanner. The scanner has 16 rings that produce 31 transaxial planes spaced 3.375 mm apart resulting in a 10.4 cm axial field of view. Two bed positions are utilized to obtain a total of 62 planes over a 21 cm total axial field of view. The in-plane (transaxial) resolution has been measured to be 6.0 to 6.5 mm (in stationary mode). The measured axial resolution is 4.7 and 5.5 mm on the central axis of the gantry and 10 cm from the axis, respectively. Prior to isotope injection, a 30-minute transmission scan is acquired for 2 bed positions (15 min each, 21 cm total axial field of view) to correct for attenuation during reconstruction of the emission scan. The emission scanning begins 40 minutes after the injection of FDG. This scan consists of 62 transverse planes spaced 3.375 mm apart, imaged parallel to the canthomeatal (CM) line. The system sensitivity was determined to be 120 kcps/uCi/ml. Once the PET image data are acquired, they are reconstructed with filtered back projection, using a Hann filter with a 0.4 cycles per pixel cutoff frequency. When the data have been transformed into Talairach space and registered, each image is resampled and displayed as 80 extrapolated with pixel size in the x, y, and z planes of 0.1720 cm.

During glucose uptake, an attentional standardization task is done, requiring a right index fingerlift response if a letter instead of a non-letter is flashed on the computer screen at fixation point. The stimulus letters and non-letters are either black or white and are presented at a rate averaging one stimulus every two seconds. All combinations of color with letter versus non-letter were equiprobable and randomly sequenced.

A single glucose run is thus obtained from each subject. By definition this image cannot be subtracted from any other so as to "isolate" a task related pattern of regional activation. This single run, however, can be compared across subjects to determine patterns of common regional covariation. Stated another way, the variation in glucose metabolic landscapes is here studied with a between-subjects reference, not a within-subject reference.

The above correlational strategy is of some interest purely for the regional covariation it might show; but that interest would be heightened if those patterns of regional covariation also showed external behavioral validation. Accordingly, behavioral phenotypes with differential genetic validity (Grigorenko et. al. 1997) were used. In particular, a phonemic awareness phenotype that focused on auditory-oral phoneme segmentation, was measured separately from phonological decoding (non-word reading) and single word reading (real words).

FACTOR ANALYSIS OF REGIONAL COVARIATION

The analyzed sample consists of the first 100 cases studied in the current term of the program project. The male-female ratio is 62/38 and the Caucasian/African-American ratio is 88/12. The mean education is 15.9 years (range 11 to 21); mean WAIS-R Vocabulary Scale Score 11.75 (range 5 to 19); mean Woodcock-Johnson (1977 version) single word reading subtest score 47.05 (range 30 to 52); and mean task d-prime 3.83 (range 1.80 to 6.0). Questionnaires were also administered with items assessing for DSM-IV attentional diagnoses (ADHD), related attentional and impulsive symptoms currently experienced as well as remembered from childhood, and behavioral history of delinquent acts.

(1) $N = 50$ normals, reading above the 25th percentile on both the Word Identification (single word reading) and Word Attack (non-word reading, i.e., phonological decoding) subtests of the Woodcock-Johnson; and

(2) $N = 50$ dyslexic or at-risk cases, specifically:

(a) $N = 31$ who had been below the 25th percentile in their childhood psychometric records, on two different reading tests at least one of which was a single word reading test;

(b) $N = 6$ unselected normals scoring below the 10th percentile on both the Word Identification and Word Attack subtests; and

(c) $N = 13$ blood relatives of an affected proband who exhibits all three behavioral phenotypes (phonemic awareness, phonological decoding, and single word reading). This proband is a phonemic awareness case with a phonological decoding phenocopy (secondary to his phonemic awareness deficit).

The regions of interest entered into the analysis are defined above. These regional values were subjected to a principal components analysis, followed by a varimax rotation. In the unrotated principal components analysis, ten factors had eigenvalues, i.e., amounts of variance accounted for that were greater than 1.0 (ranging from 7.756 to 1.060), so these were selected for rotation. The varimax-rotated factors had amounts of variance accounted for ranging from 4.3591 to 1.5414.

The varimax-rotated factors are shown in table II as factor loadings and in figure 1 as schematically mapped by their major loadings onto a brain outline. The first nine factors are defined by more than one region and are readily interpretable. (Note above that Factor 7 is best defined by four positive loadings: not only right hippocampus and lingual gyrus, but left of both regions as well. The negative left Broca's area loading is less strong, even though it is stronger for this factor than for any other).

Given nine interpretable factors, it is then relevant to consider their behavioral correlates. For this purpose, three genetically differentiable phenotypes (defined and tested in Grigorenko et. al. 1997) were assessed. These phenotypes are defined by cut scores that identify about 15% of the normal population as affected. The phenotypes were: (1) Phonemic Awareness, tested by auditory-oral tasks requiring phonemic segmentation; (2) Phonological Decoding, tested by non-word reading; and (3) Single Word Reading, tested by real word calling. The behavioral style factors represented clusters of symptoms in a standardized interview for DSM-IV symptoms and related symptoms. (Copies of the interview are available from the authors at nominal cost.) For purposes of analysis, any individual having the Phonemic Awareness phenotype was so defined, regardless of the presence of any other phenotype. Likewise, all Single Word cases were defined as having the Single Word phenotype, whatever their overlap with other phenotypes (and all Single Word cases had either the Phonemic Awareness or Phonological Decoding phenotypes as well, but not always both). Although there were many overlap cases between Phonemic Awareness and Phonological Decoding, however, in this analysis only those possessing the Phonological Decoding phenotype without the Phonemic Awareness phenotype were defined as having the Phonological Decoding phenotype. These cases could still possess the Single Word phenotype, and many did.

The correlations between factors and behavioral correlates are presented in table III. As is clear, there is considerable differentiation in

Table II.   Varimax-Rotated Factor Loadings for the N=100 sample. (See notes at end of table identifying the ROI labels).

ROI	FACTOR 1	FACTOR 2	FACTOR 3	FACTOR 4	FACTOR 5
SUP2R	0.80768	−0.13954	0.07438	0.08829	0.03951
SUP2L	0.78411	0.19909	−0.08244	0.14399	−0.08389
SUP1R	0.77403	0.16676	0.09918	−0.10861	0.06605
SUP1L	0.74454	−0.23329	0.19684	−0.01714	0.17204
ANC	0.71273	−0.07163	−0.05989	−0.03014	0.13263
INFR	0.55100	−0.14152	0.51205	−0.00384	0.12549
PITL	0.06658	0.81001	0.03957	0.21232	0.11502
A37L	0.02102	0.76502	0.11601	0.20349	0.04579
ITSL	−0.06687	0.72210	0.07603	−0.02260	−0.06230
STSL	−0.06110	0.57169	−0.03382	0.42692	0.09934
HGL	−0.08947	0.55323	−0.00442	0.18185	0.23582
LIN1L	−0.05075	0.53874	−0.13836	0.32047	0.11694
HIPL	−0.26579	0.46695	0.19351	−0.07555	0.23154
ITSR	−0.05130	0.08355	0.77714	−0.01365	−0.08161
PITR	0.04436	0.09947	0.70346	0.08857	−0.05867
A37R	0.19126	0.15955	0.68500	0.14897	0.09159
STSR	−0.01851	0.00489	0.62474	0.23162	0.28720
HGR	0.00885	−0.01846	0.59957	0.13331	0.37534
BROR	0.10919	−0.13885	0.59726	−0.06044	0.33716
CALR	0.10099	0.11921	0.05189	0.80164	−0.17924
CALL	0.00568	0.26902	0.04455	0.72559	−0.05959
LIN2L	0.00949	0.26348	0.00805	0.68350	0.18122
LIN2R	0.26500	0.08732	0.23923	0.62490	0.13663
POSR	−0.12306	−0.03165	0.27750	0.56926	0.17738
POSL	−0.14560	0.25604	0.01096	0.52356	0.20547
CAUL	0.10558	0.20144	−0.08355	−0.01894	0.76661
CAUR	0.08197	−0.02472	0.00892	−0.10060	0.75800
PUTR	0.05577	−0.02422	0.17823	0.19211	0.73768
PUTL	0.09226	0.24596	0.16784	0.00652	0.69048
IPSL	0.29013	0.07569	−0.03835	0.10442	0.01221
ANGL	0.35286	0.25689	−0.04899	−0.19177	0.02758
ANGR	0.35323	−0.13197	0.27632	0.07741	−0.11640
IPSR	0.39873	−0.24753	0.24526	0.19115	−0.02046
HIPR	0.01899	0.08347	0.16841	0.00353	0.06853
LIN1R	−0.05222	0.01219	0.19945	0.40623	0.05565
BROL	0.13698	0.37123	−0.10902	0.21923	0.25509

continued

Table II.   Varimax-Rotated Factor Loadings for the N=100 sample. (See notes at end of table identifying the ROI labels), *continues*

ROI	FACTOR 1	FACTOR 2	FACTOR 3	FACTOR 4	FACTOR 5
THAR	–0.18494	0.14830	0.20318	0.12632	0.32084
THAL	–0.02882	0.05576	0.09080	0.19085	0.40052
ORFR	0.17528	0.03985	0.28669	0.07050	0.11929
ORFL	0.22479	0.45933	0.02124	0.07063	–0.06241
INFL	0.44957	0.36184	–0.08743	–0.08172	0.05233

ROI	FACTOR 6	FACTOR 7	FACTOR 8	FACTOR 9	FACTOR 10
SUP2R	0.10406	–0.00616	–0.07200	0.15573	–0.13349
SUP2L	0.11408	–0.07617	–0.02656	0.05204	–0.03355
SUP1R	0.06421	0.00693	–0.07485	–0.13152	0.24013
SUP1L	0.15526	0.07842	0.03586	0.13588	–0.19780
ANC	0.21534	–0.02052	–0.04970	0.13102	0.16537
INFR	0.15589	–0.17044	–0.00852	0.00823	0.26046
PITL	0.13356	0.07555	–0.06745	0.01579	–0.02534
A37L	–0.13599	0.09768	0.09752	–0.07936	0.06876
ITSL	–0.03743	0.03715	0.20307	0.11306	0.04245
STSL	0.08109	–0.10462	–0.19333	0.15489	0.14878
HGL	0.31879	–0.30539	0.03752	0.10748	0.18840
LIN1L	0.08228	0.41300	0.08302	0.03900	–0.13944
HIPL	–0.04151	0.43607	–0.08673	0.05880	0.04869
ITSR	–0.06104	0.27535	0.15558	0.01346	–0.06677
PITR	0.02010	0.27915	0.19648	0.05653	–0.16408
A37R	–0.07488	0.28740	0.11911	0.02291	0.15677
STSR	0.30435	–0.15699	–0.09456	0.17008	–0.36203
HGR	0.42544	–0.09610	–0.06002	0.09696	0.07708
BROR	–0.00772	–0.27559	–0.18555	0.26782	0.20732
CALR	0.13007	–0.01839	0.16044	0.02332	–0.07373
CALL	–0.06254	–0.08037	0.29306	0.00373	0.09046
LIN2L	–0.12333	0.24818	–0.04905	–0.15969	–0.14009
LIN2R	–0.08616	0.33439	–0.17976	0.22373	–0.11202
POSR	0.30056	0.01226	0.03708	0.21212	0.40937
POSL	0.25304	–0.02970	0.15024	0.18487	0.41868
CAUL	0.01732	0.14602	0.11676	0.17355	–0.10782
CAUR	–0.03961	0.28128	0.00141	0.14833	0.09292
PUTR	–0.02556	–0.07884	0.23244	–0.06533	0.08452
PUTL	0.08450	–0.17163	0.20106	–0.21005	0.01564
IPSL	0.77083	0.03560	–0.07357	–0.04154	0.12539
ANGL	0.68319	–0.05822	0.06656	0.15885	0.04953

continued

Table II.   Varimax-Rotated Factor Loadings for the N=100 sample. (See notes at end of table identifying the ROI labels), *continues*

ROI	FACTOR 6	FACTOR 7	FACTOR 8	FACTOR 9	FACTOR 10
ANGR	0.60160	−0.06520	0.24354	−0.01200	−0.22059
IPSR	0.43567	0.09755	0.21573	0.05678	0.12041
HIPR	−0.06622	0.76411	0.05170	−0.10268	0.11855
LIN1R	0.13058	0.62072	0.00831	0.05141	−0.18518
BROL	0.17147	(−0.39798)	−0.07324	0.30906	0.24933
THAR	0.05268	0.07248	0.71550	0.10429	−0.06908
THAL	0.08302	0.02592	0.70766	0.10510	0.10949
ORFR	0.09160	−0.14171	0.10329	0.75083	−0.01080
ORFL	−0.00623	0.09752	0.13319	0.61288	0.06279
INFL	0.11051	−0.02981	0.01451	0.00168	0.61554

Notes on Table II.
L and R suffixes are left and right;
1 and 2 suffixes are anterior and posterior placements of a given region

A37 = area 37
ANC = anterior cingulate
ANG = angular gyrus
BRO = Broca's area
CAL = calcarine fissure
CAU = caudate
HG = Heschl's gyrus
HIP = hippocampus
INF = inferior frontal
IPS = intraparietal sulcus

ITS = inferior temporal sulcus
LIN = lingual/fusiform gyrus
ORF = orbital frontal
PIT = posterior inferior temporal sulcus
POS = parieto-occipital sulcus
PUT = putamen
STS = superior temporal sulcus
SUP = superior frontal
THA = thalamus

Loadings sharing a noteworthy portion of variance on a given factor, notwithstanding that they load moderately more highly on other factors, are marked by underlining.

the behavioral correlates of these regional brain activation factors. We note especially the separation of the three phenotypes: Phonemic Awareness, Phonological Decoding, and Single Word Reading—associating differentially strongly with inferior temporo-occipital, right central-frontal, and thalamic activity, respectively. This would seem to suggest the important prospect that these clusters of regional brain activation may represent different aspects of reading disability, perhaps subtypes. The factor analyses are necessarily global, overriding small but potentially important distinctions, but they certainly do raise hypotheses deserving of further test and validation across the genetic, imaging and behavioral range.

Equally deserving of test are the associations with attentional and behavioral style. It is entirely plausible that the phenotypes are not cognitive only, and that heretofore uncharacterized factors may operate to bias a given genotype toward either a cognitive or behavioral style outcome, both of which may be what the genotype creates risk for.

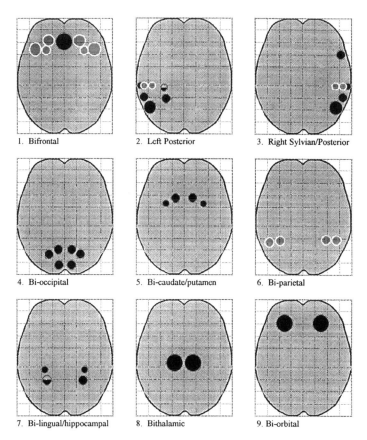

Figure 1.   Factor structure of regional covariation in the N = 100 sample.
Notes: The lighter circles, with white borders, are on the dorsolateral aspect.
The darker circles, with gray borders, are relatively ventral or medial. Broca's
area, the inferior and posterior inferior temporal sulcus, and area 37 are all
coded as ventral; superior temporal and Heschl's gyrus are coded as dorsolateral (all illustrated in Factor 3 above).

COMMENTS

1. These factors, with their associated correlates, have the advantage
   of being unbiased, i.e., not subjected to statistical procedures that
   seek the best fit between regions and correlates. The correlates of
   interest above are found to be associated with patterns of regional
   covariation that were derived without reference to those correlates; these significant associations mean that the correlates partly
   describe patterns of regional covariation that are otherwise salient
   in their own right (i.e., account for noteworthy portions of the

Table III. External correlations of factor scores in the $N = 100$ sample.

	Factor Score								
	1	2	3	4	5	6	7	8	9
Subject Characteristics:									
Age:	−46*							29*	
Gender:									
Education:									
WAIS Vocabulary:	−26								
Performance Characteristics:									
State anxiety:									
Task D-prime:									26
Reading Phenotypes:									
Phonemic:			−23				22		
Pure Decoding:			27						
Single Word:							26		
Behavioral History Features:									
Impulsivity:	−26								−22
Inattention:							28		
Delinquency:								−20	

Note: All printed correlations are $p < .05$; correlations with * are $p < .005$

metabolic variance in this diverse sample before any attention is paid to correlates).

2. An anatomical model (stressing diverse cognitive and behavioral style consequences from local hypometabolism) is supported by the above findings. The model is therefore promising as a rationale for further investigations.

3. Many of the correlations above are neurobehaviorally expected (diminished frontal activity with impulsivity). Others are newer, including:

   a. The lingual-hippocampal relation both to inattention and phonemic awareness. The prospect is raised that inattentive symptoms (perhaps approaching the DSM-IV inattentive-only subtype of ADHD) may have a more posterior, arguably sensory-perceptual quality. Also, even the auditory-oral operations defining phonemic awareness may burden extra-striate visual cortex.

   b. The thalamic relation both to single word reading and delinquency. Its neurobehavioral rationale is not immediately obvious, but makes for speculative hypothesis generating and testing.

   c. The right hemisphere relation to "pure" decoding. Because this construct is defined as having normal phonemic awareness but poor decoding, it is not surprising that it is negatively correlated with the phonemic awareness construct in the table. It will be interesting if the further data bear out the possibility that this construct relates to right hemisphere functioning because it only involves integration or synthesis of elements (phonemes) when those elements themselves are not the problem.

EDITOR'S COMMENTS

This chapter achieves two goals. First, it presents a comprehensive review of previous PET studies of anatomic regions concerned with cognitive functions that might be pertinent to reading disorders. Second, it presents a remarkable PET study of brain regions of interest using a word identification task that not only distinguishes three subgroups of reading disorder (namely phonological decoding, phonemic awareness, and single-word reading), but also provides insights into potential correlations with behaviors as complex as delinquency and anxiety. This provocative investigation may stimulate a plethora of studies about the relationships between emotional states and academic achievement.

—DDD

REFERENCES

Alexander, G. E., DeLong, M. R., and Strick, P. L. 1986. Parallel organization of functionally segregated circuits linking basal ganglia and cortex. *Ann. Rev. Neurosci* 9:357–81.

Bench, C. J., Faith, C. D., Grasby, P. M., Friston, K. J., Paulesu, E., Frackowiak, R. S. J., and Dolan, R. J. 1993. Investigations of the functional anatomy of attention using the Stroop test. *Neuropsychologia* 31(9): 907–22.

Bookheimer, S. Y., Zeffiro, T. A., Blaxton, T., Gaillard, W., and Theodore, W. 1995. Regional cerebral blood flow during object naming and word reading. *Human Brain Mapping* 3:93–106.

Carpenter, M. B. 1991. *Core Text of Neuroanatomy.* Baltimore: Williams & Wilkins.

Caretta, M., Miezin, F. M., Dobmeyer, S., Shulman, G. L., and Petersen, S. E. 1991. Selective and divided attention during visual discriminations of shape, color, and speed: Functional anatomy by positron emission tomography. *Journal of Neuroscience* 11(8):2382–2402.

Diamagnet, J. F., Price, C., Wise, R., and Frackowiak, R. S. J. 1994a. A PET study of cognitive strategies in normal subjects during language tasks. Influence of phonetic ambiguity and sequence processing on phoneme monitoring. *Brain* 117:671–82.

Diamagnet, J. F., Price, C., Wise, R., and Frackowiak, R. S. J. 1994b. Differential activation of right and left posterior sylvian regions by semantic and phonological tasks: A positron-emission tomography study in normal human subjects. *Neuroscience Letters* 182:25–28.

Duane, D. D. (ed.). 1991. *The Reading Brain.* Parkton, MD: York Press.

Eden, G. F., VanMeter, J. W., Rumsey, J. M., Maisog, J. M., Woods, R. P., and Zeffiro, T. A. 1996. Abnormal processing of visual motion in dyslexia revealed by functional brain imaging. *Nature* 382:66–69.

Ernst, M. and Rumsey, J. (eds.), In press. *Functional Neuroimaging in Child Psychiatry: Conceptual Issues and Comorbidity.* New York, NY: Laurence Erlbaum.

Evans, A. C., Marrett, S., and Collins, L. 1989. Anatomical-functional correlative analysis of the human brain using three dimensional imaging systems. *Proceedings SPIE* 1092:264–74.

Fahey, F. H., Wood, F. B., Flowers, D. L., Eades, C. G., Gage, H. D., and Harkness, B. A. 1998. Evaluation of brain activity in FDG PET studies. *Journal of Computer Assisted Tomography* 22(6):953–61.

Fiez, J. A., Raichle, M. E., Miezin, F. M., Petersen, S. E., Tallal, P., and Katz, W. F. 1995. PET studies of auditory and phonological processing: Effects of Stimulus characteristics and task demands. *Journal of Cognitive Neuroscience* 7(3):357–75.

FitzGerald, J. M. T. 1996. *Neuroanatomy: Basic and Clinical.* London: W.B. Saunders Co., Ltd.

Flowers, D. L., Wood, F. B., and Naylor, C. E. 1991. Regional cerebral blood flow correlates of language processes in reading disability. *Archives of Neurology* 48:637–43.

Frith, C. D., Kapur, N., Friston, K. J., Liddle, P. F., and Frackowiak, R. S. J. 1995. Regional cerebral activity associated with the incidental processing of pseudo-words. *Human Brain Mapping* 3:153–60.

Goldman-Rakic, P. S. 1987. Architecture of the prefrontal cortex and the central executive. *Annals New York Academy of Sciences* 769:71–83.

Grigorenko, E. L., Wood, F. B., Meyer, M. S., Hart, L. A., Speed, W. C., Shuster, A., and Pauls, D. L. 1997. Susceptibility loci for distinct components of developmental dyslexia on chromosomes 6 and 15. *American Journal of Human Genetics* 60:27–39.

Gross-Glenn, K., Duara, R., Barker, W. W., Loewenstein, D., Chang, J. Y., Yoshii, F., Apicella, A. M., Pascal, S., Boothe, T., Sevush, S., Jallad, B. J., Novoa, L., and Lubs, H. A. 1991. Positron emission tomographic studies during serial word-reading by normal and dyslexic adults. *Journal of Clinical and Experimental Neuropsychology* 13(4):531–44.

Guyton, A. C. 1991. *Basic Neuroscience: Anatomy and Physiology.* London: W. B. Saunders Co., Ltd.

Haines, D. E. 1997. *Fundamental Neuroscience.* New York: Churchill Livingstone.

Haxby, J. V., Horwitz, B., Ungerleider, L. G., Maisog, J. M., Pietrini, P., and Grady, C. L. 1994. The functional organization of human extrastriate cortex: A PET-rCBF study of selective attention to faces and locations. *The Journal of Neuroscience* 14(1):6336–53.

Hazeltine, E., Grafton, S. T., and Ivry, R. 1997. Attention and stimulus characteristics determine the locus of motor-sequence encoding. A PET study. *Brain* 120:123–40.

Heinze, H. J., Mangun, G. R., Burchert, W., Hinrichs, H., Scholz, M., Munte, T. F., Gos, A., Scherg, M., Johannes, S., Hundeshagen H., Gazzaniga, M. S., and Hillard, S. A. 1994. Combined spatial and temporal imaging of brain activity during visual selective attention in humans. *Nature* 372:543–46.

Hoehne, K. H., and Hanson, W. A. 1992. Interactive 3D segmentation of MRI and CT volumes using morphological operations. *Journal of Computer Assisted Tomography* 16:285–94.

Howard, D., Patterson, K., Wise, R., Brown, W. D., Friston, K., Weiller, C., and Frackowiak, R. 1992. The cortical localization of the lexicons. *Brain* 115:1769–82.

Hynd, G. W., and Semrud-Clikeman, M. 1989. Dyslexia and brain morphology. *Psychological Bulletin* 106:447–82.

Ingvar, M., Greitz, T., Eriksson, L., Stone-Elander, S., Trampe, P., and Euler, C. 1993. Developmental dyslexia studied with PET. *Human Brain Mapping* 1:22–31.

Karbe, H., Wurker, M., Herholz, K., Ghaemi, M., Pietrzyk, U., Kessler, J., and Heiss, W. D. 1995. Planum temporale and Brodmann's area 22. *Archives of Neurology* 52:869–74.

Kiyosawa, M., Inoue, C., Kawasaki T., Tokoro, T., Ishii, K., Ohyama, M., Senda, M., and Soma, Y. 1996. Functional neuroanatomy of visual object naming: A PET study. *Graefes Archive for Clinical & Experimental Ophthalmology* 234(2):110–15.

Liotti, M., Laberge, D., Jerabek, P. A., Martin, C. C., and Fox, P. T. 1995. A PET study of focused visual attention to letter shapes. *Human Brain Mapping Supplement* 1(2):271.

Livingstone, M., Rosen, G. D., Drislane, F. W., and Galaburda, A. M. 1991. Physiological and anatomical evidence for a magnocellular deficit in developmental dyslexia. *Proceedings of the National Academy of Sciences, USA* 88:7943–47.

Lou, H. C., Henriksen, L., Bruhn, P., Borner, H., and Nielsen, J. B. 1989. Striatal dysfunction in attention deficit and hyperkinetic disorder. *Archives of Neurology* 46:48–52.

Lubs, H. A., Smith, S., Kimberling, W., Pennington, B., Gross-Glenn, K., and Duara, R. 1988. Dyslexia subtypes: genetics, behavior, and brain imaging. In F. Plum (ed.) *Language, Communication, and the Brain.* New York: Raven Press.

Menard, M. T., Kosslyn, S. M., Thompson, W. L., Alpert, N. M., and Rauch, S. L. 1996. Encoding words and pictures: A positron emission tomography study. *Neuropsychologia* 34(3):185–94.

Moscovitch, M., Kapur, S., Kohler, S., and Houle, S. 1995. Distinct neural correlates of visual long-term memory for spatial location and object identity: A positron emission tomography study in humans. *Proceedings of the National Academy of Science* 92:3721–5.

Ono, M., Kubik, S., and Abernathey, C. D. 1990. *Atlas of the Cerebral Sulci.* New York: Thieme Medical Publisher, Inc.

Pardo, J. V., Pardo, P. J., Janer, K. W., and Raichle, M. E. 1990. The anterior cingulate cortex mediates processing selection in the Stroop attentional conflict paradigm. *Proceedings of the National Academy of Science* 87:256–59.

Paulesu, E., Frith, C. D., and Frackowiak, R. S. J. 1993. The neural correlates of the verbal component of working memory. *Nature* 362:342–44.

Paulesu, E., Frith, U., Snowling, M., Gallagher, A., Morton, J., Frackowiak, R. S. J., and Faith, C. D. 1996. Is developmental dyslexia a disconnection syndrome? Evidence from PET scanning. *Brain* 119:143–57.

Petersen, S. E., Fox, P. T., Posner, M. E., Mintun, M. A., and Raichle, M. E. 1988. Positron emission tomographic studies of the cortical anatomy of single-word processing. *Nature* (London) 331:585–89.

Petersen, S. E., Fox, P. T., Posner, M. I., and Raichle, M. E. 1989. Positron emission tomographic studies of the processing of single words. *Journal of Cognitive Neuroscience* 1:153–70.

Petersen, S. E., Fox, P. T., Snyder, A. Z., and Raichle, M. E. 1990. Activation of extrastriate and frontal cortical areas by visual words and word-like stimuli. *Science* 249:1041–4.

Porrino, L. J., and Lucignani, G. 1987. Different patterns of local brain energy metabolism associated with high and low doses of methylphenidate relevance to its action in hyperactive children. *Biological Psychiatry* 22:126–38.

Porrino, L. J., Lucignani, G., Dow-Edwards, D., and Sokoloff, L. 1984. Correlation of dose-dependent effects of acute amphetamine administration on behavior and local cerebral metabolism in rats. *Brain Research* 307:311–20.

Price, C. J., Wise, R. J. S., Watson, J. D. G., Patterson, K., Howard, D., and Frackowiak, R. S. J. 1994. Brain activity during reading. The effects of exposure duration and risk. *Brain* 117:1255–69.

Roland, P. E., and Gulyas, B. 1995. Visual memory, visual imagery, and visual recognition of large field patterns by the human brain: Functional anatomy by positron emission tomography. *Cerebral Cortex* 1:79–93.

Rumsey, J. M., Andreason, P., Zametkin, A. J., Aquino, T., King, A. C., Hamburger, S. D., Pikus, A., Rapoport, J. L., and Cohen, R. M. 1992. Failure to activate the left temporoparietal cortex in dyslexia. An oxygen 15 positron emission tomographic study. *Archives of Neurology* 49:527–34.

Rumsey, J. M., Nace, K., Donohue, B., Wise, D., Maisog, J. M., and Andreason, P. 1997. A positron emission tomographic study of impaired word recognition and phonological processing in dyslexic men. *Archives of Neurology* 54:562–73.

Sadato, N., Campbell, G., Ibañez, V., Deiber, M., and Hallett, M. 1996. Complexity affects regional cerebral blood flow change during sequential finger movements. *Journal of Neuroscience* 16(8):2691–700.

Schneider, W., Casey, B. J., and Noll, D. 1993. Functional MRI mapping of stimulus rate effects across visual processing stages. *Human Brain Mapping* 1:1–17.

Sergent, J., Ohta, S., and MacDonald, B. 1992. Functional neuroanatomy of face and object processing. *Brain* 115:16–36.

Small, S. L., Noll, D. C., Perfetti, C. A., Hlustik, P., Wellington, R., and Schneider, W. 1996. Localizing the lexicon for reading aloud: Replication of a PET study using fMRI. *NeuroReport* 7:961–65.

Talairach, J., and Tournoux, P. 1988. *Co-Planar Stereotaxic Atlas of the Human Brain: 3-Dimensional Proportional System: An Approach to Cerebral Imaging.* George Thieme Verlag Stuttgart: New York.

Tamas, L. B., Shibasaki, T., Horikoshi, S., and Ohye, C. 1993. General activation of cerebral metabolism with speech: A PET study. *International Journal of Psychophysiology* 14(3):199–208.

Thatcher, R. W., Lyon, G. R., Rumsey, J., and Krasnegor, N. (eds.). 1996. *Developmental Neuroimaging; Mapping the Development of Brain and Behavior,* Academic Press; New York, NY.

Vandenberghe, R., Price, C., Wise, R., Josephs, O., and Frackowiak, R. S. J. 1996. Functional anatomy of a common semantic system for words and pictures. *Nature* 383:254–55.

Van Horn, J. D., Berman, K. F., and Weinberger, D. R. 1996. Functional lateralization of the prefrontal cortex during traditional frontal lobe tasks. *Biological Psychiatry* 39(6):389–99.

Warburton, E., Wise, R. J. S., Price, C. J., Weiller, C., Hadar, U., Ramsay, S., and Frackowiak, R. S. J. 1996. Noun and verb retrieval by normal subjects. Studies with PET. *Brain* 119:159–79.

Wood, F. B. 1990. Functional neuroimaging in neurobehavioral research. In A. A. Boulton, G. B. Baker, M. Hiscock (eds.). *Neuromethods:* Vol. XVII. Clifton, NJ: Humana Press.

Woods, R. P., Cherry, S. R., and Mazziotta, J. C. 1992. Rapid automated algorithm for aligning and reslicing PET images. *Journal of Computer Assisted Tomography* 16:620–33.

Woods, R. P., Mazziotta, J. C., and Cherry, S. R. 1993. MRI-PET registration with automated algorithm. *Journal of Computer Assisted Tomography* 17:536–46.

Zatorre, R. J., Meyer, E., Gjedde, A., and Evans, A. C. 1996. PET studies of phonetic processing of speech: review, replication, and reanalysis. *Cerebral Cortex* 6:21–30.

APPENDIX 1: MANUAL PLACEMENT OF ROIs

Thalamus

It is not possible to isolate individual nuclei within this sensory gating structure; nor is it possible to define the limits of the structure lying adjacent to white matter. There is usually only a single peak of activation in each hemisphere. Therefore, we attempt only to position a sphere encompassing as much of the structure as possible without overlapping the nearby striatal structures. Some overlap into the ventricles can be tolerated if necessary since thresholding will de-limit pixels of predominately CSF. Place a 2.5 cm diameter (or smaller, if necessary) sphere within the thalamus located from a midline view, meeting these criteria.

Calcarine Fissure

Area 17 is located by first finding the calcarine fissure from a midline sagittal view. Then position a 2.0 cm diameter sphere entirely within the occipital pole, its center in the calcarine fissure but moved laterally so that it is not extending across the midline. (Note that due to the common asymmetry of the posterior occipital cortex, these spheres are frequently not found to be centered in the same coronal plane.)

Parietal-Occipital Sulcus

Moving laterally from the midline in the sagittal plane, the prominent parietal-occipital sulcus (POS) and calcarine fissures are clearly evident within the occipital lobe. Place a 2.0 cm sphere centered at the junction of the POS and the calcarine fissure. Move the sphere laterally until it is entirely within brain tissue.

Collateral Sulcus/Anterior and Posterior Parahippocampal Lingual Fusiform Gyri

To locate the anterior ROI: After locating the hippocampus and placing its sphere, identify the collateral sulcus from a sagittal view. Place a 2.0 cm diameter sphere within the collateral sulcus about half way along the visible length at that sagittal plane. (Usually a portion of the lateral ventricle will be seen at about this point.) Confirm from the coronal and axial planes that the center of the sphere is in the sulcus and supratentorial, adjusting as necessary. The sphere may overlap into the ventricle.

To locate the posterior ROI: Place a second 2.0 cm diameter sphere within the collateral sulcus, posterior to the first and tangent to it. Verify from all planes that the sphere is supratentorial and well centered in the sulcus.

Hippocampus

From a midbrain axial view, locate the anterior commissure (AC). Draw a horizontal line passing through the AC. This will place a vertical plane just anterior to the third ventricle. From the coronal view at this plane, index in the posterior direction to the first indication of the third ventricle. The amygdala can be identified as an almond shaped body of gray matter on the medial aspect of the temporal lobe. (The temporal horn of the lateral ventricle is often just visible.) After locating the amygdala, index in a posterior direction on the coronal planes until the configuration of the hippocampus is clearly visible. Place a 1.5 cm diameter sphere in the center of the hippocampus such that it does not overlap with the amygdala ROI.

Area 37

Index medially from an extreme lateral sagittal plane that passes through the inferior temporal gyrus watching for the occipital notch (preoccipital incisura), a short vertical-going sulcus located in the gyrus. It is often apparent from the sagittal view when the lateral aspect of the cerebellar lobe can first be visualized. The occipital notch usually T intersects with the occipitotemporal sulcus and this intersection can be located by indexing through the axial planes in this region. Center a 2.5 cm diameter sphere on the intersection, placing it high enough so that it is entirely within the cerebrum.

Posterior Inferior Temporal Sulcus

After placing the area 37 ROI, a second 2.5 cm sphere is placed tangent to it and within the inferior temporal sulcus. Verify in all planes that the sphere does not overlap with the smaller inferior temporal sulcus ROI, described below.

Heschl's Gyrus

From a coronal view through the posterior Sylvian fissure, adjust the anterior-posterior direction to locate the first evidence of Heschl's gyrus as it emerges from the medial aspect of temporal planum. (If doubled, choose the most medial.) Advance forward approximately five slices in the coronal plane. Verify from all views that the gyrus is fully evident and at about the midpoint along the horizontal plane of the Sylvian fissure. Locate the center of a 1.5 cm sphere at the superior surface of the gyrus.

Superior Temporal Sulcus

After placing the Heschl's gyrus ROI, and on the same coronal plane, the superior temporal sulcus is the next most inferior invagination evident from the coronal view. Because the superior temporal sulcus is sometimes interrupted, it may be necessary to adjust the coronal slice slightly in a posterior direction to identify it. Place a 1.5 cm sphere centered midway into the sulcus. Be sure that the sphere is within the cerebrum and does not overlap with the Heschl's gyrus ROI.

Inferior Temporal Sulcus

After locating the placement of the superior temporal sulcus ROI, and on the same coronal plane, the inferior temporal sulcus is the next most inferior invagination evident from the coronal view. Because the inferior temporal sulcus is usually interrupted, it may be necessary to adjust the coronal slice slightly to identify it. Place a 1.5 cm sphere centered midway into the sulcus. Be sure that the sphere is within the cerebrum and does not overlap with the superior temporal sulcus ROI, moving caudally if necessary.

Angular Gyrus

From the sagittal view, locate the superior temporal sulcus. Follow it to its termination. This will usually be just posterior to the primary intermediate sulcus, a short supplementary sulcus off the intraparietal sulcus. The posterior termination most often ends as the angular sulcus around which the angular gyrus folds (84% on the right, 92% on the left). When the terminus is branched the superior segment is used (occasionally it may meet the IPS). From the axial view, the ending of the STS is verified and the cursor is moved about five slices inferiorly from that point so that a 2.0 cm diameter sphere centered there is entirely within the brain.

Intraparietal Sulcus

From an axial view, locate the IPS in the parietal lobe, oriented at about a 45° angle between the postcentral sulcus and the transverse occipital sulcus (it may communicate with either or both). (The central and post central sulci may be verified by following them dorsally and ventrally and simultaneously viewing the sagittal plane. The primary intermediate sulcus will often be visible from the sagittal view.) Locate the most posterior aspect of the IPS and place a 2.0 cm diameter sphere on the coronal plane, midway between the cortical surface and the depth of the sulcus, adjusting as necessary to be entirely within the brain.

Broca's Area

Select a sagittal view through the transverse plane of the Sylvian fissure where Heschl's gyrus is clearly visible in the posterior aspect. Place a 2.0 cm sphere within the anterior aspect of the operculum, centered between the ascending and horizontal rami of the Sylvian fissure.

Dorsolateral Prefrontal Cortex—Inferior

From the midline sagittal view, place a horizontal marker tangent to the genu of the corpus callosum. The coronal view at this location affords an advantageous view of the superior, middle (when present), and inferior sulci. The inferior sulcus is easily located as a nearly horizontal feature and can be verified from the sagittal view. A 2.5 cm diameter sphere is centered within the sulcus at this coronal plane and adjusted medially if necessary so that the lateral edge of the sphere is within the cortex.

Dorsolateral Prefrontal Superior Sulcus—1 (Anterior) and 2 (Posterior): Two spheres are placed within this sulcus.

To place the anterior ROI: From the coronal plane used for location of the inferior frontal sulcus (see above), the superior sulcus is easily located as the first deep, vertical sulcus lateral to the medial longitudinal fissure. Once located, its anterior terminus is found by indexing ventrally through the axial planes. When the terminus is located, it will be necessary to back up a few slices so that a 2.5 cm diameter sphere will fit within the sulcus and as near to the cortical surface as possible. There are usually several regional peaks; thus, a sphere of this size will typically encompass at least one of them.

To place the posterior ROI: The second 2.0 cm diameter sphere is placed within the same sulcus as above, but posterior to it. The second sphere should be tangent to the first and all planes must be checked to assure that the entire sphere is within the cerebrum.

Orbital Frontal Cortex

Beginning from a low axial view, travel upward until the orbital frontal bone is visualized around the eye orbits. Place a coronal plane through both orbits. From the coronal view, the most medial ventral gyrus will be the gyrus rectus. Going laterally, the next gyrus will be the orbital frontal gyrus. A 2.5 cm diameter sphere is placed in the center of the gyrus so that the edges of the sphere take in both sulci surrounding the gyrus but avoid muscle artifact above the eyes, adjusting the axial plane accordingly. There are several sulci in this region, the most medial of which is oriented in an anterior-posterior position; however, other short sulci may be in the same region, one of which may appear to be a laterally directed branch. These short sulci will likely be included within the sphere. (The associated PET activity usually has only one maximum pixel.)

Head of Caudate Nucleus

This rostrally positioned, large gray matter structure is easily visualized from either the axial or coronal plane. From a midbrain axial view, index through the slices choosing the one judged to contain the "fullest" representation of the head of the caudate nucleus. Place a 2.0 diameter sphere at the center, insuring by inspection of all views that the sphere is not infringing upon the putamen. It may extend into the lateral ventricle.

Putamen

From an axial view through the striatal cortex, locate the slice where the putamen is the densest (i.e., has the fewest apparent white striations). In the coronal view, the caudate and putamen will be approximately of the same area. Center a 1.5 cm diameter sphere in the most anterior aspect, taking care that it does not overlap into the head of the caudate nucleus or extend into the insula.

Anterior Cingulate

Beginning on a midline sagittal slice, find the intersection of two planes tangent to the anterior edge and the dorsal surface of the corpus callosum. On the coronal plane thus selected, place a 2.5 cm diameter sphere adjusted to straddle midline.

Chapter • 9

Linkages Between Attention Deficit Disorders and Reading Disability

*Ann C. Schulte, C. Keith Conners,
and S. S. Osborne*

Reading disabilities and attention disorders are two of the most common problems of childhood. Prevalence estimates for both disorders vary, with conservative estimates for the prevalence of attention disorders at 3% to 5%, and for reading disorders at 5% to 10% (American Psychiatric Association 1994; Barkley 1990; Hallahan, Kauffman, and Lloyd 1996). Although a range of outcomes are possible for individuals with either disorder, both disorders have potential long-term consequences. Reading disabilities are associated with grade retention, dropping out of school, and lowered educational and occupational attainment (Blackorby and Wagner 1996; Rutter et al. 1976). Attention disorders are associated with lowered academic achievement, antisocial behavior, dropping out, and substance abuse (Barkley 1990; Barkley et al. 1990).

That these two common, but debilitating, disorders tend to co-occur in children has been noted for many years (e.g., Lambert and Sandoval 1980; Rutter 1974). An association between reading disabilities and attention disorders has been found in studies that differed in type of sample (epidemiological vs. clinical), age of children studied, method of defining both disorders, and country of origin (Holborow and Berry 1986; Lambert and Sandoval 1980; McConaughy, Mattison, and Peterson 1994; McGee et al. 1986; Rutter 1974).

Despite the frequency with which an association between reading disabilities and attention deficit disorders has been reported, we do not have a clear understanding of why the two disorders co-occur and the implications of this comorbidity for treatment and long-term outcomes for children. In this chapter, we examine a number of issues related to reading disabilities/attention disorders comorbidity. In the first section, we examine the comorbidity prevalence rates that have been reported in the literature and hypotheses concerning the relationship between the two disorders. In the second section, we discuss the few existing studies that examine the impact of attention problems on outcomes for children with reading disorders. We then reexamine the longitudinal data from the Carolina Learning Disabilities Project (McKinney, McClure, and Feagans 1982; McKinney and Speece 1986) to determine whether early attention problems affect academic outcomes for children in this sample. In the third section, we examine points of possible overlap between the cognitive processes associated with attention and reading that may help explain the links between the two disorders. Posner's delineation of three attention networks (Posner 1988; Posner and Peterson 1990) is used as the basis of a discussion of emerging research findings that suggest there may be a subtype of attention disorders that includes reading difficulties as part of its symptoms. We conclude with a section discussing future directions for research regarding the linkages between these two common childhood disorders.

A Note on Terminology

In this chapter, we have chosen to use the terms "reading disabilities" and "attention disorders," rather than more precise terms, such as "dyslexia" and "attention deficit hyperactivity disorder" (ADHD) to reflect the wide variation in definitions employed in the studies discussed here. As one group of researchers (Shaywitz, Fletcher, and Shaywitz 1994) noted, no two studies appear to have used the same criteria for defining either disorder. This situation is unfortunate, as it is quite possible that the pathways or linkages between attention disorders and reading disabilities may vary depending on how each disorder is defined. For example, inattention as manifested in classroom behavior and reflected in teacher ratings, may have a different relationship to reading than inattention as measured by parent ratings, or inattention measured by a continuous performance task.

COMORBIDITY OF READING DISABILITY AND ATTENTION DISORDERS

There is general agreement that reading disabilities and attention disorders tend to co-occur, but the extent to which they overlap is a matter of debate (Hinshaw 1992). Comorbidity prevalence rates must be considered from two perspectives: the prevalence of reading disabilities in children with attention disorders and the prevalence of attention disorders in children with reading disabilities. Whether comorbidity rates are elevated in only one direction, or both, has important implications for causal hypotheses. For example, elevated rates of reading disabilities in children with attention deficit disorder, but no corresponding increase in the rate of attention disorders in children, suggest a different set of causal hypotheses than elevated rates in both directions. Given the critical role that comorbidity prevalence rates play in determining how reading disabilities and attention disorders are related, it is important that these estimates be precise and variables that influence comorbidity be well understood.

Although determining the extent to which these two disorders co-occur would appear to be a relatively straight-forward endeavor, in practice, it is quite difficult. Table I provides a sample of the range of estimates that have been reported in the literature. As is clear, even from the small number of studies summarized in the table, comorbidity estimates vary considerably.

Table I. Reading disability (RD), learning disability (LD), and attention disorder (AD) comorbidity rates reported in the research literature

Study	Type of sample	Overlap	
		% AD w/ RD/LD	% RD/LD w/ AD
Frick et al. (1991)	Referred	13%	—
Holborow and Berry (1986)	School-based epidemiologic	27%	41%
Lambert and Sandoval (1980)	School-based epidemiologic	16%	—
McConaughy et al. (1994)	Referred	—	28%
Semrud-Clikeman et al. (1992)	Referred	23%	—
Shaywitz and Shaywitz (1988)	School-based epidemiologic	11%	33%
Shaywitz et al. (1994)	School-based epidemiologic	36.4%	15%
Silver (1981)	Referred	92%	—

There are a number of possible reasons for this variation. First, co-morbidity rates are likely to differ because of age-related changes in: (a) skills and expectations, (b) the precision with which both attention and reading can be measured, and (c) the relation between the two domains. Second, the stringency and manner in which each disorder is defined affects its prevalence and the association observed between the disorders. For example, Shaywitz and Shaywitz (1988) and Shaywitz et al. (1994) (see table I) each derived their prevalence figures from the same epidemiological sample, but used somewhat different definitions of reading disabilities and attention disorders. In the Shaywitz and Shaywitz (1988) study, a regression-based IQ/achievement discrepancy definition and a 1.5 *SD* cut-off was used to classify children as learning disabled. Despite the fact that children could evidence a discrepancy in *either* reading or math to be classified as learning disabled, the comorbidity prevalence rates in both directions were low. There was clear evidence of elevated comorbidity in only one direction, with the prevalence of attention disorders in children with learning disabilities exceeding the population rate (33% vs. 23%; Shaywitz and Shaywitz 1998), but the prevalence of learning disabilities in children with attention disorders similar to the rate found in the general population (Pennington 1991). In the second study, Shaywitz et al. (1994) looked only at reading disabilities, but broadened their criteria for reading disability to include children with IQ/achievement discrepancies *or* reading achievement below the 25th percentile. With this definition, the prevalence rate of reading disabilities in the general population was much higher (23% for reading disabilities *alone* in comparison to the approximately 10% rate for reading *and* math disabilities in the earlier study), and the rate of attention disorders in children with reading disabilities increased markedly. This shift in comorbidity rates also changed the nature of the association found between the disorders. Although there was a one-way association in Shaywitz and Shaywitz (1988), there was a two-way association in Shaywitz et al. (1994), with reading disabilities in children with attention disorders, and attention disorders in children with reading disabilities occurring at about two times the rate observed in the general population.

Finally, the use of an epidemiological versus a clinical sample has been found to affect comorbidity rates markedly (DuPaul and Stoner 1994; Hinshaw 1992; Shaywitz et al. 1994). Children are much more likely to be referred and treated for one disorder in the presence of the second disorder. Thus, when clinical samples are used, the estimates of the extent to which the two disorders overlap are inflated. For example, Shaywitz et al. (1994) reported that 15% of children with reading disabilities in an epidemiological sample exhibited problems with attention, although over 40% of children in a referred sample of children with reading disabilities met the same criteria for diagnosis of an attention disorder.

In general, comprehensive reviews (DuPaul and Stoner 1994; Hinshaw 1992; Semrud-Clikeman et al. 1992) of attention disorders/ reading disabilities comorbidity studies conclude that comorbidity between the two types of disorders occurs beyond the level expected by chance, but at a much lower rate than studies using clinic samples would suggest. Conservative estimates of the overlap fall in the range of 10% to 20% (Hinshaw 1992), with less conservative estimates in the range of 20% to 40% (DuPaul and Stoner 1994). There is some evidence that the prevalence of attention disorders in children with reading disabilities is higher than the prevalence of reading disabilities in children with attention disorders (DuPaul and Stoner 1994; Pennington 1991), but this finding is not consistent across studies (e.g., Shaywitz et al. 1994).

HOW ARE ATTENTION DISORDERS AND READING DISABILITY RELATED?

In his comprehensive review of the research regarding the relationship between externalizing behavior problems and reading disability, Hinshaw (1992) discusses four possible causal models that explain the relationship between reading disabilities and attention disorders: (a) poor reading leads to attentional problems, (b) attentional problems lead to poor reading, (c) both domains lead to the other, and (d) underlying variables result in both problem domains. Support for each of these models can be found in the research literature, but there have been few rigorous tests of alternative causal models (Hinshaw 1992; McGee and Share 1988). Research related to each of the four models is summarized in the remainder of this section.

Reading Disabilities Lead to Attention Disorders

Reading difficulties may cause children to be less attentive in school. McGee and Share (1988) are perhaps the strongest proponents of this causal model, arguing that most attention disorders are a consequence of learning difficulties at school. They suggest that attention disorders might best be considered as disorders of conduct in the classroom that occur when children are unable to participate successfully in school activities because of skill deficits. Findings they use to support their position include the limited effect of psychostimulant, cognitive, and behavioral treatments for attention disorders on achievement[1]; the

---

[1]Although more recent evidence suggests that interventions for attention disorders can have an impact on achievement (DuPaul and Stoner 1994).

difficulty finding specific cognitive deficits reliably associated with attention disorders; and the increase in behavior problems over time for children with reading disabilities (McGee et al. 1986). They acknowledge that direct evidence for their position is limited and call for longitudinal research examining changes in both domains over time.

Pennington and his colleagues (Pennington 1991; Pennington, Groisser, and Welsh 1993) also propose that reading disabilities lead to attention disorders, but only in a subset of the children with reading disabilities. Unlike McGee and Share, who maintain that attention disorders cannot be linked to specific cognitive deficits, Pennington (1991) maintains that attention disorders and reading disabilities are generally the result of unique and separate sets of cognitive deficits (phonological processing deficits for reading disabilities and executive functioning deficits for attention disorders). In some cases, however, reading disabilities may result in the symptoms of attention deficit hyperactivity disorder without the underlying cognitive deficits. In other words, reading disabilities can produce a phenocopy of an attention disorder. In a study examining this hypothesis, Pennington et al. (1993) examined four groups of children: those with attention disorders only, those with reading disabilities, those with both disorders, and a control group with neither disorder. They found a double dissociation between the reading disability and attention disorders groups, with the reading disability group showing deficits only in tasks related to phonological processes, and the attention disorders group showing deficits only in tasks related to executive functions. Consistent with their model, the comorbid group resembled the reading disabled group in terms of cognitive deficits. Compared to the reading disability only group, the comorbid group had a lower maternal education level, more mother-only households, more family members with alcohol and drug abuse problems, and higher special education rates.

To explain this pattern, Pennington et al. (1993) proposed that the prototypical pathway between reading disability and attention disorder begins with children who have a congenital, mild language disability born into a household with stressed single parents. These children's language difficulties interact with their environment, which does not provide adequate structure and support for development of language and socialization for school. They show mild attentional problems as they enter school, failing to listen to the teacher and shifting activities frequently. As reading demands grow, these children experience increased frustration and their attention and behavior problems in the classroom increase. By later elementary school, they show all the behavioral characteristics of attention deficit hyperactivity disorder, but their behavior is the result of environmental circumstances rather than deficits in executive functioning.

Supporting Pennington's model, a number of other studies (e.g., Felton and Wood 1989; Hall et al. 1997; McGee et al. 1989) failed to find the unique cognitive deficits associated with attention disorders in reading disabled/attention disordered samples. A study by Felton et al. (1987), employing a multi-group design similar to Pennington's, however, found cognitive deficits unique to reading disabilities and attention disorders, but their comorbid group displayed *both* sets of deficits. The conflicting findings across studies are difficult to interpret, but may be related to differences in definitions and stringency of diagnostic criteria across studies.

Attention Disorders Lead to Reading Disabilities

Attention disorders may make it more likely that a child has difficulty learning to read. It is clear that many of the behaviors that define inattention in the classroom, such as high rates of off-task behavior, also interfere with the acquisition of reading skills, or with opportunities for the extended practice required to achieve reading fluency.

Support for this view has been found by Fergusson and Horwood (1992). Using a structural equation approach and data from a large epidemiological sample of children in New Zealand studied at ages 10 and 12 years, their data suggest that attention influences reading achievement, but reading achievement does not affect attention. It is interesting that this one-way relationship was observed in the upper grade levels. Most children are fluent decoders by the close of elementary school and much of the growth in reading is related to the development of more sophisticated comprehension strategies. It is just these processes in reading that other researchers have suggested are the most vulnerable to attentional processes (Forness et al.; Swanson 1992; Shaywitz, Fletcher, and Shaywitz 1994).

An alternative, more cognitively based hypothesis within this class of causal models is that children with attention disorders are poor readers because they have difficulty allocating attentional resources. Using event related potential measures (ERP), Segalowitz, Wagner, and Menna (1992) found that measures of poor readers' Contingent Negative Variation attentional ERP collected during a vigilance task were strongly related to their reading comprehension. They suggested that some children have difficulty recruiting the attentional resources to coordinate the linguistic and graphemic processes necessary to learn to read, perhaps due to immaturity of the frontal lobe/limbic system. The small number of subjects in their study (11 poor readers and 16 good readers), their mean age of 15 years, and the fact that only reading comprehension was assessed, however, limit the conclusions that can be drawn from this study about the role of attention in learning to read.

In sum, longitudinal studies that chart growth in decoding and comprehension skills across the early elementary years and their relationship to attentional behaviors and cognitive processes are needed to fully evaluate this causal model. However, the relatively low rate of reading disabilties in children with attention disorders suggests that the pathway between attention disorders and reading disabilities must be more complex than a simple, direct "interference hypothesis."

Attention Disorders and Reading Disabilities Are Reciprocally Related

Attention disorders and reading disabilities may influence each other. Children with attention disorders may have more difficulty acquiring reading skills, and poor reading skills may increase the likelihood that a child has difficulty attending, particularly in academic settings.

Rowe and Rowe's (1992) study of inattentiveness in the classroom and reading achievement provides strong data to support this view. In a cross-sectional study of 5,000 students drawn from elementary and secondary schools, they found that students' inattentiveness was negatively related to their reading achievement and that lowered reading achievement contributed to inattentiveness in the classroom.

This model explains many of the findings supporting pathways in both directions between reading disabilities and attention disorders discussed in previous sections. Such a model predicts that the overlap between reading disabilities and attention disorders increases with age. Again, longitudinal studies of reading acqusition and attention are needed to evaluate this model.

Underlying Variables Result in Both Attention Disorders and Reading Disability

The repeated finding that inattention and poor reading readiness are associated even before the onset of formal schooling strongly suggests that there may be underlying variables that disrupt both domains (Hinshaw 1992). Poor language or verbal skills are one possibility, as these difficulties may lead to deficits in reading as well as deficits in verbal mediation which, in turn, could affect children's self control. Such an explanation could not account for the presence of reading disabilities that are defined in terms of ability/achievement discrepancies, but could account for high rates of overlap when reading disabilities are identified on the basis of low reading achievement alone. Family environment might play a role in this hypothesized causal chain with child rearing practices that contribute to poor self control also contributing to low levels of reading readiness.

Another hypothesis that fits within the underlying variable classification is the possibility that some neurocognitive deficit, other than attention, may underlie both disorders (DuPaul and Stoner 1994; Hinshaw 1992; Keogh 1971). However, current neuropsychological models of reading disabilities and attention suggest little overlap between the cognitive deficits that characterize each disorder (Shaywitz, Fletcher, and Shaywitz 1994), with current conceptualizations of the disorders positing a core deficit in phonological processing in reading disorder (Pennington 1991; Wagner and Torgesen 1987), and executive functions in attention disorders (Barkley 1997; Pennington 1991).

Despite the fact that current models of reading disabilities and attention disorders point to unique neurocognitive deficits for each disorder, there is evidence from two different lines of research that there may be a common etiology for the two disorders, at least for a subset of the children with both disorders. Light et al. (1995), in a study of identical and same-sex fraternal twins, found that about half of proband deficit in reading was due to genetic factors that also influenced attention disorders. In addition, Halperin et al. (1997) suggested that there may be two distinct subgroups of children with attention disorders, one of whom is characterized by both attentional difficulties and reading problems.

Building on Posner's work (discussed in more detail later in this chapter) delineating multiple attention systems in the brain (Posner 1988; Posner and Peterson 1990) and models that suggest that noradrenergic (NA) mechanisms play a role in ADHD symptoms and treatment, Halperin et al. (1997) suggested that there may be two distinct subgroups of children with attention disorders, one whose attentional difficulties arise due to deficits in the frontal attentional system, and one whose difficulties arise due to deficits in the posterior attentional system. Children with attentional problems caused by deficits in the posterior attentional system are also likely to have reading difficulties. They speculate that dysregulation or overreactivity of the "NA-rich" (p. 1688) locus coeruleus activity disrupts the posterior attention system and the regions of the posterior cortex and thalamic regions that are related to auditory reception and language processing in one subgroup of children. In contrast, reduced activity in the locus coeruleus leads to inhibitory control and executive function deficits in a second group of children with attention disorders.

Consistent with their model, Halperin et al. (1997) found that ADHD children with RD had higher plasma levels of the noradrenergic metabolite 3-methoxy-4-hydroxyphenylglycol (MHPG) than ADHD children without RD.

Halperin et al.'s (1997) model predicts that children with ADHD with and without RD would show unique patterns of deficits on tasks tapping different attentional systems. The model could also account for Pennington et al.'s (1993) finding that children with reading disabilities and attention disorders did not show the same executive function deficits found in the attention disorder only group.

Causal Models Summary

It is clear that the observed relationship between reading disabilities and attention disorders has generated much speculation and relatively little consensus. Although the body of evidence supporting difficulties with phonological processing as the core deficit in reading disabilities is now quite strong (Torgesen and Wagner 1998; Wagner and Torgesen 1987), the difficulty finding a consistent cognitive deficit (or deficits) underlying attention disorders limits our understanding of how the two disorders are related. Furthermore, it seems likely that there are multiple pathways that link the two disorders. Longitudinal studies that begin with a preschool sample and include precise measurement of both reading skill development and attention are needed. Furthermore, to examine hypothesized relationships between behavioral and cognitive constructs of attention, it is important that measures of both domains be included.

The possibility that there may be a subtype of attention disorder that is accompanied by a reading disorder is intriguing. Data from studies employing behavioral genetic (Light et al. 1993), physiological (Halperin et al. 1997), and neuropsychological (Pennington et al. 1993) approaches, although limited, are consistent with this view. The presence of a subtype with a second locus for attentional difficulties other than the frontal executive system would help explain the inconsistent findings across studies concerning the cognitive deficits associated with attention disorders, and may have implications for treatment. We will return to this topic in a subsequent section, but first complete our discussion of comorbidity issues with an examination of the research concerning the impact of attention disorders on outcomes for reading disabilities.

DO ATTENTION DISORDERS AFFECT OUTCOMES FOR CHILDREN WITH READING DISABILITIES?

Children with both an attention disorder and reading disability evidence a "double deficit." As both disorders have long-term outcomes, it seems reasonable to hypothesize that the presence of both disorders would affect children's responses to academic remediation and long-term outcomes. Surprisingly, there has been little longitudinal research on this topic.

Wood and Felton Studies

Wood and Felton (1994) examined the issue of whether the presence of an attention disorder affects outcomes for children with reading disorders using data from three longitudinal samples. The first sample was a group of 204 first graders, drawn from an epidemiological study of reading disabilities, who were assessed again in grades three and five. The authors examined the extent to which cognitive, achievement, and attentional characteristics predicted third and fifth grade reading achievement. Word identification and passage comprehension skills were measured with the Woodcock-Johnson Psycho-educational Battery. Attention disorder in the first grade was assessed with the parent portion of the Diagnostic Interview for Children and Adolescents (DICA; Herjanic 1983). Children were placed into four categories based on total number of symptoms parents reported: (a) serious ADD, (b) borderline, (c) normal, and (d) supernormal. For this sample, first-grade ADD status did not predict word recognition scores in first, third, or fifth grade.

Wood and Felton also followed a reading impaired, epidemiologically derived sample of 60 children from third to eighth grade. Almost half the sample (45%) was classified as ADHD in the third grade using DSM-III R criteria. As in the first sample, ADHD status was not related to either word recognition in fifth or eighth grade, or to passage comprehension in either grade. The authors noted the difficulty of understanding that attention disorder could have so little impact on reading achievement. They suggested that reading, as measured on the Woodcock-Johnson, may be highly sensitive to incidental learning, which is less likely to be impaired in children with ADHD than intentional learning. They also suggested that the one-to-one nature of the testing environment with an unfamiliar examiner for the Woodcock-Johnson may have elicited better performances from the children than reading tasks conducted under more typical circumstances.

Wood and Felton's third sample was a group of adults who had been evaluated as children in a clinic for the assessment and treatment of reading disorders. Archival records of childhood problems and adult outcomes were available for these adults. Although not all the children had been assessed with the same measures of reading, Wood and Felton developed a procedure for classifying children as reading disabled if they fell in the bottom 9% of the standardization sample for each test. They also used the clinical interview notes that were part of each case to classify children as attention disordered based on DSM-III criteria.

In order to examine the impact of attention disorders on adult outcomes for children with reading disabilities, Wood and Felton used multiple regression to examine the relationship of childhood reading disability status and attention disorder status on adult reading achievement (assessed as single word reading on the Wide Range Achievement Test) and on years of high school and post-high school education. They found that childhood reading disability strongly predicted adult reading achievement, with 43.6% shared variance. Childhood Verbal IQ also made a significant contribution. In terms of educational attainment, attention disorder and reading disability jointly predicted number of years of high school and post-high school education, with attention disorder and reading disability status each accounting for approximately 15% of the variance. Gender, childhood socioeconomic status, and childhood Verbal IQ were unrelated to educational outcome. They suggested that attention disorder may impair the task persistence needed for educational attainment far more than it affects reading.

In their discussion of the findings from the three samples, Wood and Felton concluded that childhood attention deficit disorder had no measurable impact on the development of single-word reading skill, either in childhood or adulthood, although it did have a deleterious effect on long-term education outcome. On the basis of their data, they argued that clinicians and educators directly treat the reading disabilities of "double deficit" children and not assume the reading difficulties will disappear when children's attentional difficulties are addressed.

Wood and Felton's failure to find any impact of attention disorders on reading is somewhat surprising. Their results run counter to the findings of both Fergusson and Horwood (1992) and Rowe and Rowe (1992), discussed earlier, who both found that attention contributes to reading achievement. A number of differences between these two studies and the Wood and Felton studies may account for the discrepant findings. First, both Fergusson and Horwood (1992) and Rowe and Rowe (1992) examined the relationship of reading and attention in large samples (n = 1,265 and 5,000, respectively) of children achieving at all levels in reading. Both studies also assessed attention as a continuous, rather than categorical, variable. Felton and Wood's samples were smaller (n < 200) and with the exception of the adult sample taken from the archives of Orton's reading clinic, restricted to children with reading disabilities. The lower power and restriction in range on both the reading and attention measures in the Felton and Wood studies may have masked the impact of attention disorders on reading disorders. In addition, both the Fergusson and Rowe studies used measures of reading that included a comprehension component, while the Wood and Felton measures only tapped word recognition and decoding skills. It may be that attention difficulties have their primary impact on reading comprehension, a possibility discussed by others (e.g., Forness et al. 1992; Shaywitz et al. 1994). Finally, Felton and

Wood depended primarily on parental report of attention problems, Rowe and Rowe used a teacher questionnaire, and Fergusson and Horwood combined teacher and parental reports. It is possible that attention problems manifested in the classroom are the only ones that influence reading outcome and parents are poor reporters of these problems. Alternatively, teachers' knowledge of students' reading problems may influence their ratings of student attention.

Carolina Longitudinal Learning Disabilities Project

The failure to find an impact of attention disorders on reading outcomes for children with reading disabilities in the Felton and Wood (1994) studies led us to examine this issue in another longitudinal sample of children with learning disabilities. The Carolina Longitudinal Learning Disabilities Project (McKinney and Feagans 1984) followed 63 first and second graders who were newly identified by the public schools as having learning disabilities for a period of five years. Each child with learning disabilities in the sample was matched with a nonidentified comparison student in terms of first-year classroom, ethnicity, and gender. Students entered the study in two waves: half entering the study in 1978; half in the following year.

Although the behavioral characteristics of this sample and their impact on outcome have been examined (McKinney and Speece 1986; Osborne, Schulte, and McKinney 1991; Speece, McKinney, and Applebaum 1985), whether the presence of attention problems in the classroom affected long-term school outcomes has not been directly addressed in any previous study. To do so, we used teacher ratings from the task orientation and distractibility scales of Classroom Behavior Inventory (CBI; Schaefer, Edgerton, and Aronson 1977) collected during the first year of the study to classify the children with learning disabilities into two groups: children with learning disabilities alone (LD) and children with learning disabilities and attention disorder (LD/AD). To form these groups, items from the distractibility and task orientation scales of the CBI were summed and z-scores created based on the mean and standard deviation of the normal comparison students on the combined scale. Students whose z-scores on the combined distractibility/task-orientation scale were below 1.5 were placed into the LD group. Students whose z-scores fell at 1.5 or above were placed in the LD/AD group. Using this strategy, 30 of the students fell in the LD group; 31 fell into the LD/AD group (behavior ratings for two students were unavailable).

In examining the impact of attention problems on achievement, we used a hierarchical linear models (HLM) analysis strategy (Bryk and Raudenbush 1987; Burchinal and Applebaum 1991) in which Peabody

Individual Achievement Test age equivalent scores in reading recognition and reading comprehension collected across four years were predicted from chronological age. Growth curves for three groups were compared: (a) children with learning disabilities (LD), (b) children with learning disabilities and attention disorders (LD/AD), and (c) the normal comparison group. Table II describes the demographic characteristics of the three groups. For these analyses, we set our age intercept at nine years. Attention group, gender, and IQ were viewed as fixed effect variables and age was viewed as a random effect variable.

An HLM analysis strategy was particularly well suited to this dataset because limited fourth-year data were collected for the students in the second wave due to funding cuts (see table II). Unlike many multivariate analysis techniques, HLM does not require complete, balanced data, only that data are missing at random rather than systematically. Given that the majority of missing data were related to the year in which the student entered the study, and placement in the first or second wave was not related to group assignment or any variable of interest, we felt comfortable including the fourth year data available in the analysis.

Figure 1 presents the population curves for the three groups on the reading recognition and reading comprehension measures (see table III for group growth curve parameter estimates and standard

Table II. Characteristics of learning disabled (LD), learning disabled and attention disordered (LD/AD) and normal comparison groups.

	LD				LD/AD				Comparison			
Year of Data	1	2	3	4	1	2	3	4	1	2	3	4
n	29*	24	22	14	30	28	26	12	59	55	51	29
Gender (% Male)	62.1				90				76.3			
Full Scale IQ												
M	95.6				95.6				108.2			
SD	12.0				10.4				14.0			
Age												
M	7.5	8.5	9.5	10.6	7.0	7.8	8.9	10.1	7.2	8.0	9.1	10.3
SD	.7	.7	.7	.7	.6	.6	.6	.7	.7	.7	.7	.7
PIAT Reading Recognition												
M	6.8	7.9	9.0	9.6	6.8	7.9	9.0	9.6	7.8	8.7	10.0	11.2
SD	.6	.7	1.4	1.6	.6	.7	1.4	1.6	1.4	1.6	1.8	2.1
PIAT Reading Comprehension												
M	7.1	7.8	9.0	9.4	7.1	7.8	9.0	9.4	7.8	8.7	9.9	11.6
SD	.5	.7	1.1	1.4	.5	.7	1.1	1.4	1.2	1.4	1.8	2.4

*28 for reading comprehension analyses due to missing Year 1 score.

errors). For reading recognition, the growth curves for all groups were linear. As expected, the normal comparison group showed a steeper rate of change than both LD groups ($F(1,149) = 14.09$, $p < .0002$). The difference in slopes between the LD and LD/AD groups approached significance ($F(1,149) = 2.63$, $p < .1068$). In terms of level of achievement, the normal comparison group again differed from both LD groups ($F(1,149) = 33.81$, $p < .0001$), and the two LD groups were significantly different from one another ($F(1,149) = 3.99$, $p < .0476$).

For reading comprehension, all three groups again showed linear growth curves. The normal comparison group showed a steeper rate of change than both LD groups ($F(1,148) = 18.04$, $p < .0001$), but there

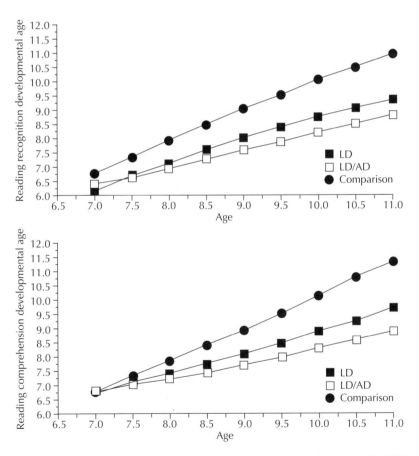

Figure 1.   Growth curves for students with learning disabilities only (LD), learning disabilities and attention disorders (LD/AD) and normally achieving comparison students (Comparison).

Table III.   Group Growth Curve Parameters

	Reading Recognition B	(SE)	Reading Comprehension B	(SE)
Intercept	5.12***	(.65)	5.56***	(.52)
Group—LD	.65*	(.32)	.59	(.33)
Group—Normal Comparison	1.71***	(.28)	1.61*	(.28)
Full Scale IQ	.03***	(.01)	.02***	(.01)
Gender (female)	.41*	(.19)	.24	(.15)
Age	.63***	(.10)	.57***	(.13)
Age X Group—LD	.21	(.11)	.19	(.17)
Age X Group—Normal Comparison	.45***	(.11)	.60***	(.15)

Note:* = $p < .05$, ** = $p < .01$, *** = $p < .001$

Presented are the results from an analysis employing a reference cell model. The reference cell consists of the boys in the LD/AD group. The group effects test whether there are group differences at nine years of age. The age slope parameters describe the rate of change in the developmental score with each additional year among children in the reference cell. The age X group parameters describe the difference in the rate of change in developmental scores for each group in comparison to the reference cell.

was no difference in rate of growth between the LD and LD/AD group ($F(1,148) = 1.23$, $p < .2687$). In terms of level of achievement, the normal comparison group differed from both LD groups ($F(1,148) = 31.11$, $p < .0001$). The LD and LD/AD group did not differ from one another, although, again, the difference approached significance ($F(1,148) = 3.30$, $p < .0714$).

We also examined whether the presence or absence of attention problems affected special education dismissal rate (see table IV). Data on special education placement were available for 41 students (20 LD and 21 LD/AD). As predicted, we found that at the study's end, children in the LD/AD group were more likely to be receiving special education services than children in the LD group ($X^2_{(1)} = 3.450$, $p < .04$, one tailed). These results suggest that attention problems affect place-

Table IV.   Special education status of students with learning disabilities (LD) and students with learning disabilities and attention disorders (LD/AD) at study endpoint in the Carolina Longitudinal Learning Disabilities Study.

Group	Dismissed from special education	Remaining in special education
LD		
N (%)	8 (40%)	12 (60%)
LD/AD		
N (%)	3 (14%)	18 (86%)

ment decisions in schools, a finding that is consistent with earlier research indicating that behavioral problems affect school identification as learning disabled (Shaywitz et al. 1990).

In sum, there are limited data about the impact of attention disorders on long-term outcomes for children with reading and other learning disabilities. Large scale studies of the relationship between reading and attention suggest that attention problems should affect reading progress. The evidence in clinical samples is not strong, however. Wood and Felton failed to find any evidence of differential outcome for reading disorders depending on the presence or absence of attention disorders. Data from the Carolina Longitudinal Learning Disabilities Study are mixed. For reading recognition, the LD and LD/AD groups were significantly different in level of achievement and differences in the rate of growth between the groups approached significance. For reading comprehension, the LD and LD/AD groups did not appear to differ in either level of functioning or rate of growth. Given that previous research (e.g., Forness et al. 1992 ; Shaywitz et al. 1994) seemed to suggest that attentional problems would have their greatest impact on comprehension processes, these results were unpredicted. The small sample size may have contributed to the failure to find differences between the LD and LD/AD group in reading comprehension and the marginal significance of the comparison between the groups in rate of growth in reading recognition.

It is unfortunate that so few studies have examined the issue of outcomes for children with comorbid reading disabilities and attention disorders. Longitudinal studies of epidemiologically based samples of reading disordered children with and without attention disorders are needed. Although parental and teacher behavior ratings are important in the diagnosis of attention deficit hyperactivity disorder, it may be that it is classroom attention that is most important in determining whether attention problems affect reading outcome. As such, it is important that both within-setting and across-setting measures of attention be employed in subsequent studies.

ATTENTION SYSTEMS AND RAPID WORD IDENTIFICATION

In the past 25 years, new techniques to measure brain activity, such as positron emission tomography (PET) and functional magnetic resonance imaging (fMRI), have led to more sophisticated models of the cognitive processes underlying human perception, memory, and behavior (Posner and Raichle 1994). In turn, these models have led to speculation and research concerning the extent to which disorders such as attention deficit hyperactivity disorder, schizophrenia, and dyslexia are explained by deficits in these cognitive systems (Posner 1988; Posner and Raichle 1994; Swanson et al. 1991). More precise descriptions of the cognitive processes and structures involved in attending and reading also make it possible to look for common mechanisms that may help explain the overlap observed between disorders in these areas (e.g., Halperin et al. 1997).

Posner and his colleagues (Posner and Peterson 1990; Posner and Raichle 1994) have described three neural networks that are thought to carry out functions important to selective attention. Each involves different areas of the brain and performs different functions. The first, the visual orienting network, is involved in the detection of visual targets and shifting of attention toward the target. This system is thought to be represented equally in each hemisphere and involve the posterior parietal lobe, superior colliculus, and pulvinar. The second, the executive attention network, is involved in the detection of objects that fulfill certain search criteria, or the conscious execution of an instruction (Posner and Raichle 1994). Although the areas involved in this system are less well understood than those for the visual orienting network (Posner 1988), they are thought to include the anterior cingulate gyrus, the lateral frontal lobe, and Wernicke's area (for language tasks) (Posner and Raichle 1994). The third, the vigilance network, is involved in sustained alertness. This network is thought to be represented primarily in the right hemisphere and to involve the posterior parietal and right frontal areas of the cortex (Posner and Raichle 1994).

Researchers in attention disorders have begun to examine the extent to which deficits in the functioning of these three attention networks may be present in persons with attention disorders (Swanson et al. 1991). For the most part, persons with attention disorders show deficits in tasks that are thought to involve the executive attention network, also referred to as the anterior or voluntary attentional system. However, as noted earlier in the chapter, there is some intriguing work by Halperin et al. (1997) that suggests that deficits in the visual orienting network, involved in the rapid, automatic processing of visual stimuli, may be implicated in some subset of children with attention disorders and reading disabilities.

Although not conducted to verify Halperin's proposal that deficits in the visual orienting network and reading are related, a study conducted at the second author's Attention Disorder Program at Duke University is relevant to this hypothesis. Conners and his colleagues examined the performance on several laboratory tasks, of a large sample of children ($n > 200$) between the ages of 6 and 18 who had been referred for problems in attention. Among the tasks completed by the children was a decision task thought to tap two of Posner's attentional networks, a letter array task that assessed children's speed of lexical access, and a variety of other tasks, including a continuous performance vigilance task, and the Rey Osterreith Complex Figure Task.

The decision task was a variant of Posner's model task for attention (Posner and Raichle 1994). This task involves fixating on a central point on a computer screen and awaiting the presentation of a target on the right or left side of the screen. When the target appears, children are to press a button as quickly as possible. Reaction time is measured from the time the target appears to the time children respond by pressing the button.

In a portion of the trials, a cue appears in the right or left visual field to alert the child that the target is about to appear. In the valid cue condition, the target appears in the same place as the cue. In the invalid cue condition, it appears on the opposite side of the screen. In addition to cue manipulation (correct cue, incorrect cue, and no cue), the task also involves an interstimulus interval manipulation. In half of the trials, the target appears 100 msec after the cue. In the other half, the target appears 800 msec after the cue.

The 100 msec interstimulus interval is so short that it is thought to allow only activation of the involuntary, or spatial, attention network. However, completion of the task with the 800 msec delay is thought to involve activation of the executive or anterior attention network (Swanson et al. 1991). Thus, by varying the interstimulus interval, different attentional systems are activated by the same task.

The array task involved comparison of two five-letter arrays, with the child indicating with two response keys whether the arrays were the same or different. Words, legal nonwords (e.g., "spart") and illegal nonwords (e.g., sxatr) were presented.

To examine the relationship between functioning of the two attention networks and performance on the remaining laboratory tasks, the mean reaction time for a child's performance at the 100 msec interstimulus interval on the Posner model task was subtracted from his or her mean reaction time for the 800 msec interval. Children's difference scores were then ordered and divided into quartiles which were used to classify children into three groups. Children in the upper quartile were classified as having deficits in automatic attention relative to voluntary attention, children in the midrange were classified as having no deficits, and children in the lower quartile were classified as having voluntary attention deficits relative to voluntary attention.

Consistent with Halperin et al. (1997), children classified as having automatic attention deficits performed more poorly than the no-deficit group on only one measure, the letter array task. In contrast, the voluntary deficit group performed more poorly than the no-deficit group on every measure but the letter array task. The finding that impairment in automatic attention is closely related to rapid processing of lexical arrays again suggests that there may be attention disorder subtypes that produce different patterns of academic impairment. Confirming the existence of these subtypes would seem to be a promising area for future research.

CONCLUSIONS

The relationship between reading disabilities and attention disorders has intrigued researchers for two decades. However, the difficulty defining and measuring core constructs in each area has led to a body of research that is confusing and contradictory. It is clear that with epidemiological samples and rigorous identification criteria, the overlap between the disorders is much smaller than is generally indicated in clinical samples. The early associations between language and attention problems that occur before children are exposed to formal instruction argue for longitudinal studies that follow children from before school entry into the middle grades to examine causal models. It is also important that laboratory and behavioral measures of attention, and multiple informants, be used in assessing attention disorders, and that reading measures be used that separate phonological skills, word recognition, and reading comprehension from one another. The use of multiple measures on the same sample may help researchers make sense of the conflicting data that exists by allowing systematic examination of how measures in each domain are related (e.g., teacher versus parent ratings, inattention versus hyperactivity) and how measures within a domain vary in their relationship to measures in the second domain (e.g., do laboratory measures of sustained attention and behavior ratings show the same relationship to word recognition?).

It is interesting that few studies have addressed the issue of whether a "double deficit" results in poorer long-term outcome. Given the serious long-term consequences of both disorders, this would appear to be a critical question. It is surprising that this issue seems to have been largely examined as a sidelight in databases designed to examine other questions, rather than as a central question that merits its own study.

Finally, progress in understanding the core deficits in both disorders and the increased sophistication of models of cognitive processes that has been brought about by advances in measuring brain activity make this an opportune time for new research into comorbidity. It is encouraging that the questions about the relationship between the two disorders are becoming more sophisticated and precise. Perhaps the next decade will bring the confusing array of findings about reading disability/attention disorders comorbidity into focus, and further our understanding of these two serious childhood disorders.

EDITOR'S COMMENTS

Both reading disorders and attention disorders are relatively common. That they both would occur in the same individual is perhaps not surprising. But, as Dr. Schulte and her colleagues show in the well-written chapter, the frequency of their association (comorbidity) is far more than chance would predict.

The association of reading and attention disorder may be biologic; and if, as we have seen in DeFries' chapter, reading disorder is often genetic, then the association may represent shared genetic site(s) or shared gene effects on brain functions that influence both reading acquisition and attention.

This "double deficit" lessens the extent of doubly-affected individuals' education by one and one-half years and increases the risk of social/emotional dysfunction. Thus, defining the mechanisms for reading and attention disorders and the means by which they can be ameliorated, educationally and medically, is a societal imperative.

ACKNOWLEDGEMENTS

The authors would like to thank Margaret Burchinal for her assistance in completing the HLM analyses.

REFERENCES

American Psychiatric Association 1994. *Diagnostic and Statistical Manual of Mental Disorders: Fourth edition.* Washington, DC: American Psychiatric Association.

Barkley, R. A. 1990. *Attention-deficit Hyperactivity Disorder: A Handbook for Diagnosis and Treatment.* New York: Guilford Press.

Barkley, R. A. 1997. Behavioral inhibition, sustained attention, and executive functions: Constructing a unified theory of ADHD. *Psychological Bulletin* 121:65–94.

Barkley, R. A., Fischer, M., Edelbrock, C. S., and Smallish, L. 1990. The adolescent outcome of hyperactive children diagnosed by research criteria: I. An 8-year prospective follow-up study. *Journal of the American Academy of Child and Adolescent Psychiatry* 29:546–57.

Blackorby, J. and Wagner, M. 1996. Longitudinal postschool outcomes of youth with disabilities: Findings from the National Longitudinal Transition Study. *Exceptional Children* 62:399–413.

Bryk, A. S., and Raudenbush, S. W. 1987. Application of hierarchical linear models to assessing change. *Psychological Bulletin* 101:147–58.

Burchinal, M. R., and Appelbaum, M. I. 1991. Estimating individual developmental functions: Various methods and their assumptions. *Child Development* 62:23–43.

DuPaul, G. J., and Stoner, G. 1994. *ADHD in the Schools: Assessment and Intervention Strategies.* New York: Guilford.

Felton, R. H., and Wood, F. B. 1989. Cognitive deficits in reading disability and attention deficit disorder. *Journal of Learning Disabilities* 22:3–22.

Felton, R. H., Wood, F. B., Brown, I. B., Campbell, S. K., and Harter, M. R. 1987. Separate verbal and naming deficits in attention deficit disorder and reading disability. *Brain and Language* 31:171–84.

Fergusson, D. M., and Horwood, L. J. 1992. Attention deficit and reading achievement. *Journal of Child Psychology and Psychiatry* 33:375–85.

Forness, S. R., Youpa, D., Hanna, G. L., Cantwell, D. P., and Swanson, J. M. 1992. Classroom instructional characteristics in attention deficit hyperactivity disorder: Comparison of pure and mixed subgroups. *Behavioral Disorders* 17:115–25.

Frick, P., Kamphaus, R. W., Lahey, B. B., Loeber, R., Christ, M. G., Hart, E., and Tannenbaum, L. E. 1991. Academic underachievement and the disruptive behavior disorders. *Journal of Consulting and Clinical Psychology* 59:289–94.

Hall, S. J., Halperin, J. M., Schwartz, S. T., and Newcorn, J. H. 1997. Behavioral and executive functions in children with Attention-Deficit Hyperactivity disorder and reading disability. *Journal of Attention Disorders* 1:235–47.

Hallahan, D. P., Kauffman, J. M., and Lloyd, J. W. 1996. *Learning Disabilities.* Boston: Allyn and Bacon.

Halperin, J. M., Newcorn, J. H., Koda, V. H., Pick, L., McKay, K. E., and Knott, P. 1997. Noradrenergic mechanisms in ADHD children with and without reading disabilities: A replication and extension. *Journal of the American Academy of Child and Adolescent Psychiatry* 36:1688–97.

Hinshaw, S. P. 1992. Externalizing behavior problems and academic underachievement in childhood and adolescence: Causal relationships and underlying mechanisms. *Psychological Bulletin* 111:127–55.

Holborow, P. L., and Berry, P. S. 1986. Hyperactivity and learning difficulties. *Journal of Learning Disabilities* 19:426–31.

Keogh, B. A. 1971. Hyperactivity and learning disorders: Review and speculation. *Exceptional Children* 38:101–9.

Lambert, N. M., and Sandoval, J. 1980. The prevalence of learning disabilities in a sample of children considered hyperactive. *Journal of Abnormal Child Psychology* 8:33–50.

Light, J. G., Pennington, B. F., Gilger, J. W., and DeFries, J. C. 1995. Reading disability and hyperactivity disorder: Evidence for a common genetic etiology. *Developmental Neuropsychology* 11:323–35.

McConaughy, S. H., Mattison, R. E., and Peterson, R. 1994. Behavioral/emotional problems of children with serious emotional disturbance and learning disabilities. *School Psychology Review* 23:81–98.

McGee, R., Share, D., Moffitt, T. E., Williams, S., and Silva, P. A. 1988. Reading disability, behaviour problems, and juvenile delinquency. In *Individual Differences in Children and Adolescents: International Perspectives*, eds. D. H. Saklofske and S. B. G. Eysenk. London: Hodder & Stoughton.

McGee, R., Williams, S., Moffitt, T., and Anderson, J. 1989. A comparison of 13-year-old boys with attention deficit and/or reading disorder on neuropsychological measures. *Journal of Abnormal Child Psychology* 17:37–53.

McGee, R., Williams, S., Share, D. L., Anderson, J., and Silva, P. A. 1986. The relationship between specific reading retardation, general reading backwardness, and behavioural problems in a large sample of Dunedin boys: A longitudinal study from five to eleven years. *Journal of Child Psychology and Psychiatry* 27:597–610.

McKinney, J. D., and Feagans, L. 1984. Academic and behavioral characteristics: Longitudinal studies of learning disabled and average achievers. *Learning Disability Quarterly* 7:251–65.

McKinney, J. D., McClure, S., and Feagans, L. 1982. Classroom behavior patterns of learning disabled and non-learning disabled children. *Learning Disability Quarterly* 5:45–52.

McKinney, J. D., and Speece, D. L. 1986. Academic consequences and longitudinal stability of behavioral subtypes of learning disabled children. *Journal of Educational Psychology* 78:365–72.

Osborne, S. S., Schulte, A. C., and McKinney, J. D. 1991. A longitudinal study of students with learning disabilities in mainstream and resource programs. *Exceptionality* 2:81–96.

Pennington, B. F. 1991. *Diagnosing Learning Disorders: A Neuropsychological Framework.* New York: Guilford.

Pennington, B. F., Grossier, D., and Welsh, M. C. 1993. Contrasting cognitive deficits in attention deficit hyperactivity disorder versus reading disability. *Developmental Psychology* 29:511–23.

Posner, M. 1988. Structures and functions of selective attention. In *Clinical Neuropsychology and Brain Function: Research, Measurement, and Practice,* eds. T. Boll and B. K. Bryant. Washington, DC: American Psychological Association.

Posner, M., and Peterson, S. E. 1990. The attention system of the human brain. *Annual Review of Neuroscience* 13:25–42.

Posner, M. I., and Raichle, M. E. 1994. *Images of Mind.* New York: W. H. Freeman.

Rowe, K. J., and Rowe, K. S. 1992. The relationship between inattentiveness in the classroom and reading achievement (Part B): An explanatory study. *Journal of the American Academy of Child and Adolescent Psychiatry* 31:357–68.

Rutter, M. 1974. Emotional disorder and educational underachievement. *Archives of Disease in Childhood* 49:249–56.

Rutter, M., Tizard, J., Yule, W., Graham, P., and Whitmore, K. 1976. Isle of Wight studies 1964–1974. *Psychological Medicine* 6:313–32.

Schaefer, E. S., Edgerton, M., and Aronson, M. 1977. *Classroom Behavior Inventory.* Chapel Hill, NC: The Frank Porter Graham Child Development Center.

Segalowitz, S. J., Wagner, W. J., and Menna, R. 1992. Lateral versus front ERP predictors of reading skill. *Brain and Cognition* 20:85–103.

Semrud-Clikeman, M., Biederman, J., Sprich-Buckminster, S., Lehman, B. K., Faraone, S. V., and Norman, D. 1992. Comorbidity between ADDH and learning disability. A review and report in a clinically referred sample. *Journal of the American Academy of Child and Adolescent Psychiatry* 31:439–48.

Shaywitz, B. A., Fletcher, J. M., and Shaywitz, S. E. 1994. Interrelationships between reading disability and attention deficit-hyperactivity disorder. In *Learning Disabilities Spectrum: ADD, ADHD, and LD,* eds. A. J. Capute, P. J. Accardo, and B. K. Shapiro. Baltimore, MD: York Press.

Shaywitz, S. E., and Shaywitz, B. A. 1988. Attention deficit disorder: Current perspectives. In *Learning Disabilities: Proceedings of the National Conference,* eds. J. F. Kavanaugh and T. J. Truss. Parkton, MD: York Press.

Shaywitz, S. E., Shaywitz, B. A., Fletcher, J. M., and Escobar, M. D. 1990. Prevalence of reading disability in boys and girls: Results of the Connecticut Longitudinal Study. *Journal of the American Medical Association* 264:998–1002.

Silver, L. B. 1981. The relationship between learning disabilities, hyperactivity, distractibility, and behavioral problems. *Journal of the American Academy of Child and Adolescent Psychiatry* 20:385–97.

Speece, D. L., McKinney, J. D., and Applebaum, M. 1985. Classification and validation of behavioral subtypes of learning disabled children. *Journal of Educational Psychology* 77:67–77.

Swanson, J. M., Posner, M. I., Potkin, S., Bonforte, S., Youpa, D., Fiore, C., Cantwell, and D., Crinella, F. 1991. Activating tasks for the study of visual-spatial attention in ADHD children: A cognitive anatomic approach. *Journal of Child Neurology* 6(Suppl):S117–S125.

Torgesen, J. K. and Wagner, R. K. 1997. Alternative diagnostic approaches for specific developmental reading disabilities. *Learning Disabilities: Research and Practice* 13:220–32.

Wagner, R. K., and Torgesen, J. K. 1987. The nature of phonological processing and its causal role in the acquisition of reading skills. *Psychological Bulletin* 101:192–212.

Wood, F. B., and Felton, R. H. 1994. Separate linguistic and attentional factors in the development of reading. *Topics in Language Disorders* 14(4):42–57.

Chapter • 10

Neurological Factors Underlying the Comorbidity of Attentional Dysfunction and Dyslexia

Kytja K.S. Voeller

Clinicians and researchers have long been aware that dyslexia and attention deficit hyperactivity disorder (ADHD) are, in some way, closely associated. However, neither the nature nor the extent of the association is understood. One possibility is that any association is merely an artifact of the relatively high prevalence of both disorders. Another possibility is that the association is a manifestation of a true neurobiological relationship.

In this chapter, I first review some of the clinical literature regarding the relationship between ADHD, dyslexia, and language disorder, and examine the broader neurological features of dyslexia. Information coming out of a recent study on the remediation of dyslexia is presented.

Finally, various hypotheses about how dyslexia and ADHD might be related at a neurobiological level are discussed.

The changing nomenclature for attention deficit hyperactivity disorder makes for terminological awkwardness. To simplify this, the term ADHD is used throughout. When an early DSM classification is referred to, this will be defined, but will then be referred to as ADHD.

ATTENTION DEFICIT HYPERACTIVITY DISORDER (ADHD) AND DYSLEXIA

Attention deficit hyperactivity disorder and dyslexia are commonly considered to be separate disorders (DSM-IV American Psychiatric Association 1994). It is generally believed that a patient who is dyslexic may or may not have ADHD, and that the association is a random one. However, many of those working in the field of learning disabilities have observed that dyslexia and ADHD are, in fact, closely associated (Douglas and Peters 1979; Levine et al. 1982). Studies attempting to assess the degree of overlap have generated remarkably variable results—the extent of the overlap has been estimated as ranging between 10% and 92% (Biederman et al. 1991). In part, this variability stems from the use of different definitions. In addition, some of the studies contain substantial methodological flaws (such as not specifying the definitions that were used, or not conducting a formal assessment of reading achievement). These methodological problems have been reviewed in considerable detail (Semrud-Clikeman et al. 1992). Semrud-Clikeman et al., also reported a study of their own involving 126 children, referred by a clinic, who were divided into those with academic problems, those with ADHD as defined by DSM-III criteria, and a random sample of normal controls. They set discrepancy criteria at different levels with rather different results. Using one method, in which reading disability was defined as a discrepancy between reading achievement (WRAT-R reading) (> 10 standard score points below full-scale IQ [FSIQ]), 38% of the ADHD subjects and 8% of normal controls were dyslexic. When reading achievement was set at 20 standard score points > FSIQ, 23% of subjects with ADHD and only 2% of the controls had reading disability. When a third criterion was used—reading achievement < 85 and > 15 standard score points below FSIQ—the number of children with ADHD who also had dyslexia dropped to 15% and none of the controls were reading disabled. In summary, depending on the particular definition of dyslexia used, the number of children with ADHD who also had dyslexia ranged from 15% to 38%, which is substantially higher than the rate in the control population.

If dyslexia and ADHD are truly separate disorders, then another relevant issue is whether children with ADHD only (ADHD pure) and ADHD plus dyslexia (ADHD + RD) have different cognitive profiles. This issue has been examined by a number of researchers. Felton et al. (1987) compared a group of children with dyslexia with and without attention deficit disorder (ADD), and controls, using a 2 x 2 matrix in which dyslexia and ADD (present or absent) were the two independent variables. Using age and intelligence as covariates, cognitive test scores were analyzed using a multivariate analysis. This analysis revealed that there was a main effect for both independent variables but no interaction. Follow-up univariate analysis revealed that there was little overlap between the dependent measures responsible for the two main effects. The ADD versus non-ADD differences involved tests of memory and measures of semantic and linguistic fluency. However, Share and Schwartz (1988) reviewed this study and observed that when subjects with ADD or reading disability and ADHD+RD were compared directly, without comparing them to controls, only two of the tests were significant at a $p < .01$ level—the *Rapid Automatized Naming* and *Boston Naming Test*. Subjects with ADD alone performed better than dyslexics on this particular subset of tests. McGee et al. (1989) also reported an overlap between these two conditions in a longitudinal study of a large sample of children in New Zealand. At age 13 years, reading scores derived from the Burt Word Reading Test-1974 were available on 26 of 27 boys with ADD. The mean reading score of boys with ADD was 62.0 with a range from 14 to 92, in contrast to 83.3 in those without ADD ($p < .05$). Half of the boys with ADD were also reading disabled, supporting the notion of a relatively large overlap. The authors examined the neuropsychological profile of these boys and failed to demonstrate any difference in their cognitive abilities.

ATTENTION DEFICIT HYPERACTIVITY DISORDER AND DEVELOPMENTAL LANGUAGE DISORDER

Developmental language disorder is strongly related to dyslexia. Some dyslexics have only a phonological awareness deficit and/or anomia, but others have substantial deficits in processing grammar and/or semantics. Thus, the extent of the overlap of ADHD and language disorder is relevant to a study of dyslexia, although the exact nature of the relationship is imperfectly understood.

A number of studies have documented a substantial overlap between ADHD and language disorder. Love and Thompson (1988) reported on 200 children ranging in age from 2.8 to 7.7 years who were referred to a mental health center. Excluding children with mental retardation or autism, the authors found that 75 (64.7%) of the 116 children in the study had a speech and/or language disorder. Of the 75 children with a speech and/or language disorder, 56 (75%) also had ADHD. The prevalence rate for the dual diagnosis of language disorder and ADHD (48.3%) was three times the rate of language disorder without ADHD (16.4%) and twice that of ADHD without language disorder. Interestingly, more boys than girls had combined language disorder and ADHD, with a ratio of 2.6:1. In those children with language disorder plus attention deficit disorder *without hyperactivity*, the ratio of boys to girls was 9:1.

Cantwell and Baker (1991) studied 600 children with language impairment (mean age 5.6, ranging from 1 to 16 years). The subjects underwent an initial evaluation and were then re-evaluated some four years later. The DSM-III ADHD diagnosis was used. Half of the 600 children had a psychiatric illness. The most common psychiatric diagnosis was ADHD (identified in 19%). Learning disability (essentially reading disability) was defined by DSM-III criteria and McLeod's formula, which employed a discrepancy criterion based on WISC-R Performance IQ, chronological age, and scores from the WRAT-R (McLeod 1978). Using this definition, 42 (only 7%) of the total cohort were identified as learning disabled (over 25% of the children of school age). In the group of children with a learning disability, ADHD was identified in 40% and was the most common psychiatric diagnosis. Nine percent had either oppositional defiant disorder or conduct disorder. Cantwell and Baker were able to re-evaluate 300 of the original 600 children four or five years later. At that time, the mean age of the group was 9.1 years. Ninety-one of 300 children had learning disability; 84% had an unspecified "psychiatric illness" compared to 49% of the matched controls. Sixty-eight percent of the children with learning disability had some form of behavior disorder, versus only 40% of controls. Attention Deficit Hyperactivity Disorder was again, by far, the most common diagnosis (present in 63% of the children with learning disability, but only 30% of the children in the matched comparison group $p <. 0001$). This study indicates the close relationship between language disorder, learning disability (reading disability), and ADHD. Moreover, it provides a longitudinal perspective. Many of the children with language impairment evolved into children with learning disabilities, and there was an increase in the number of children with ADHD from the first to the later study.

Tirosh and Cohen (1998) identified 166 children with ADHD out of a cohort of 3208 (5.2%) school-aged children (6- to 11-years of age) identified as ADHD by their teacher. Of the 166 children, 27 (16.2%) were already on medication. Of this group of 27, only 5 children could be withdrawn from the medication so that they could participate in the study. An additional 24 parents declined participation. After excluding other children for comorbid behavioral disorders, 101 children were evaluated on both language and reading tests. Nearly half of the ADHD children (45%) were identified as being impaired in at least one area of language. There was a higher proportion of girls in the group of ADHD children who were also language impaired than in the group of children with ADHD alone. The mean WISC-R Full-Scale IQ was lower in the ADHD plus language impaired group than in the group with only ADHD, but both were in the average range. They noted that children with both disorders appeared to have great difficulty with short-term verbal memory.

An excellent summary of studies regarding the association of language disorders and ADHD appears in Tannock and Schachar (1996). These authors suggest that the executive dysfunction associated with ADHD ". . . impedes the development of internalized self-directed talk and self-regulation, which in turn has a negative effect on the development and use of these higher-order cognitive processes" (p. 147). However, other models, which take into consideration developmental neurobiological data, are possible. For example, genetically programmed neuronal anomalies in the temporal lobe could give rise to developmental language disorders in the young child. These same anomalies may disrupt the normal development of the dopaminergic systems, which, in turn, might result in clinical ADHD. (To support this concept, a study by Saunders et al. (1998) reported that medial temporal lobe lesions in neonatal monkeys disrupt the prefrontal regulation of striatal dopaminergic activity in later development.) Thus, an underlying anomaly of brain development could be a common cause for the emergence of both ADHD and language disorder.

ATTENTION DEFICIT HYPERACTIVITY DISORDER, DYSLEXIA, AND MOTOR SYSTEM DYSFUNCTION

Denckla and Rudel (1978) reported that children with ADHD, without any evidence of motor dysfunction on neurological examination, manifested deficits on a quantified examination of motor coordination. In a second study involving a group of children with reading disability, (Denckla et al. 1985) noted more subtle motor deficits in the group that also had ADHD. The study involved comparing two groups of children with reading disability. One group consisted of children who did not meet criteria for ADHD, and the other group (matched in other characteristics) was hyperactive. The hyperactive subjects performed more slowly on five of the six timed tests on both sides of the body, and, on some tasks, the younger children had more dysrhythmia and overflow movements. Thus, the information from these two studies suggests that motor coordination deficits are associated with hyperactivity, and, to the extent that a dyslexic is hyperactive, one might expect associated motor deficits. It is not clear if attention deficit, without hyperactivity, is associated with as significant a coordination impairment.

Share, McGee, and Silva (1986) reported on 95 dyslexic children, subjects drawn from the Dunedin Multidisciplinary Health and

Development Study, an extensive longitudinal study on nearly 1000 children. The dyslexic subjects were divided into high- and low-ADD groups. Using several different standardized measures of motor development, as well as articulation tests, the children were examined every two years from age 5 to age 9. Articulation deficits were present in both the low- and high-ADD dyslexic groups. The groups differed only on the leg coordination scale from the McCarthy Scale for Children's Abilities at age 5 years. To some extent, this study contradicts the studies by Denckla and colleagues described above. However, there are substantial differences in the types of motor tasks that were employed in these two studies. Denckla's tasks involved internally generated repetitive movements that were meticulously timed in contrast to other motor tasks that were judged in terms of non-temporal parameters. In addition to the measurement issues, internally generated movements place heavier demands on the prefrontal system than external pacing (Gerloff et al. 1998). Interestingly, Share et al. (1986) suggested that the association between ADD and dyslexia might be due to a "fundamental rate-processing deficit." (p. 318)

Wolff and colleagues have conducted a number of studies on motor coordination in subjects with dyslexia, using sophisticated, quantitatively measured motor tasks. They demonstrated that half of the subjects with dyslexia and members of their families are impaired in timing control and the performance of coordinated motor actions in comparison to less than 10% of controls. Moreover, family members who showed motor coordination deficits made significantly more dysphonetic spelling errors than family members who had dyslexia without motor deficits. Children of parents with motor coordination deficits also made more dysphonetic spelling errors (Wolff, Melngailis, and Kotwica 1996).

The motor impairments described in dyslexics by Wolff and colleagues consisted of greater variability of inter-response interval (IRI), which became particularly apparent at faster speeds. To repeat rhythmic patterns accurately, it is necessary to anticipate the distribution of temporal duration or stress assignments in the production of rhythmic patterns and the proportional or relative timing of components that confer a rhythmic structure on the sequence. In general, these deficits were identified only on bimanual tasks. Normal subjects show relatively low IRI variability during finger tapping. After a very brief period of external cueing with the metronome (lasting for only two to three stimuli) normal subjects could anticipate the intervals and the lag time between the anticipated response and the next external signal within a range of 30 to 35 msec. They could proportionately scale IRI and tap duration within measures. Although subjects with dyslexia can also anticipate metronome signals, their anticipation time, (interval between their response and the next metronome signal) was three to six times longer than controls and it took them much longer to learn a new tapping pattern. The constraints imposed by the metronome seemed to place an extra burden on the individuals with dyslexia. Synchronizing motor response to a metronome signal and reproducing rhythmic patterns was difficult for individuals with dyslexia, even when it was at their preferred rate. Wolff discounts the possibility that this is a purely cerebellar deficit as dyslexics performed as well as controls on unimanual tasks. Moreover, as the subjects with dyslexia grew older, the differences in performance compared to controls disappeared on certain tasks. Nine- and 10-year-old subjects with dyslexia could not perform bimanual synchronous tapping as well as controls, but by 11 to 13 years the difference had disappeared. Adolescents with dyslexia did not perform as well on bimanual alternation tasks as did controls, but in adulthood there were no differences. There was no correlation between performance on tests of academic achievement and on the motor coordination tasks. Wolff observes that the impaired bimanual coordination seen in subjects with dyslexia resembles that observed following callosectomy.

Other studies have supported the notion of motor deficits in dyslexics. In a study of Finnish individuals with dyslexia, Byring and Pulliainen (1984) noted deficits in sequential finger opposition that persisted into adulthood. Kinsbourne et al. (1991) also observed that there was a strong relationship between educational variables and right-sided sequential finger opposition and the right heel-toe tests, which correlated more strongly than numerous language variables. (Here again, sequential movements are internally generated and self-paced.)

Leslie, Davidson, and Batey (1985) studied motor performance using the Purdue Pegboard in right-handed, language-impaired subjects with dyslexia with a naming deficit, and matched controls (age 9 to 11 years). The subjects with dyslexia had difficulty on the unimanual task, particularly with the left hand, but not on the bimanual task. Gladstone et al. (1989) on a bimanual coordination task using a modified Etch-A-Sketch toy concluded that children with dyslexia had evidence of impairment in interhemispheric information transfer as well as a deficit in ipsilateral motor pathways. Moore et al. (1995) studied adults with dyslexia using the same task and noted that they were slower in unimanual knob turning, less accurate in bimanual performance, with particular difficulty in asymmetric hand movements. Eliminating visual feedback did not change the magnitude of the difference. No differences were present in speed of bimanual responding. Performance on these motor tasks correlated with scores on the WAIS-R Block Design subtest but not on a Rhyme Fluency task. The pattern of deficits in this series of experiments is similar to that described in subjects who have undergone callosectomy. Moore and colleagues have suggested that this pattern of impaired bimanual coordination may reflect a callosal system deficit, in that the left hemisphere motor control system cannot effectively control premotor and motor systems of the right hemisphere. Wolff, Cohen, and Drake (1984) pointed out that dyslexic symptoms are not part of the post-callosectomy syndrome.

A possible cerebellar deficit was postulated by Nicolson, Fawcett, and Dean (1995) after finding evidence of impaired balance in subjects with dyslexia.

Motor performance also involves articulatory movements. It would be reasonable to expect, given the link between articulation and phonological processing (Heilman, Voeller, and Alexander 1996; Liberman and Mattingly 1985; Rizzolatti and Arbib, 1998), that individuals with dyslexia would perform rapid articulatory movements less well than controls. In support of this hypothesis, Wolff, Michel, and Ovrut (1990) provided evidence that adolescents and adults with dyslexia performed articulatory movements (that is, repeating /pa/ta/ka) more slowly than controls and had greater difficulty synchronizing with the metronome at faster speeds than controls. Subjects with dyslexia also made more syllable sequencing errors. Wolff (1993) observed that, although there is no obvious or direct causal relation between bimanual coordination and learning to read, there is strong evidence that there is a commonality between the neuronal mechanisms controlling timing precision and serial order in speech and language and the temporal organization of motor behaviors.

DYSLEXIA, ATTENTION AND THE VISUAL SYSTEM

The acts of fixating on a small segment of text, making a saccade to the next segment, and extracting relevant information are components of the reading process that require both motor control and attention. Although an effortless process in good readers, subjects with dyslexia complain that they transpose letters and that words move around on the page. An adequate reader must integrate visual, oculomotor, and attentional functions while simultaneously processing phonological and semantic information. Therefore, it is not surprising that impaired attentional processing can result in perturbations of the reading process. For example, there have been a few cases of *selective attentional* or *neglect dyslexia* reported in adults with acquired parietal lesions (Ellis, Flude, and Young 1987, Patterson and Kay 1982; Shallice and Warrington 1977). Rayner et al. (1989) described a similar case in which a bright adult with a history consistent with developmental dyslexia (with phonologic awareness deficits) also manifested prominent visuospatial/perceptual and attentional deficits.

A number of studies have demonstrated low-level dysfunction in the visual system of subjects with dyslexia (Martos and Vila 1990; Pavlidis 1981; Zangwill and Blakemore 1972). Martin and Lovegrove (1987) described a slow flicker fusion rate in subjects with dyslexia. Impaired vergence amplitudes were noted by Stein and Fowler (1981). These studies have been hotly contested, and replications have been inconsistent (Black et al. 1984; Brown, Haegerstrom-Portnoy, and Adams 1983; Olson, Kliegl, and Davidson 1983; Stanley, Smith, and Howell 1983). One weakness of these early studies is that the criteria by which subjects with dyslexia were selected are poorly defined, and it is not clear if they were studying persons with poor reading with phonological deficits or some other more unusual form of reading disorder.

Studies indicating some form of dysfunction in the magnocellular system of individuals with dyslexia have come from both researchers studying the visual system and clinicians. Lehmkuhle et al. (1993) conducted a visual evoked potential (VEP) study in which low- and high-spatial frequency targets were presented in either a steady or flickering background to subjects with dyslexia and controls. The flickering field reduced the amplitude of the VEP in subjects with dyslexia more than in controls, suggesting some sort of dysfunction in the magnocellular system, but not the parvocellular system. Livingstone et al. (1991) reported a VEP study using a binocularly presented checkerboard pattern at low and high contrast. There was no difference between the groups at high contrast. At low contrast, they found the early negative wave of the VEP present in all controls but either missing or delayed in subjects with dyslexia. The investigators interpreted this early negative wave as reflecting incoming thalamocortical activity in layer 4C of V1. Neuropathological studies of the lateral geniculate bodies of five subjects with dyslexia and five controls revealed that there were changes restricted to the magnocellular layers of the lateral geniculate bodies. The lateral geniculate bodies of the subjects with dyslexia contained smaller cells and fewer neurons than those of normal readers. The parvocellular layers were normal in appearance. Examining steady-state visual evoked potentials at a variety of contrast levels, they found that at high contrast there was no difference, but at 15 Hz, using low-contrast stimuli, there was a reduction in the responses of normal subjects but responses were virtually absent in the subjects with dyslexia. These findings have been contested by Victor et al. (1993) who criticized the Lehmkuhle study and reported that they were unable to replicate Livingstone's findings (Victor et al. 1993).

Preclinical studies in macaques have provided support for the idea of magnocellular dysfunction, because there is a substantial decrease in luminance contrast sensitivity for stimuli of high temporal frequency and lower spatial frequency following lesions of the magnocellular lateral geniculate system.

Neuroimaging studies in subjects with dyslexia also have supported the concept of some sort of visual involvement (e.g., fMRI study of visual processing in subjects with dyslexia by Eden et al. 1996). The positron emission tomography (PET) study reported by Horwitz, Rumsey, and Donohue (1998), showed failure of activation and functional connectivity between the left angular gyrus and the occipital-temporal region (visual areas V5/MT) suggesting some sort of dysfunction of the magnocellular system in individuals with dyslexia.

In response to the concern about selection of subjects with dyslexia, investigators also modified selection criteria so that they were closer to current standards and in some cases, also identified phonologic deficits in the subjects with dyslexia who were studied. Moreover, some studies have demonstrated that the auditory and visual systems of subjects with dyslexia do not process rapidly presented visual or auditory information as well as controls. Cornelissen et al. (1995) demonstrated that subjects with dyslexia (defined on the basis of an IQ-reading level discrepancy using a regression formula) had impaired visual motion sensitivity even when high contrast and illumination levels were present. This finding was supported by Eden et al. (1995) who examined individuals with dyslexia, "backward readers," and controls on two tasks involving brief presentations of visual stimuli. They found a positive correlation between a measure of phonologic awareness and task performance, as well as the fact that one of the tasks, along with verbal IQ, and chronological age accounted for 73% of the variance in reading ability. They attributed this to difficulty in speed of information processing. Cornelissen et al. (1998) looked for a correlation between motion thresholds and letter detection errors, rather than contrasting dichotomous groups of normal and disabled readers. Children who performed well on the motion detection task made fewer letter detection errors than those who performed poorly. This correlation held up even when children who met a standard discrepancy criterion definition of "reading disabled" were excluded. They constructed a polynomial model using letter errors, phonologic awareness—as measured with a spoonerism task—and motion detection. Moreover, they indicated that deficits in either the phonological or magnocellular visual system can produce the same pattern of impairment in terms of mapping orthographic to phonological units. Farmer and Klein (1993) compared subjects with dyslexia and controls on tasks of temporal processing in both the auditory and visual modalities. They found evidence of a temporal processing deficit in subjects with dyslexia, who required longer inter-stimulus intervals to segregate clicks perceptually and were less accurate in perceiving temporal order of tones. The visual temporal processing deficit was not as obvious, but there was a trend suggesting impairment. Slaghuis, Lovegrove, and Davidson (1993) also demonstrated that both auditory and visual deficits coexisted in subjects with dyslexia, and persisted into adulthood (Slaghuis, Twell, and Kingston 1996). Nicolson and Fawcett (1993) also noted that when a learning task involved integrating visual and auditory information, children with dyslexia took much longer than controls to master the information successfully.

Dyschronia

The above studies, which provide support for a deficit in processing both rapid auditory and visual stimuli, as well as in generating rapid bimanual motor output have given rise to the concept that the pathophysiology of dyslexia involves a much more basic deficit in timing, and represents a dyschronia (Llinás 1993). A dyschronia results from a cellular dysfunction that modifies "the normal properties of neuronal circuits responsible for temporal aspects of cognition" so that the nervous system is allowed to function in a relatively normal fashion only within particular temporal windows. Llinás postulates that for some reason these neurons are unable to generate sharp enough ensemble oscillations at higher frequencies and reset such rhythmicity following close-interval sensory stimulation. In addition, the concept of dyschronia does not, at this point, specify a particular locus of dysfunction. Certainly, it is broader than a specific hemisphere, cortical, or subcortical area.

COMMENTARY AND PERSONAL RESEARCH

These studies of the overlap between ADHD and dyslexia indicate that, indeed, a certain degree of comorbidity between ADHD and dyslexia does exist, but the extent of the overlap depends heavily on the diagnostic criteria that are employed. The study described above by Semrud-Clikeman et al. (1992) clearly indicates the impact of varying definitions of reading disability on the extent of the comorbidity.

All these previous studies employed the DSM categorical diagnosis of ADHD and the discrepancy criterion definition of dyslexia. These approaches are, of course, well accepted and widely used in both clinical and research settings. However, the current categorical definition of ADHD, which relies on the presence of behavioral descriptors (which can mean different things to different people), and requires inference on the part of the observer is not without some problems (Fletcher, Morris, and Francis 1991). The definition does not look below the surface at the biological factors that underlie ADHD. As a result, individuals with specific behavioral characteristics will be defined as ADHD. The grouping may include persons with different genetic makeup, but the same behavioral phenotype. Moreover, persons with the same genetic traits may not be categorized as ADHD, if the manifestations are sufficiently mild. Currently, an acceptable scheme for a dimensional diagnosis of ADHD, or one based on biological features, has yet to be developed.

With regard to dyslexia, the discrepancy criterion diagnosis has been the subject of extensive criticism (Fletcher et al. 1992; Francis et al. 1996). The same genotype-phenotype problem exists as it does with ADHD, which in turn makes it difficult to identify associations between ADHD and dyslexia.

The data presented here involves a somewhat different approach to the diagnosis of both dyslexia and ADHD. Although the majority of the subjects also meet the standard categorical diagnosis of ADHD and the discrepancy criterion-based diagnosis of dyslexia, neurocognitive tasks that provide a parametric and dimensional approach were also administered. The diagnosis of dyslexia was based on the presence of a phonological awareness deficit that has been shown to be characteristic of phonological dyslexia, the most common type of dyslexia. In addition to standard DSM criteria, subjects were also tested on neurocognitive laboratory studies, which involve assessment of attentional and intentional behaviors. In addition, therapists who had received some training in monitoring attention also observed the subjects closely over a long period of time.

Study 1: Methods.

The intensive remediation study was conducted by Dr. Alexander and myself at the Morris Center in Gainesville as part of the NICHD-funded grant on Prevention and Remediation of Reading Disabilities (HD30988A; J. Torgesen, PI;). The 62 children who were recruited into the study had all been classified by the school system as learning disabled and were attending SLD classes. They were identified by their teachers as the most difficult to instruct in single word decoding and as a group they were severely dyslexic. During the instructional period, two children dropped out of the study, so the final sample contains 60 subjects. The mean age of this group was 118 (STD = 12) months. There were 17 girls and 43 boys.

After obtaining informed parental consent and the children's assent, subjects underwent a series of assessments that included WISC-3 IQ, an extensive series of tasks assessing phonological awareness,

Rapid Automatized Naming tasks, academic achievement, various tests of reading, valuations of language—the *Clinical Evaluation of Language Fundamentals, Revised* (CELF-R), and the *Boston Naming Test*. A pediatric neurological history and examination were performed. Each child was screened for ADHD using multiple assessment techniques. The SNAP (a DSM-III ADHD checklist) (Pelham et al. 1984) was completed by the parents and the therapists. After completing the SNAP, following initial work with the child, therapists kept daily notes of the child's behavior, including observations about activity level, ability to attend to the task at hand, and impulsivity. In addition, therapists also re-assessed the child two weeks after treatment had been underway. Classroom teachers completed the *Multiple Grade Inventory for Teachers* (Shaywitz personal communication) and the *Conners Teacher Rating Scale* (Conners 1973). Each of the two rating scales was reviewed using an item-by-item analysis and DSM-III items were extracted and compiled to arrive at the classroom teacher's rating for DSM-III ADHD.

In addition, children were evaluated on neuropsychological tests of attentional and intentional function. The attentional task was a letter cancellation task, which, when adapted for use in children, strongly discriminates between children with attention deficit disorder and controls (Voeller and Heilman 1988). The task consists of nine pages of block capital letters, 3/8" high (36 pt Franklin Gothic). The target letters (A, E, or I) were scattered randomly among other non-target letters. There were three pages each in which the target letters were A's, E's, and I's. The target letters were arrayed so that they were equally distributed in all four quadrants. The page was placed so that the center of the test was squarely in the midline of the subject's body, but any obvious struggle over paper placement was avoided as this might increase arousal. The test was timed but time did not enter into the scoring. Errors consisted of the sum of all omitted target letters.

The ocular response task (a contra-saccade task) has been shown to detect deficits in response inhibition in adults with right frontal lesions (Guitton, Buchtel, and Douglas 1985; Butter et al. 1988). A modification of this task was developed for children (Voeller, Alexander, and Heilman 1990). The task consisted of presenting a series of 48 stimuli, 24 delivered in a randomized pattern to the left and right temporal visual fields. The child was instructed to fixate on the examiner's nose during the presentation of the stimulus. The examiner's hands were positioned at an angle of 20° laterally. The child was instructed not to look at the stimulus, but rather look *away* from the stimulus. A practice session was administered so that it was clear that the child understood the "rules." The task was videotaped so that it could be accurately scored after it had been administered. Errors consisted of the total number of glances towards, rather than away from, the stimulus.

Both tasks were normed on a group of 8- to 10-year-old control subjects who had undergone an elaborate diagnostic procedure to rule out ADHD or dyslexia. These tasks proved to have extremely high diagnostic efficiency in terms of discriminating between control and ADHD groups (Voeller 1996). They appear to measure two different aspects of ADHD: predominantly attentional capacity (stimulus detection) and intentional capacity (the control of motor aspects of attention, deficits which result in impulsivity and distractibility).

After the evaluation phase was completed, the children were randomly assigned to one of two instructional conditions—the *Auditory Discrimination in Depth* program, (Lindamood and Lindamood 1975) and the *Embedded Phonics* program developed by Elaine Rose, M.A. (unpublished), which provides a more traditional approach to reading remediation. *Embedded Phonics* involves explicit instruction in a stringent phonics approach, coupled with reading in context, reinforced with a rich array of meaningful writing and reading experiences. Both treatment programs involved one-to-one therapy in a quiet room, allowing for movement, and managing behavior with reinforcers. The therapy required some degree of attentional capacity and focus to be effective. The cognitive load was never frustrating and was carefully gauged to the instructional level of the student. If the child continued to be inattentive or distractible in this setting, medication was recommended, but behavioral management was always used first. Children in each condition received eighty 50-minute sessions (total 67 hours) of one-to-one intensive remediation delivered in two sessions a day (with a ten-minute break between the two sessions), five days a week, over an 8- to 10-week period. They also received a one-hour session each week for the following 8 weeks to help them generalize their newly developed reading skills to classroom assignments. Follow-up assessments were also conducted but will not be discussed here.

Going into this study, Dr. Alexander and I anticipated that approximately half of the subjects might have ADHD and about half of those might be on medication. To our surprise, only seven subjects (11.7%) had been formally diagnosed as having ADHD and had been treated with psychostimulant medication. Even though they were "treated," they often remained symptomatic because they were receiving subtherapeutic doses or were not taking the medication in a consistent fashion.

Study 1: Results

The subjects enrolled in this study were indeed severely reading disabled and language impaired. As a group, they were of normal intelligence, but manifested difficulty in phonological awareness, deficits in both receptive and expressive language, and significant impairment in academic skills. There were no significant differences in the demographic or cognitive characteristics of the two treatment groups— *Auditory Discrimination in Depth* and *Embedded Phonics*.

Parent ADHD Ratings. Attention Deficit Hyperactivity Disorder ratings were available for 45 (8 parent ratings were never completed; 7 children who had been previously diagnosed as ADHD were also excluded). Parents endorsed ADHD criteria for at least one of the subscale criteria in 29 (64.4%) of the children.

Classroom Teacher ADHD Ratings. Teacher ratings were available for 41 children. When two teachers rated a student, the student was rated as meeting ADHD criterion if at least one of the teachers endorsed one or more of the subscale criteria. The teachers rated 16 (39.0%) as having ADHD. In 15 cases, ratings were available from two teachers. In 10 of these (66.6%), the teachers agreed; in 5 they did not.

Therapists' Initial ADHD Ratings. After working with the child for about two weeks, the therapists completed a SNAP rating. Therapists' ratings were available on all 60 subjects, but 7 were excluded because they had been on medication. The therapists identified 29 (54.7%) of the 53 children as meeting criteria for at least one of the ADHD subscales.

Therapists' Later ADHD Ratings. Meticulous records were kept during each individual treatment session noting the child's ability to stay awake and focused on the task, motor activity, restlessness characterized by difficulty staying in seat, excessive talkativeness, and impulsive responses. After spending several more weeks with the children, the therapists indicated that additional children met criteria for ADHD. In these later ratings, all 60 children were assessed, but the 7 who had been previously diagnosed and treated were excluded. On the second assessment, the therapists substantially increased the number of children rated as meeting ADHD criteria, ultimately identifying 41 (77.4%) as having the disorder.

Comparison of Parent ADHD Ratings with Teacher and Therapist Ratings. There was only modest agreement between the parents and classroom teachers: they agreed on 20 of the 36 (55.5 %) cases on which ratings were available from both, and disagreed on 16 (44.4%). Agreement was defined as identifying a given child as meeting DSM-III criteria for at least one of the three ADHD subscales (hyperactivity, impulsivity, or inattention). It was not required that they agree on a specific subscale. For example, if a parent rated a child as meeting hyperactivity subscale criteria and a teacher rated the child as meeting inattention criteria, this would be considered as indicating that they agreed that the child had ADHD. The number of cases agreed on was close to that in which there was disagreement, and this was reflected in poor agreement over chance agreement (kappa = .175) (Cohen 1960).

The same criteria were used for defining agreement between parents' and therapists' initial rating. In 28 of 45 cases (62%) there was agreement and in 17 (37%) there was disagreement between the parent and therapist. In 19 cases, both observers agreed that the child did indeed meet ADHD criteria: in 9 cases, both felt that the child did not. Parents rated 10 children as having ADHD, whereas the therapist did not agree, and in 7 cases, the parent did not perceive the child as having ADHD, whereas the therapist did. The kappa coefficient was +0.12, which indicates limited agreement over chance.

When the parent's initial rating was contrasted to the therapists' later ratings, both agreed on 23 of 45 (51.1%) and disagreed on 22. This is actually a lower level of agreement than the earlier ratings, which was accounted for by the therapists' increased ratings of ADHD, which resulted in shifting children out of the parent "no"/therapist "no" category into the parent "no"/ therapist "yes" category.

When the classroom teacher and early therapist's ratings were compared, the two raters agreed on 29 (70%) and disagreed on 12 of 41 (29.3%). The kappa coefficient was .42, which falls below the .60 criterion recommended by (Hartmann 1977). When the classroom teacher and the therapist were contrasted on the therapist's later evaluation, the kappa was even lower (0.04). This was again due to the fact that the therapists shifted the initial "ADHD-no" rating to an "ADHD-yes" rating, increasing the extent of disagreements.

The way in which parents, teachers, and therapists rated the seven children who were on medication at the time of entrance into the study was also instructive. The parents rated six of them as meeting DSM-III ADHD criteria. However, the classroom teacher did not identify any of the five children that they provided ratings for as having ADHD. Even more interesting was the fact that initially the therapists rated only two of these children as "ADHD-yes," and the other five as "ADHD-no." Many of these children were under-aroused, sleepy, and not at all active, thus fitting into the earlier ADD or "predominantly inattentive" type. The "ADHD-no" ratings were not necessarily due to the fact that these children were medicated, as they were often undermedicated and/or receiving the medicine only intermittently. The later ratings by the therapists classified all seven children as "ADHD-yes."

Neuropsychological Tests for ADHD. The Cancellation Task identified 43 children out of 57 (6.1%) as falling 1 *SD* or more below the mean or being unable to perform the task (the two children were not tested and one was on medication and was excluded). On the

Ocular Response task, 41 of 58 (70.1%) of the children performed at or below 1 *SD* from the mean. These tasks measure somewhat different aspects of attention: the Cancellation Task is sensitive to stimulus detection errors (attention deficit) and the Ocular Response task is sensitive to deficient stimulus response inhibition (distractibility). Fifty-one of 57 children (89.4%) performed below -1 *SD* on one or both tasks. The tasks were congruent in the classification of 35 children: "ADHD-yes" for 35 (66.0%), "ADHD-no" for 5 (9%) (excluding children who performed in the normal range because they were on medication). Roughly equal numbers (8 classified as "yes" by the ocular response task but "no" by the cancellation and 10 classified as "no" by the ocular response and "yes" by the cancellation task). This suggests that these measures indeed assess different aspects of attention.

There was little agreement between the laboratory tests combined and the parent, classroom teacher, or initial therapist ratings. As far as the later therapist ratings, there was still a low level of agreement (kappa = +.118), which reflected the fact that the therapists rated 10 children as "ADHD-no" whereas the test identified them as "ADHD-yes." The tests appear more sensitive to these manifestations of inattention/distractibility than the therapist.

Treatment of ADHD. Out of the 60 children enrolled in the program, seven had been formally diagnosed and started on psychostimulant medication at some time before entry into the study. However, only two children were on medication at the time they enrolled in the study. It proved to be very difficult to start children on medication, even when there was a high degree of consensus about the diagnosis. By the half-way point of therapy (40 hours) only 11 children had been started on medication, and only a fraction of those were adequately medicated. In several instances, it was apparent that they were getting medication in a very inconsistent fashion. Medication was started on an additional five children after the half-way point. After therapy was completed, the parents of two additional children requested that they be treated.

Study 2

Based on the information that we gleaned from Study 1, it was apparent that a large number of children with dyslexia also had some degree of attentional and intentional disorders. In some cases, it was not possible to manage this with purely behavioral methods and environmental adaptations. Treatment with psychostimulants, when necessary, vastly improved the children's abilities to benefit from the remediation programs. It was the impression of the therapists that the children with ADHD were slower to respond to therapy because much time was taken up trying to get them focused on the learning task, but the data is still under analysis.

A second issue had to do with the effect of psychostimulant treatment on the child's performance on some of the phonological awareness tasks. We had previously observed that, without specific treatment addressing phonologic weakness, some children improved on these tasks even without specific interventions, once they were started on medication. In these cases, they no longer met the criteria for phonological impairment. It is, however, unclear what effect medication alone would have on their overall reading ability.

There are a variety of ways to approach this question. One method is to have two groups of children with dyslexia and ADD—one group to be treated and the other not. There are two problems with this: first, we cannot ethically withhold offering treatment once the diagnosis is made, and, secondly we cannot prevent parents from seeking treatment elsewhere. In addition, some parents steadfastly refuse treatment for their children. After considering all the alternatives, we decided that the best approach was to inform parents that, if their child was diagnosed as having ADD, we would arrange for treatment. Treatment would include medical as well as behavioral interventions. Parents would be expected to attend group meetings in which they learn about ADD and are given instructions for management. Because of the delays in starting patients on medication, we attempted to eliminate some of the problems encountered in Study 1 by identifying and treating subjects *before* they were enrolled in the remedial treatment phase.

If parents did not agree to follow through with both aspects of this multimodal approach to treatment, we would not enroll them in the study. Since financial limitations may well affect some of the families, we paid for the medication and other aspects of the therapy during the course of the study. Moreover, the children who improved on medication to the point that they no longer met the criteria for admission into the program would be continued on medication and monitored closely.

To answer these questions, we embarked on a small pilot study.

Study 2: Methods

Kindergartners who were identified by their teachers as potentially having a reading-disability were enrolled in the study. After informed consent was obtained, including the explanation regarding the medication issue, the children were evaluated on Letter-Sound, Sound Elision and Rapid Digit Naming tasks. Based on these three scores, the risk for reading disability by the second grade was computed, using the protocol developed by Wagner and Torgesen (1987) and Wagner, Torgesen, and Rashotte (1994). Before entering the children into the assessment phase, parents were again advised of our intent to evaluate and treat children at risk for reading disability, and it was explained that if the child had ADHD, they would be enrolled in the treatment phase only if they were on medication. If parents did not feel comfortable with undertaking a trial of medication, the child was not enrolled.

The children then underwent intellectual screening, academic testing, language assessment, pediatric neurological history and examination, and attention screening before entrance into the program. Children who meet the diagnostic criteria for ADHD were then started on medication that was titrated so that symptoms were relatively well controlled before the remediation phase was undertaken. The three baseline tasks were readministered on a dose of methylphenidate 0.3mg/kg. If the magnitude effect of test on medication exceeded 0.8, the child would then remain on medication but not undergo the treatment program.

Study 2: Results

Fourteen children were enrolled in the study. The diagnosis of ADHD was based on DSM-IV criteria. Three children did not meet diagnostic criteria for ADHD. Four children were already on psychostimulant medication at the time they entered the study, although not all were on effective doses. The children were taken off the medication for one week and tested on the three baseline tasks—*Rapid Digit Naming* (average of two trials), *Letter-Sound Task* (the child was asked to name letters and provide associated sounds), and Sound Elision ("say tulip without saying lip")—as well as some of the baseline attention/intention tasks. After treating the child with psychostimulant medication, these tasks were repeated. Of the seven children who were tested on and off medication, one showed an effect magnitude of 0.8 or above. This boy was continued on medication, retested periodically, but did not enter the remediation study. Six children entered the treatment phase and continued to receive medication. Four other children with ADHD were not entered into the test-retest assessment, because their parents were reluctant to start them on medication.

The mean age of the seven children who were treated with combined psychostimulant medication and the educational segment of the study was 79.0 (*SD* = 7.0) months. Three were girls; four were boys. Intelligence Quotient estimates (based on the Stanford-Binet Vocabulary subtest) were 106 (*SD* = 9.5), the mean Peabody Picture Vocabulary Test-R) score of 101.5 (*SD* = 8.9). (See Table I.)

Table I.   Study 2: Prevention. Baseline Test Scores and Scores Before and After Psychostimulant treatment

#/Sex	Age in months	Stanford-Binet Vocabulary (IQ)	PPVT-R	Rapid Digit Naming # digits/sec		Letter-Sound (% correct)		Elision	
				Off meds	On meds	Off meds	On meds	Off meds	On meds
#1M	90	120	104	1.10	0.86	71	69	5	7
#2M	78	108	88	1.34	1.49	34	60	8	7
#3F	84	98	112	2.40	1.03	71	89	5	4
#4F	83	94	105	2.33	1.03	51	57	9	7
#5M	70	112	98	1.13	1.21	22	68	6	7
#6M	74	112	93	1.96	2.31	57	54	5	7
#7F	74	98	111	1.11	1.11	63	74	5	3
Mean	70.0	106.0	101.6						
S.D.	7.0	9.5	8.9						

There was considerable variability between subjects in their off-on medication performance. On the Rapid Digit Naming Test, three children decreased their correct words/second rate and three increased it. One did not change. The Letter-Sound Task appeared to be much more responsive to the medication effect: six of the seven children improved their performance. On a paired t-test, the Letter-Sound Task was the only off/on medication task that showed a weak trend toward improvement ($p = .08$). The Elision Task was the most variable, with four declining in performance and two showing an improvement. Four subjects (all boys) showed improvement on at least two of the three tasks, but only one of them (who improved on all three tasks) showed an effect size large enough to move him into the "non-impaired" group. In this study our ability to manipulate medication dosages was limited, and it is possible that either larger or smaller doses would have shown more of an effect. A particularly puzzling feature was that two of the three girls showed a decline in performance on medication on two of the three tests. In a subsequent study, it will be important to assess test-retest performance in both medicated and non-medicated subjects to ascertain the variability in the test-retest situation. It does suggest that psychostimulant treatment has some effect on a child's ability to perform tasks that involve processes underlying reading disability.

DISCUSSION

The first question addressed in this paper has to do with the extent of the overlap between ADHD and dyslexia. Our findings would suggest that very few individuals with dyslexia do not have ADHD of some degree. The current study differed from previous reports in several different ways. (1) The subjects as a group were probably more severely dyslexic than many in previous studies. (2) The selection of subjects was based not only on a discrepancy criterion (which was necessary for classification by the school system as learning impaired and is typical of this type of study), but they also met criteria for phonologic awareness deficit. The fact that all subjects in this study had documented severe phonologic awareness deficit represents a different way of defining a child as learning disabled and is a departure from previous studies. (3) In addition to ratings by parents and classroom teachers, the subjects were also observed in a one-to-one situation for a total of 67 hours by a therapist who was in an excellent position to monitor the child's level of motor activity, as well as the child's ability to sustain attention, inhibit impulsive responding and distractibility. The therapy situation was structured so that the child was always working below his or her frustration level. Finally, (4) in addition to the standard parent ratings, classroom teacher ratings, and those by the therapist, the children were tested on a series of measures that assess attention and intention. These measures provide a quantitative estimate of inattention and impulsivity, which has high diagnostic validity.

Classroom teachers identified 39.7% of children as having ADHD, but there was agreement on only two-thirds of the children rated by two classroom teachers. There was little agreement between the classroom teachers, the parents (who identified a few more children), and the therapists. The relatively low rate of identification by these groups is further supported by the fact that only a small number of children had been previously diagnosed and treated for ADHD. The Morris Center therapists, as a group had had considerable experience with children with ADHD. In their initial assessments, they identified more children as having ADHD (54.7%) than the classroom teachers (39%) but not as many as the parents (64.4%).

Although all the raters identified approximately half of the children as meeting ADHD criteria, the agreement between any pair of raters was uniformly poor. When two classroom teachers rated the same children, they did not agree in a third of the cases.

The therapists who worked with these children were in a good position to identify children with significant attention deficits because they could observe the child closely over a long period of time. The difference in the number of children identified as ADHD on their first rating (54.7%) and their second ratings (77.4%) (in both cases, children already diagnosed were not included) reflects the effect of the long and intense observation period.

The neuropsychological test battery also identified a substantial number of children as having deficits over 1 *SD* from the mean on measures of inattention and response inhibition. It is difficult to find precise equivalents on the laboratory measures with the DSM-IV subtypes, and the laboratory measures are quite sensitive to deficits in this sphere. The agreement between the therapists' second assessment and the laboratory measures was better than any other rating, although the kappa still fell below +.60. This would support the concept that there is a very high degree of attention deficit hyperactivity disorder in the dyslexic population, much higher than previous estimates.

What possible explanations are there for such a strong association between ADHD and dyslexia? There are numerous points at which attentional functions intersect with the process of reading. The process of reading involves a complex combination of phonological analysis, visual/attentional functioning with integrated ocular movements. Reading requires not only an initial step of visual-perceptual processing of orthographic stimuli, but the effective conversion of these stimuli into phonological code, maintaining this information in an auditory buffer, and then extracting relevant semantic information. Because effective reading is heavily dependent on attentional and intentional factors, it is not hard to understand why many children with dyslexia might also have some degree of attentional dysfunction. It is not clear at this point whether attentional dysfunction is separate from the reading problem or is an intrinsic part of it. However, it is likely that if an individual has a phonological awareness deficit, the process of extracting phonologic information is extremely demanding of attention. In a severe case in which there is a dense phonological awareness deficit, the affected individual might be essentially unaware of the salient features of orthography. It would be analogous to a blind person being unable to pay attention to visual stimuli. It is likely that there is a spectrum of attentional dysfunction, ranging from something bordering on unawareness to simply very effortful attending that drains attentional capacity.

The suggestion that dyslexia is a "dyschronia" also fits in with this observation. Earlier in this chapter I discussed the relationship of motor, language and visual dysfunction to dyslexia which seems to involve some aspect of processing rapidly changing sensory stimuli and certain sorts of motor output. One can view attention deficit as another manifestation of a dyschronia. Attention is an active process by which sensory stimuli are processed by the brain in a fashion that selectively enhances information that is of high relevance to the organism (Voeller 1998). The speed of this enhancing function must be at least as rapid as the incoming sensory stimuli, so that any slowness in the process would have a significant effect on attention.

The major point to be made here is that there may be a substantial overlap between dyslexia and ADHD, particularly if attentional/intentional dysfunction is not viewed from the restrictive perspective of a categorical classification scheme that is based on observations by potentially fallible raters.

EDITOR'S COMMENTS

In Anderson's chapter, the possible anatomic basis for the co-occurrence of attention disorder and dyslexia was discussed. Voeller now shows behaviorally, how often these two disorders commingle, with perhaps the majority of those with reading disorder having some form of attention deficit. She notes the CNS processing deficits are multi-system and may reflect cellular dyschronia affecting auditory, visual, tactile-kinesthetic, and motor performance.

Her own research in Florida points out the many complexities of treating attention disorders medically and educationally, i.e., difficult to do one without the other. Finally, the defining of a complex behavioral disorder by non-research-trained observers is not without hazard and may lead to erroneous classification. All the more reason why biologic and/or neuropsychologic markers are needed to define these disorders of attention and reading.

REFERENCES

American Psychiatric Association. 1994. *Diagnostic and Statistical Manual of Mental Disorders.* Fourth ed. Washington, DC: American Psychiatric Association.

Biederman, J., Newcorn, J., and Sprich, S. 1991. Comorbidity of attention deficit hyperactivity disorder with conduct, depressive, anxiety, and other disorders. *American Journal of Psychiatry* 148:564–77.

Black, J. L., Collins, D. W. K., DeRoach, J. N., and Zubrick, S. 1984. A detailed study of sequential saccadic eye movements for normal and poor reading children. *Perceptual and Motor Skills* 59:423–34.

Brown, B., Haegerstrom-Portnoy, G., and Adams, A. 1983. Predictive eye movements do not discriminate between dyslexic and control children. *Neuropsychologia* 21:112–28.

Butter, C. M., Rapcsak, S., Watson, R. T., and Heilman, K. M. 1988. Changes in sensory inattention, directional motor neglect and "release" of the fixation reflex following a unilateral frontal lesion: A case report. *Neuropsychologia* 26:533–45.

Byring, R., and Pulliainen, V. 1984. Neurological and neuropsychological deficiencies in a group of older adolescents with dyslexia. *Developmental Medicine and Child Neurology* 26:765–73.

Cantwell, D. P., and Baker, L. 1991. Association between attention-deficit hyperactivity disorder and learning disorders. *Journal of Learning Disabilities* 24:88–95.

Cohen, J. 1960. A coefficient of agreement for nominal scales. *Educational and Psychological Measurement* 20:37–46.

Conners, C. K. 1973. Rating scales for use in drug studies with children. *Psychopharmacology Bulletin* 9:24-84; 219–22.

Cornelissen, P. L., Richardson, A. J., Mason, A. J., and Fowler, M. S. 1995. Contrast sensitivity and coherent motion detection measured at photopic luminance levels in dyslexics and controls. *Vision Research* 35:1483–94.

Cornelissen, P. L., Hansen, P. C., Hutton, J. L., Evangelinou, V., and Stein, J. F. 1998. Magnocellular visual function and children's single word reading. *Vision Research* 38:471–82.

Denckla, M. B., and Rudel, R. G. 1978. Anomalies of motor development in hyperactive boys. *Annals of Neurology* 3:231–33.

Denckla, M. B., Rudel, R. G., Chapman, C., and Krieger, J. 1985. Motor proficiency in dyslexic children with and without attentional disorders. *Archives of Neurology* 42:228–31.

Douglas, V. I., and Peters, K. G. 1979. Toward a clearer definition of the attentional deficit disorder of hyperactive children. In *Attention and Cognitive Development*, ed. G. A. Hale and M. Lewis. New York: Plenum Press.

Eden, G. F., Stein, J. F., Wood, H. M., and Wood, F. B. 1995. Temporal and spatial processing in reading disabled and normal children. *Cortex* 31: 451–68.

Eden, G. F., VanMeter, J. W., Rumsey, J. M., Maisog, J. M., Woods, R. P., and Zeffiro, T. A. 1996. Abnormal processing of visual motion in dyslexia revealed by functional brain mapping. *Nature* 382:66–69.

Ellis, A. W., Flude, B. M., and Young, A. W. 1987. "Neglect dyslexia" and the early visual processing of letters in words and nonwords. *Cognitive Neuropsychology* 4:439–64.

Farmer, M. E., and Klein, R. 1993. Auditory and visual temporal processing in dyslexic and normal readers. *Annals of the New York Academy of Sciences* 682:339–41.

Felton, R. H., Wood, F. B., Brown, I. S., Campbell, S. K., and Harter, M. R. 1987. Separate verbal memory and naming deficits in attention deficit disorder and reading disability. *Brain and Language* 31:171–84.

Fletcher, J. M., Morris, R. D., and Francis, D. J. 1991. Methodological issues in the classification of attention-related disorders. *Journal of Learning Disabilities* 24:72–77.

Fletcher J. M., Francis D. J., Rourke B P., Shaywitz S. E., Shaywitz B. A. 1992. The validity of discrepancy-based definitions of reading disabilities. *Journal of Learning Disabilities* 25:555–61.

Francis, D. J., Fletcher, J. M., Shaywitz, B. A., Shaywitz, S. E., and Rourke, B. P. 1996. Defining learning and language disabilities: conceptual and psychometric issues with the use of IQ tests. *Language, Speech, and Hearing Services in Schools* 27:132–43.

Gerloff, C., Richard, J., Hadley, J., Schulman, A. E., Honda, M., and Hallett, M. 1998. Functional coupling and regional activation of human cortical motor areas during simple, internally paced and externally paced finger movements. *Brain* 121:1513–31.

Gladstone, M., Best, C. T., and Davidson, R. J. 1989. Anomalous bimanual coordination among dyslexic boys. *Developmental Psycholology* 25:236–46.

Guitton, D., Buchtel, H. A., and Douglas, R. M. 1985. Frontal lobe lesions in man cause difficulties in suppressing reflexive glances and in generating goal-directed saccades. *Experimental Brain Research* 58:455–72.

Hartmann, D. P. 1977. Considerations in the choice of rater observer reliability estimates. *Journal of Applied Behavior Analysis* 42:937–47.

Heilman, K. M., Voeller, K., and Alexander, A. W. 1996. Developmental dyslexia: A motor-articulatory feedback hypothesis. *Annals of Neurology* 39:407–12.

Horwitz, B., Rumsey, J. M., and Donohue, B. C. 1998. Functional connectivity of the angular gyrus in normal reading and dyslexia. *Proceedings of the National Academy of Science, USA* 95:8939–44.

Kinsbourne, M., Rufo, D. T., Gamzu, E., Palmer, R. L., and Berliner, A. K. 1991. Neuropsychological deficits in adults with dyslexia. *Developmental Medicine and Child Neurology* 33:763–75.

Lehmkuhle, S., Garzia, R. P., Turner, L., Hash, T., and Baro, J. A. 1993. A defective visual pathway in children with reading disability. *New England Journal of Medicine* 328:989–96.

Leslie, S. C., Davidson, R. J., and Batey, O. B. 1985. Purdue pegboard performance of disabled and normal readers: Unimanual versus bimanual differences. *Brain and Language* 24:359–69.

Levine, M. D., Busch, B., and Aufsuser, C. 1982. The dimension of inattention among children with school problems. *Pediatrics* 70:387–95.

Liberman, A. M., and Mattingly, I. G. 1985. The motor theory of speech perception revised. *Cognition* 21:1–36.

Lindamood, C. H., and Lindamood, P . 1975. *Auditory Discrimination in Depth.* Allen, TX: DLM/Teaching Resources.

Livingstone, M. S., Rosen, G. D., Drislane, F. W., and Galaburda, A. M. 1991. Physiological and anatomical evidence for a magnocellular defect in developmental dyslexia. *Proceedings of the National Academy of Science, USA* 88:7943–47.

Llinás, R. 1993. Is dyslexia a dyschronia? *Annals of the New York Academy of Sciences* 682:48–56.

Love, A. J., and Thompson, M. G. G. 1988. Language disorders and attention deficit disorders in young children referred for psychiatric services: Analysis of prevalence and a conceptual synthesis. *American Journal of Orthopsychiatry* 58:52–64.

Martin, F., and Lovegrove, W. 1987. Flicker contrast sensitivity in normal and specifically disabled readers. *Perception* 16:215–21.

Martos, F. J., and Vila, J. 1990. Differences in eye movement control amongst dyslexic, retarded, and normal readers in the Spanish population. *Reading and Writing: An Interdisciplinary Journal* 2:175–88.

McGee, R., Williams, S., Moffitt, T., and Anderson, J. 1989. A comparison of 13-year-old boys with attention deficit and/or reading disorder on neuropsychological measures. *Journal of Abnormal Child Psychology* 17: 37–53.

McLeod, J. 1978. Psychometric identification of children with learning disabilities. University of Saskatchewan, Saskatoon: Institute of Child Guidance and Development Monograph.

Moore, L. H., Brown, W. S., Markee, T. E., Theberge, D. C., and Zvi, J. C. 1995. Bimanual coordination in dyslexic adults. *Neuropsychologia* 33:781–93.

Nicolson, R. I., and Fawcett, A. J. 1993. Children with dyslexia automatize temporal skills more slowly. *Annals of the New York Academy of Sciences* 682:390–92.

Nicolson, R. I., Fawcett, A. J., and Dean, P. 1995. Time estimation deficits in developmental dyslexia: Evidence of cerebellar involvement. *Proceedings of the Royal Society of London. Series B: Biological Sciences* 259:43–47.

Olson, R. K., Kliegl, R., and Davidson, B. J. 1983. Dyslexic and normal readers' eye movements. *Journal of Experimental Psychology: Human Perception and Performance* 9:816–25.

Patterson, K., and Kay, J. 1982. Letter-by-letter reading: Psychological descriptions of a neurological syndrome. *Quarterly Journal of Experimental Psychology* 34A:411–41.

Pavlidis, G. T. 1981. Do eye movements hold the key to dyslexia? *Neuropsychologia* 18:57–64.

Pelham, W. E., Atkins, M. S., Murphy, H. A., and Swanson, J. M. 1984. A rating scale for the diagnosis of the diagnosis of attention deficit disorders: Teacher norms, factor analyses, and reliability. Unpublished manuscript.

Rayner, K., Murphy, L. A., Henderson, J. M., and Pollatsek, A. 1989. Selective attentional dyslexia. *Cognitive Neuropsychology* 6:357–78.

Rizzolatti, G., and Arbib, M. A.: 1998. Language within our grasp. *Trends in Neurosciences* 21:188–94.

Saunders, R. C., Kolachana, B. S., Bachevalier, V. and Weinberger, D. R. 1998. Neonatal lesions of the medial temporal lobe disrupt prefrontal cortical regulation of striatal dopamine. *Nature* 393:169–71.

Semrud-Clikeman, M., Biederman, J., Sprich-Buckminster, S., Lehman, K., Faraone, S. V., and Norman, D. 1992. Comorbidity between ADDH and learning disability: A review and report in a clinically referred sample. *Journal of the American Academy of Child and Adolescent Psychiatry* 31:439–48.

Shallice, T., and Warrington, E. K. 1977. The possible role of selective attention in acquired dyslexia. *Neuropsychologia* 15:31–41.

Share, D. L., McGee, R., and Silva, P. A. 1986. Motor function in dyslexic children with and without attentional disorders. *Journal of Human Movement Studies* 12:313–20.

Share, D. L., and Schwartz, S. 1988. A note on the distinction between attention deficit disorder and reading disability: Are there group-specific cognitive deficits. *Brain and Language* 34:350–52.

Shaywitz, S. E., Shaywitz, B. A., Pugh, K. R., Fulbright, R. K., Constable, R. T., Menci, W. E., Shankweiler, D. P., Liberman, A. M., Skudlarski, P., Fletcher, J. M., Katz, L., Marchione, K. E., Lascadie, C., Gatenby, C., and Gore, J. C. 1998. Functional disruption in the organization of the brain for reading in dyslexia. *Proceedings of the National Academy of Science, USA* 95:2636–41.

Slaghuis, W. L., Lovegrove, W. J., and Davidson, J. A. 1993. Visual and language processing deficits are concurrent in dyslexia. *Cortex* 29:601–15.

Slaghuis, W. L., Twell, A. J., and Kingston, K. R. 1996. Visual and language processing disorders are concurrent in dyslexia and continue into adulthood. *Cortex* 32:413–38.

Stanley, G., Smith, G. A., and Howell, G. A. 1983. Short-term visual information processing dyslexics. *Child Development* 44:841–44.

Stein, J. F., and Fowler, M. S. 1981. Visual dyslexia. *Trends in Neurosciences* 4:77–80.

Tannock, R., and Schachar, R. 1996. Executive dysfunction as an underlying mechanism of behavior and language problems in attention deficit hyperactivity disorder. In *Language, Learning, and Behavior Disorders: Developmental, Biological, and Clinical Perspectives*, ed. J. H. Beitchman, N. J. Cohen, M. M. Konstantareas, and R. Tannock. Cambridge: Cambridge University Press.

Tirosh, E., and Cohen, A. 1998. Language deficit with attention-deficit disorder: A prevalent comorbidity. *Journal of Child Neurology* 13:493–97.

Victor, J. D. 1993. Defective visual pathway in reading-disabled children. *New England Journal of Medicine* 329:579.

Victor, J. D., Conte, M. M., Burton, L., and Nass, R. D. 1993. Visual evoked potentials in dyslexics and normals: Failure to find a difference in transient or steady-state responses. *Visual Neuroscience* 10:939–46.

Voeller K. K. S., and Heilman K. M.: 1988. Attention deficit disorder in children: A neglect syndrome? *Neurology* 38:806–8.

Voeller, K. K. S. 1996. Impulsivity in ADHD: Neurological features, test measures, response to medication, and diagnostic efficiency. Presented at the Society for Research in Child and Adolescent Psychopathology, Santa Monica CA January 1996.

Voeller K. K. S. 1998. Attention-Deficit/Hyperactivity Disorder I: Neurobiological and clinical aspects of attention and disorders of attention. In *Textbook of Pediatric Neuropsychiatry*, ed. E. Coffey and R. Brumbach. Washington, DC: American Psychiatric Association Press, Inc.

Voeller, K. K. S., Alexander, A., and Heilman, K. M. 1990. Defective response inhibition in attention deficit hyperactivity disorder [abstract]. *Neurology* 40(S1):410.

Wagner, R. K., and Torgesen, J. K. 1987. The nature of phonological processing and its causal role in the acquisition of reading skills. *Psychological Bulletin* 101:192–212.

Wagner, R. K., Torgesen, J. K., and Rashotte, C. A. 1994. Development of reading-related phonological processing abilities: New evidence of bidirectional causality from a latent variable longitudinal study. *Developmental Psychology* 30:73–87.

Wolff, P. H., Cohen, C., and Drake, C. 1984. Impaired motor timing control in specific reading retardation. *Neuropsychologia* 22:587–600.

Wolff, P. H., Melngailis, I., and Kotwica, K. 1996. Family patterns of developmental dyslexia, Part III: Spelling errors as behavioral phenotype. *American Journal of Medical Genetics* 67:378–86.

Wolff, P. H., Michel, G., and Ovrut, M. 1990. The timing of syllable repetitions in developmental dyslexia. *Journal of Speech and Hearing Research* 33:281.

Zangwill, O., and Blakemore, C. 1972. Dyslexia: Reversal of eye movements during reading. *Neuropsychologia* 10:371–73.

Chapter 11

The Abilities of Those with Reading Disabilities: Focusing on the Talents of People with Dyslexia

Thomas G. West

Perhaps my early problems with dyslexia made me more intuitive: when someone sends me a written proposal, rather than dwelling on detailed facts and figures, I find that my imagination grasps and expands on what I read.

Richard Branson, *Losing My Virginity.*

Don Winkler has a brain for the 21st century. A dyslexic brain. As other managers struggle to 'think outside the box,' Mr. Winkler has no other way of thinking. . . . In five years he has built the finance arm of Banc One Corp. from an industry also-ran to $26 billion in assets. How he did so says a lot about Mr. Winkler and the value of quirky thinking in a chaotic business world.

Thomas Petzinger, Jr., *Wall Street Journal.*

His thoughts often seem to progress in a nonlinear fashion, which McCaw says stems from [his] dyslexia. . . . He has difficulty absorbing lengthy written documents and usually avoids them. That leaves time for him to do what he prefers anyway, which is to think and to stand back and take in the big picture. . . .

Andrew Kupfer, *Fortune.*

I've always felt that I have more of an ability to envision, to be able to anticipate where things are going, to conceive a solution to a business problem than people who are more sequential thinkers.

Charles Schwab, explaining that his dyslexia seems to have compensations, quoted in *Business Week*.

THE SMARTEST LAD

In 1896, in the first description of developmental reading disability in the medical literature, it was noted that a certain student could not learn to read in spite of "laborious and persistent training." However, his headmaster observed that this student "would be the smartest lad in the school if the instruction were entirely oral" (Morgan 1896). The study of reading disability has frequently had to consider the often striking inconsistencies between high intelligence and ability and surprisingly poor reading and writing skills. However, most research focuses mainly on the problems to be corrected rather than the hidden potential to be identified and developed.

The quotations concerning the four highly successful individuals above would suggest that there is something about the dyslexic mind that sometimes confers significant and consequential benefits. This kind of mind can indeed have a great deal to contribute if educators and parents understand that the talents and special abilities exhibited by such individuals are often quite different from the most highly valued talents and abilities in a conventional or academic context. What is true for creativity in business, is often also true for the arts, technology, and the sciences as well.

Reading disabilities and dyslexia are not always seen as closely associated with talent and high accomplishment. One of our problems, then, should be to figure out why some succeed in such dramatic ways while others never seem to realize a small fraction of their potential. Perhaps those who have already succeeded at this complex task may be the best guides in helping researchers and people with dyslexia understand how to create success where there is often failure. It may be better, initially, to look at highly individualized personal reports and case histories to see if we can learn new ways of approaching old problems.

REAL PROBLEMS, REAL TALENTS

Some researchers argue that the gifts and talents seen among highly successful people with dyslexia are merely more noticeable because of the striking contrast between exceptional capabilities and highly specific disabilities. They argue that a properly constructed study would probably show that the proportion of gifted people with dyslexia is likely to be no greater than the non-dyslexic population.

Others, following the approach of the late Dr. Norman Geschwind, argue that the nature and variety of talents are directly related to different brain structures seen in people with dyslexia, and that the problems and unusual strengths come together in a package that is difficult to separate into parts. That is, the same microscopic, structural brain changes that produce reading difficulties and other problems, may often produce brain changes and differences that can be highly beneficial in certain areas of work and life. It might be said that it is not so much the frequency and extent of talent within this group that is of greatest interest, but the kinds and degrees of talent, and whether these are unusually beneficial in different fields. In other words, perhaps not all people with dyslexia can be shown to be highly gifted in some way, but those who are highly gifted may have gifts that are unusual and somehow distinctive, because theory would suggest that, in this population, neurological mechanisms may produce distinctive talents as well as distinctive difficulties. This perspective also suggests that there may be important talents in this population that are difficult to assess with conventional instruments. Some argue that individuals with dyslexia are often judged by the wrong criteria so that many talented individuals are being cast out of the system—depriving them of their useful roles, and depriving the larger society of their distinctive contributions (Geschwind 1982, 1884; Geschwind and Galaburda 1987; Frey 1990; West 1997).

Still others argue that the areas of proficiency often noted among people with dyslexia, such as visual and spatial talents (among others), happen to be just those talents that are now in great demand. It is no small matter, perhaps, that the *Wall Street Journal* article and others like it indicate that these talents seem to be more and more highly regarded in the business world where performance is so important, in contrast to other worlds where credentials often seem more important than performance. The particular talents that many people with dyslexia seem to have are seen as well timed for the newest computer graphic and information visualization technologies, even though many educators and professionals are unaware of this trend and of what it will eventually mean. Consequently, the problem for some people with dyslexia is not so much their inability to do what is expected in school, but their inability to persuade those in authority that their particular talents have growing value, while their particular difficulties are becoming rapidly less and less important (West 1992).

Many people see themselves as strong visual thinkers. Although not all of these are dyslexic, many have had educational difficulties and have family members who are either dyslexic or have a similar history of educational difficulties. Although many members of this group have succeeded in business, science, global politics, and other areas, they are very much aware that their way of thinking is quite different from that of most people around them. They find it difficult to explain their visually based ideas to non-visual people. They also find that they can rapidly identify and establish rapport with other strong visual thinkers, communicating with great ease and fluency. Individuals in this group feel that an understanding of such patterns will greatly benefit those with reading problems as well as many others (Dreyer 1997; Gleick 1992; J. K. 1997).

For some time, professionals have felt that looking at the gifts and talents thought to be associated with dyslexia would be a distraction from the serious business of correcting deficits in literacy skills. More recently, however, there has been a growing awareness among certain professionals and researchers that it is time for a serious scientific look at this other side of dyslexia.

This chapter is intended to provide a preliminary rationale for a program of systematic scientific study focusing on various strengths and talents that are believed to be closely associated with developmental reading disability. Profiles of a few highly successful people with dyslexia are provided to underscore the high level and variety of talent sometimes displayed. Reference is made to a recent revival of interest in visual and spatial talents, their links to dyslexia, and their links to extreme giftedness in science and mathematics. Finally, there is some discussion of recent research looking at giftedness among individuals with dyslexia. This discussion includes some consideration of methodological problems, since effective study of this population may require innovative use of advanced technologies as well as novel approaches to studying a highly heterogeneous population.

HIDDEN TALENTS

As we look for hidden talents instead of obvious weaknesses, it seems worthwhile to look first at highly successful people to try to see patterns—to try to understand what may be in store for the larger population. When we look at such examples, it appears that many strengths that are often not recognized in school or university, come to be recognized in work and in life. By seeing the longer-term implications we become aware that we need to find ways of seeing and developing the gifts and talents hidden under the difficulties.

When we look at highly successful individuals with dyslexia, we see that they succeed by following their substantial gifts, not by focusing on their difficulties. Accordingly, it is clear that we need to find ways of bringing traditional education more in line with the changing requirements of work and life. The more we are able to do this, the more likely we will help people with dyslexia and others like them. We may also find ways to help non-dyslexic individuals in the larger society as well.

Achieving the Impossible—Richard Branson

Richard Branson is not well known by the general public in the United States, but in the United Kingdom and much of Europe, he is probably one of the best known and most popular media figures. Some may have heard of him as the wealthy hot-air balloonist who tried several times, unsuccessfully, to circle the globe. In the business world he is best known as one who operates (for the most part very successfully) over 150 businesses as diverse as airlines, recording companies, railroads, soft drinks, and investment services. It is no surprise that he has developed a distinctive management style, emphasizing informality and unconventionality, high employee motivation, and decentralized enterprise control. Even his management philosophy is seen by many as backward. While other companies seek "shareholder value," Branson seeks happy and "cheery" employees, reasoning that if employees are happy and having fun, then the customers will be pleased as well and will come back. He is also a master at doing a variety of unconventional stunts to gain free media coverage for each of his new ventures (Jackson 1994; Strong 1998).

In a recent autobiography and in magazine interviews (Branson 1998; Strong 1998) and a series of television programs (Channel Four 1999), Branson has begun to talk publicly about his own dyslexia and the connections it may have to his remarkably successful and varied career. When asked to define himself, he makes reference to traits and attitudes often observed among people with dyslexia. He explains:

> 'I always loved the play Peter Pan, and I've never wanted to grow up. I'm a bit of a maverick. I love people, I love challenge, I love taking on the establishment. I love turning things upside down and having fun while doing it. I love motivating people, I love to achieve the impossible. I don't want to waste a moment of my life. I judge people within seconds of meeting them, within 30 seconds' (Strong 1998).

True to patterns familiar among persons with dyslexia,

> Branson never made it beyond [his boarding school]. He couldn't get past his entrance exams for university. He attributes this largely to his sense that education was less than essential, but his lousy math and Latin skills—and a mild form of dyslexia—played a part as well. 'I'm not dramatically

dyslexic, but I come out with some strange words sometimes,' he says. 'I have a little trouble telling left from right. . . . That's why I paint my parachute release bright red, because I accidentally pulled it once instead of the rip cord and the chute came off.'

Many people with dyslexia note that they need to learn from observation and by doing—not from books and lectures. Branson sounds a similar theme:

'I think the most interesting thing about Britain is that most of the entrepreneurs left school at around 15,' he says. 'Very few of them if any went on to university or college. I think the advantage of leaving school at 15 and starting up in business is that you don't have anything to lose. . . . You learn to become street savvy. And learning how to survive and learning from your mistakes is a lot better than trying to learn in some sterile setting' (Strong 1998).

Ridiculous Questions—Don Winkler

One of the advantages that many people with dyslexia seem to have in the world of business (and in science and technology) is the ability to find innovative solutions to difficult problems—the more unexpected and the more unconventional the better. Part of Don Winkler's dyslexia is his propensity to perceive things in reverse. Yet, this same propensity seems to have contributed directly and indirectly to his ability to see novel solutions. Banc One had hired Winkler to run a "sleepy" consumer lending affiliate called Finance One. According to a *Wall Street Journal* columnist,

. . . seeing things backward yielded deep insights. Like any lender, Banc One rejects a proportion of personal-loan applications as sub-standard. . . . Winkler recognized that these unqualified bank borrowers were perfect candidates for the debt-consolidation and home-equity loans that his unit provided. So he set about turning Banc One's rejects into Finance One's referrals (Petzinger 1998).

Winkler now "instructs colleagues in 'breakthrough thinking' with backwardness at its heart." He speaks with personal authority beyond that of the usual motivational speaker, when ". . . he tells people that failures are stepping stones to success, that breakdowns can lead to breakthroughs. . . . " According to Winkler, the most essential element is ". . . asking the most ridiculous questions possible, a practice he encourages by passing out clown noses. As he puts it, 'The dumber the question—the more people laugh at you—the more likely it will lead to breakthroughs.' " (It is noteworthy that medical essayist Lewis Thomas once observed that you could be sure that wonderful results were on the way when people in the laboratory started to laugh at the ridiculous, unexpected, and impossible findings [West 1997].)

It may tell us a lot about the current state of business thinking and reporting that a *Wall Street Journal* columnist asserts that Winkler has ". . . a brain for the 21st century. A dyslexic brain." It is commonplace for business managers to be told to "think outside the box"—to think in truly novel ways. So it is seen as a considerable advantage to have "no other way of thinking"—thus honoring "the value of quirky thinking in a chaotic business world." It is interesting to note that the *Wall Street Journal* columnist ended his piece with this request to his readers: "*What can dyslexics teach managers? Please send your ideas to tom@pet-zinger.com.*" We may well wonder whether such business writers are just pursuing an odd and entertaining story, or, instead, are setting forth observations that some day can be tested in order to learn valuable and broadly applicable lessons about learning and creativity.

Dyslexic Visionary—Craig McCaw

Another notable example of business reporting that puts a positive light on dyslexia is the May 1996 cover article for *Fortune* magazine in which cellular telephone entrepreneur Craig McCaw is described as a "dyslexic visionary." For some, this cover article may be seen as a major event in the evolution of attitudes about dyslexia in the business world. It is significant that such a phrase should be used by a major business publication, especially one focusing on the interests of senior corporation executives who, presumably, have little interest in apparent weaknesses that have no clear advantages in the competitive world of business (Kupfer 1996).

It is also significant that the cover text links McCaw's dyslexia quite specifically to his business interests: "Craig McCaw's Cosmic Ambition—The Dyslexic Visionary who Fathered Cellular Looks to Launch an Even Bigger Industry." Although the article deals mostly with McCaw's innovative ideas about a global communications network, it also discusses McCaw's remarkable ability to anticipate trends. The writer points out that Bill Gates was persuaded to invest over $10 million of his own money in McCaw's new venture because Gates said that "Craig . . . thinks ahead of the pack and understands the communications business and where it's going better than anyone I know."

The article portrays McCaw's dyslexia as a clear advantage in his entrepreneurial business environment:

> His thoughts often seem to progress in a nonlinear fashion, which McCaw says stems from [his own] dyslexia. . . . He has difficulty absorbing lengthy written documents and usually avoids them. That leaves time for him to do what he prefers anyway, which is to think and to stand back and take in the big picture. . . . McCaw [says] that he is good at seeing

circumstances from the other person's point of view, or at least in a different way from most. That helps him do what great entrepreneurs do, which is not to invent, but to see the hidden value of an idea already in plain sight, a value that seems obvious as soon as it is given voice. McCaw didn't discover wireless communications—he was merely the first to truly understand what it was worth.

Envisioning Solutions—Charles Schwab

Charles Schwab is another example of a highly talented person with dyslexia in the business world. He is the founder of the highly successful stock brokerage company of the same name. Schwab often refers to his own dyslexia in press interviews, which is a great benefit in helping to change public attitudes about the links between talent and various learning problems, especially in the business community. In addition, he and his wife Helen have established a foundation that has worked for years to help parents understand the problems once experienced by Schwab and others (Robbins 1992).

Schwab had real difficulties in school and at the university with reading and spelling, but he attributes his business success, in part, to the special perspectives that seem associated with his dyslexia. He explains, "I've always felt that I have more of an ability to envision, to be able to anticipate where things are going, to conceive a solution to a business problem, than people who are more sequential thinkers." Like Craig McCaw and Richard Branson, Schwab is described by his associates as a big-picture thinker who can anticipate what will be wanted but leaves the detailed implementation to others—a combination that seems to work well in keeping his company at the forefront (Mitchell 1995).

Indeed, well into mid-1999, Schwab showed the ability to anticipate trends and take advantage of new technologies ahead of others. Schwab to increased his customer base and company value by being the first large brokerage house to serve fully the Internet stock trader. Many companies seem to operate on only one or two good ideas and then, in time, are gradually overtaken by others with newer and fresher ideas. The Schwab organization is remarkable for maintaining something like a perpetually youthful point of view, seeing each new trend and technological change, not as a threat to an established position, but as an opportunity to be innovative and to take major risks once again. This extended youthful view is not at all uncommon among highly successful people with dyslexia, in many different fields. The Irish poet, William Butler Yeats, for example, found that he had more and more wonderful ideas as he became older—using a delightfully apt (if dated) metaphor, "one poem leading to another as if he were smoking, lighting one cigarette from another" (quoted in West 1997).

Accordingly, the Schwab company, which has already created a new kind of brokerage firm seems to be well on its way to establishing a new kind of Internet company. A recent analysis of the Schwab company's role in becoming a major player among emerging Internet companies is especially instructive about how well they have adapted to fast-changing conditions. A reporter for the *Red Herring*, a small-circulation magazine written for the venture capital industry, explains why it included Charles Schwab in its June 1999 listing of the 100 top "electronic economy" companies:

> Last year Charles Schwab was not even a remote consideration for the *Red Herring* 100. Analysts and *Herring* Editors were busy focusing their attention on pure play Internet investment companies . . . and didn't consider Schwab to be part of the digital universe. We have reconsidered. Although Schwab may not be a traditional Internet company, its Net strategy is playing a big part in the company's success. It's not only the largest discount brokerage in the country; it's the largest online brokerage: in January 1999 the company reported that it was averaging 153,000 online trades worth $2.6 billion per day. Schwab understands the Internets two main attractions for consumers: easy access to information and a wide range of products. . . . In March Schwab announced that its net income for the first quarter of the year would be . . . close to double that of the first quarter of 1998. Although the company may take great pride in its redefinition of the brokerage business, we give it credit simply for delivering what the investor wants (Semansky 1999).

The MIT Disease—Nicholas Negroponte

The varied talent seen in many people with dyslexia seems to be especially well recognized in the world of computers, as well as entrepreneurial business. Both are areas in which performance is measured by demonstrating working systems (rather than writing reports) and where anticipating technological trends is more highly valued than traditional academic skills and paper credentials. One of the leading visionary thinkers in the computer field is Nicholas Negroponte, the dyslexic founder of the Media Lab at the Massachusetts Institute of Technology (MIT). More than a decade ago, he and others started work to form the Media Lab, which was to be based on the idea that major industries—such as publishing, telecommunications, television, feature film, and computers—would all converge over time, until at a certain point, it would be hard to tell which was which. Of course, now these predictions are seen as splendidly and universally justified, as we are daily confronted by the reality of these expectations.

In 1995, Negroponte published *Being Digital*, a book of essays, based on a series of columns in the magazine *Wired*, about the varied longer-term effects of the computer revolution. Because the book is so explicitly focused on computers, it is quite remarkable that the first and last sentences of his *Introduction: The Paradox of a Book* refer not to computers at all—but instead to his own dyslexia and his difficulties with reading. The book begins: "Being dyslexic, I don't like to read books." And pages later: "So why [have I written] an old-fashioned book . . . especially one without a single illustration?" He gives several reasons. Among these are the advantages inherent in the vagueness of words. When you read, he notes, more is left to the imagination and more is drawn from your own personal experience. In contrast, he observes that "like a Hollywood film, multimedia narrative" provides such detailed and realistic representations of things that "less and less is left to the mind's eye." Consequently, finishing his introduction, he says: "You are expected to read yourself into this book. And I say that as someone who does not like to read" (Negroponte 1995).

Thus, Negroponte provides a remarkable example of one of the leading and most prescient communicators of the digital revolution, referring in his book, repeatedly, to his own reading problems. It is also notable that during his book tour for *Being Digital*, Negroponte commented that links between dyslexia and high talent are often observed at MIT—indeed, these observations are so frequent that, on campus, dyslexia is called "the MIT disease."

Some months after his book came out, Negroponte was featured on the cover of *Wired* magazine to celebrate the first ten years of the Media Lab. Playing on the title of Negroponte's book, the *Wired* article begins: "Being Nicholas—The Media Lab's visionary founder . . . is the most wired man we know (and that is saying something)." During the interview, Negroponte was asked whether he would rather read text on a computer screen or on paper. His answer reveals the matter-of-fact, by-the-way manner many successful people with dyslexia have come to use when speaking of their difficulties:

> I don't read long articles period. I don't like to read. I am dyslexic and I find it hard. When people send me long [electronic-mail] messages, I ignore them. The only print medium I read every day is the front page of the *Wall Street Journal*, which I scan for news of the companies I am interested in. All the rest of my reading is on screens, and often not very good screens, because I travel so much (Bass 1995).

Ancient Stigma Removed—Lee Kuan Yew

Cross-cultural comparisons can be valuable tests of the broad applicability of certain observations. Accordingly, some researchers have felt the need to identify examples of highly respected individuals from non-Western cultures who would fit the larger patterns of high ability with some form of dyslexia or related learning problems. It is difficult enough to discuss things that are perceived as defects in Western cultures, especially among men who learn early the cost of showing any sign of weakness. As difficult as these discussions are in Western groups, they are often much more difficult in Asian and Middle Eastern groups. Foreign students who are tested for dyslexia and learning disabilities in American universities, for example, seem to have an unusually difficult time getting past their own personal denial. Apparently, they perceive a social stigma that seems to be much greater than that experienced by many Westerners.

Accordingly, it is of some importance that a series of newspaper articles in Hong Kong and Singapore announced early in 1996, that Lee Kuan Yew—perhaps the most respected senior statesman throughout all of Asia—revealed that he had "mild dyslexia." According to an account in a Hong Kong newspaper,

> Singapore's elder statesman, Lee Kuan Yew, known as an intellectual heavyweight in world political circles, has revealed he suffers from mild dyslexia. . . . The 72-year-old former premier and Cambridge-educated lawyer said he was tested by a British expert . . . 10 years ago at the suggestion of his neurologist daughter Lee Wei Ling, who has the same problem. . . . ' I am pretty proud of him, all considered,' [Dr. Lee] said of her iron-willed father who, as premier for more than three decades, transformed Singapore from a British colonial port into an Asian economic power.

The reason for the testing was, as the elder Lee explained, "I had complained that I could not read fast without missing important items." Lee's daughter had learned of her own dyslexia as part of her medical training in Boston and realized that her father seemed to have similar problems (Agence France Press 1996, Yeo 1996).

These revelations were made as part of an announcement that royalties for a new CD-ROM of Lee Kuan Yew's life would be donated to the Dyslexia Association of Singapore. The association chairman noted that "now that S[enior] M[inister] Lee has admitted to having dyslexia, the stigma is removed and parents will no longer think that it is something to be ashamed about." Lee's daughter serves as a consultant to the Singapore dyslexia organization (Hussin 1996). Lee Kuan Yew's personal revelation makes us wonder at possible connections between his dyslexia and his visionary and long-standing political leadership.

Seeing What Others Don't See—Jack Horner

An example of a highly talented and innovative person with dyslexia working in science is John R. (Jack) Horner. Well known to young enthusiasts of dinosaur films and to professional paleontologists, Jack

Horner was written up in the "Scholarship" section of the *Chronicle of Higher Education*, trade tabloid newspaper for university professors. The article seems an odd choice for the *Chronicle*, since Jack Horner is about as far from the traditional scholar as anyone can imagine. It is true that he has an honorary doctorate and now supervises 12 doctoral candidates, but Horner never completed an undergraduate degree nor any graduate work, having flunked out of the University of Montana six times. Yet, in spite of this, as the *Chronicle* article explains, after he had established himself, "his brilliant synthesis of evidence . . . forced paleontologists to revise their ideas about dinosaur behavior, physiology, and evolution" (McDonald 1994).

Horner never earned an undergraduate degree because he failed "just about all his science courses, and never [completed] his undergraduate work." Although he had great difficulty with his college work, it is clear that, at a deeper level, he was continuously absorbing the knowledge needed to revolutionize a field. As Horner tells the story, his difficult beginnings helped him to take risks.

> 'Back in the days when I was growing up, nobody knew what dyslexia was. . . . So everybody thought you were lazy or stupid or both. And I didn't think I was, but I wasn't sure. I had a lot of drive, and if somebody told me I was stupid, that usually helped—it really helped me take a lot more risks. For someone that everybody thinks is going to grow up to pump gas, you can take all the risks you want. Because if you fail, it doesn't matter.'

But the risks paid off. According to the curator of the museum of vertebrate paleontology at the University of California at Berkeley: "A lot of people have tended to underestimate Jack because he hasn't come through the traditional academic route. But he is, without question, one of the two or three most important people in the world today studying dinosaurs." Horner is able to see things differently and he observes things others do not see. For example, he believes that it is really of little interest to find the fossil bones of a very large adult dinosaur. What he is interested in finding are fossils of many dinosaurs of many sizes, in their environment, in order to understand the life of the animals and the way they interacted with other animals in that environment. Horner is known not only for his markedly different way of looking at things, but also his unusual ability to see, in the field, the tiny fossil bones of baby dinosaurs that other experts cannot find. According to another researcher: "He has a gift. . . . He can see things the rest of us don't see."

Horner's life is especially worth noting because, in spite of his persistent academic failures, eventually he came to be acknowledged as one who transformed some of the fundamental thinking in his field. His story forces us to reconsider what is really important in one's work and what is not. Horner proved to have extraordinary difficulties with things that are largely peripheral to his discipline—reading, composition, test taking. However, he also proved to be unusually gifted in those things that lie at the heart of his discipline—being unusually observant while searching for fossil bones in the field, being able to interpret the surprising patterns that emerge from the evidence, thinking his way beyond and around his associates, and developing innovative and persuasive arguments based on looking at the raw data in a very different way.

Titanic Talent —Valerie Delahaye

In recent years, a French television program was shown in Canada about the "brain drain" from France. At about the same time, there were newspaper articles about scientists and engineers leaving France because of apparently limited opportunities, coupled with their belief that they would always be known for the schools they attended rather than for how well they performed their work. One story was of special interest because the TV program told of a young computer graphics artist, Valerie Delahaye, who could not find work or be properly educated in France because of her dyslexia. However, she found that she was warmly received by computer graphics companies in the United States. They were interested in her artistic and computer skills and thought the dyslexia was not a problem, especially since they already knew that many artists are dyslexic to some extent. She has since worked on and had major responsibilities, in many projects, including the feature films *The Fifth Element* and *Titanic*. With an enormous career boost from having had a major role in a film that won many Academy Awards, she has more recently moved on to help start a new computer graphics company in Montreal, Canada (Delahaye 1997, 1998; West 1998).

Delahaye's personal estimate is that about half of all computer graphics artists are probably dyslexic. Some may think her estimate is exaggerated until it is compared with a study of first year students in a London art school which reported a rate of fully 75% (*Independent*). In France, Valerie's difficulties with writing and working under pressure had kept her from passing exams—even those required to enter art school. In the United States, however, she was able to benefit from testing accommodations so that she could finally receive a professional education in her area of strength. She was not forced to be judged in areas that were largely irrelevant to her work and talent. However, she has expressed concern that the educational system in France still has done very little to address these problems and misconceptions (West 1998).

Delahaye's work experience is especially revealing in trying to understand the complex relationship between dyslexia and talent.

Valerie was the 3D manager at James Cameron's computer effects company Digital Domain. On the 3D team, she was aware that many of the artists were dyslexic. She observed that these artists seemed to be unusually talented in their ability to come up with some of the most brilliant and advanced ways of visualizing whole scenes. They were able to accomplish the daunting task of creating the ship, the water, the sky, and the human figures using only computer graphics. She observed that many dyslexics seem to be unusually able in visualizing very complex scenes and ideas. Of course, this ability was extraordinarily useful in making *Titanic* because they had to recreate scenes that had never been photographed, the only record being the oral reports given by survivors.

In hiring her staff, Delahaye found she had to pull videotapes out of the trash in the personnel office. The personnel staff would reject applicants based on their paper credentials and would not always bother to look at the videos. In contrast, Delahaye would not look at the résumés. She looked only at the video samples of their work. For example, she saw one tape in which the animation was poor but the lighting was great. So, she hired the one who had done the lighting. She also noted that the team members were easy to work with because they were so highly motivated. After so much failure in school, when given a chance, they wanted to show what they could really do. Also, they never had to read anything. When you are pushing the technology and the software to the limits, you cannot consult a manual or a handbook. You have to ask your co-workers. It is an entirely oral culture—perfect for people with dyslexia. Those who are responsible for education and hiring need to understand that many of the old rules do not apply when you are on the edge of the really new.

TRANSFORMING OCCUPATIONS

Delahaye's story highlights for us the great changes that some occupations are going though at this time, and the increasingly evident inconsistencies between the skills valued in the old verbal technological context and the skills more highly valued in the emerging technologies of images and visualization. The old world of the book and writing required one set of talents and skills, while the expanding world of moving images and visualized information seems to require quite a different set. It would be wrong, however, to see these changes as relevant only to the graphic arts. Rather, there are good reasons to believe that the new technologies and techniques will, in time, spread to virtually all areas—from science and technology to business and politics. These technologies will provide a powerful set of new tools to analyze and manipulate all forms of information about ever more varied subject matter. And as these techniques spread and alter the ways that we work and learn, it is expected that it is only a matter of time before visual talents are perceived as more highly valued.

Some might argue that the move to images is quite superficial, as it would appear to shift attention and effort from basic verbal literacy. However, a more persuasive argument can be made that, especially for the young, visual literacy will be as important, or possibly more important, than verbal literacy. Of course, you want proficiency in both areas as much as possible, but we should not allow visual talent to be dropped by the wayside just because of verbal difficulties. In addition, a case can be made that the Delahaye experience may be very close, indeed, to the experience of scientists and engineers generally. More and more, groups are coming to a rediscovered awareness of the importance of visual and spatial abilities—not only in art and design, but also in engineering, medicine, other sciences, mathematics, and related disciplines. Despite strong conventions of thought and common belief, we are seeing a gradual reawakening of interest in spatial abilities that were formerly thought to be relatively unimportant.

All forms of work are changing more rapidly and more extensively than most individuals and institutions are aware. Of course, we are aware that many of the more routine functions of the copy editor, bank clerk, and bookkeeper are already being done more rapidly and more cheaply by machines. However, many are not aware that in similar fashion, it may not be very much longer before "expert" computer systems and artificial life "agents" learn to replicate reliably the more routine professional judgments of attorneys, engineers, physicians, and investment bankers. Referring to the work of Stanford University economist Paul Krugman, *The Economist* magazine observed: "Lawyers and Accountants . . . could be today's counterparts of early-19th-century weavers, whose incomes soared after the mechanisation of spinning only to crash when the technological revolution [finally] reached their own craft" (*Economist* 1995). Accordingly, not only are the new technologies changing the ways of doing high-level work, they are also eating away large chucks of what used to be considered high-level work. Both trends are likely to benefit the talents that many dyslexics have, as they make their varied difficulties become increasingly unimportant.

More of those people working at the edge of these new technologies, in the sciences as well as business or the professions, are coming to recognize the implications of these unexpected trends. For example, Dr. Larry Smarr, a physicist, astronomer, and director of a supercomputer center, commented:

> I have often argued in my public talks that the graduate education process that produces physicists is totally skewed to selecting those with analytic skills and rejecting those with visual or holistic skills. I have

claimed that with the rise of scientific visualization as a new mode of scientific discovery, a new class of minds will arise as scientists. In my own life, my 'guru' in computational science was a dyslexic and he certainly saw the world in a different and much more effective manner than his colleagues. . . . (Smarr 1994).

Some 50 years ago, Norbert Weiner, one of the originators of the computer revolution, warned that it was only a matter of time before the computer eliminated the value of lower brain functions, just as the steam engine eliminated the value of unskilled labor (Weiner 1948, 1961). Accordingly, we may well look to the supercomputer centers for evidence of trends that will shortly effect our whole economy and educational system—very possibly for the benefit of many people with dyslexia.

Rediscovering Spatial Abilities at Johns Hopkins

With these changes, it is all the more important to understand that the assessment of abilities other than verbal and mathematical abilities has been widely neglected in education. They simply were thought to be unimportant. Fortunately, this has begun to change as some research groups are gradually rediscovering the value of assessing visual and spatial capabilities. Researchers at Johns Hopkins University, for example, provide us with a look at what a few researchers are now doing—and how views are changing in a few institutions in ways that would seem sympathetic to strong visual thinkers and to people with dyslexia. These researchers are trying to improve methods of identifying scientific talent at various educational levels and to better predict performance in science education before college. They have seen that the conventional verbal and mathematical reasoning measures are not enough and they have determined that what is needed is a good way to assess spatial reasoning as well (IAAY 1997; Mills 1998; Stumpf and Klien 1989).

In their words:

> . . . Spatial ability has been given only token attention as an important dimension of cognitive functioning. Research on the structure, identification, and development of spatial ability has been conducted by a few researchers . . . around the world and often ignored by the psychological and educational community. In addition, spatial ability has played only a modest role in educational assessment and instruction.

The Hopkins researchers are aware that they are, to some extent, breaking new ground. Of course, assessments of spatial abilities have been around for a long time. But they have nearly always been treated as tangential to the more conventional measures of academic abilities. The Hopkins researchers note that although there are other research programs similar to theirs, they are the only ones so far using measures of spatial ability in a serious way. The use of computers in the Hopkins testing program is of special interest. One obvious benefit of computer use in spatial testing is that it allows the actual rotation of objects on the screen—objects such as blocks, twisted cables, or molecule structures.

The Other Side of Extreme Giftedness

It is noteworthy that the Hopkins researchers have also found that to deal effectively with the most highly talented students, one must be ready to deal with dyslexia and other learning disabilities as well. The idea that it is not unusual for smart people to have dyslexia or some form of learning disability is especially hard for many conventional educators to understand. It is to the credit of the Hopkins researchers that early on they began to understand that they were seeing patterns of mixed abilities in their students—patterns that many thought could not and should not exist. This is the reason that an explicit item on their six-point research agenda is: "Explore the benefits of using spatial tests to identify academic ability in students with learning disabilities. . . ." (IAAY 1997). The Hopkins researchers explain that they are investigating "the relationship between the development of spatial reasoning and specific learning disabilities. Although there is much speculation about such a relationship," they point out that, "little empirical research has been conducted to establish its existence. This line of research would help us to better understand individuals with learning disabilities and assist educators as they plan appropriate educational interventions. . . ." Accordingly, they feel that "one possibility is the development of teaching approaches that utilize a spatial orientation for . . . students who possess strong spatial skills and who have difficulty learning in other modalities."

It is worth noting that the Hopkins researchers come out of a tradition started in the 1970s when they were dealing with only the most highly gifted students, in the beginning focusing mainly on mathematical talent. Indeed, for some time they have dealt with, as they say, the "one-out-of-10,000" gifted not the usual "one-out-of-20" gifted. In order to find these students, they traditionally have given a college entrance examination (the SAT) to students five or six years early—testing students on a good deal of material they have never been taught. Then, they would take into their program only those students who received the highest scores out of very large numbers of students nation-wide (Benbow 1993; Mills 1998). Consequently, the Hopkins researchers had, as their early focus, the most extremely gifted children.

It is therefore all the more noteworthy that their research focus has moved toward spatial abilities, toward learning difficulties, and toward the integral use of computer graphics in their assessment tools. This progression is seen as singularly important in gaining a sophisticated understanding of the patterns that contain so many unexpected connections and links between things that were formerly thought to be worlds apart. Perhaps the researchers at Hopkins have been moving through a gradual learning process that might be reflected, over time, in our culture and institutions at large. But we may wonder how long it will take before most organizations and conventional educational institutions begin to think along similar lines.

The Hopkins researchers see their newly developed spatial tests as timely. They note that "spatial tests have been around for years, but have not been as widely administered as are tests of verbal or mathematical reasoning." However, "today," they observe, "some educators are intrigued by their potential. What" they ask "if spatial tests were added to the regular program of standardized assessment? Could they flag abilities that currently go undetected?" Could they "identify promise in students who now pass more or less unnoticed? That, at least, is the hope," in their view (IAAY 1997).

SEARCHING FOR TALENTS

Although dyslexia research has long been focused on difficulties rather than talents, this direction has begun to shift. A number of studies are beginning to appear that address this new concern with talent, yielding mixed results so far. A careful review and analysis of these studies needs to be carried out. However, although this chapter is not the appropriate place for such a review, several preliminary observations and comments may be helpful in pointing out some of the possibilities and problems that need to be considered in future research.

One recent study, conducted by John Everatt and his associates at Surrey University in the United Kingdom has been "looking at various possible positive aspects, but the one that was most promising . . . was a relationship between dyslexia and creativity." The study has employed "several different measures of creativity (alternative uses, figural creativity, insight problems, and a questionnaire about thinking innovatively)." Generally, the study has found "consistent evidence of the dyslexic adults . . . scoring higher than matched controls, although the same was not the case for dyslexic children on the figural task." Everatt wants to assess his findings further, wondering "why the effect occurs in adults but not children." It is noteworthy that

Everatt's "own data on visual abilities has been less positive." However, he notes that work by others at Hull University in Britain and Gdansk in Poland "has provided some evidence for a relationship between visual abilities and dyslexia" (Everatt 1998). Consistent with expectations, the study Everatt refers to does, in fact, suggest that people with dyslexia generally prefer visual-spatial methods of work and that they tend to prefer simultaneous ("random") over "sequential" styles of learning (Wszeborowska-Lipinska and Singleton 1998).

Another recent study carried out by Winner, French, Seliger and others, investigated the association between dyslexia and spatial talents, mainly among students at Boston College (Winner et al. 1999). In two studies, they "tested the hypothesis that dyslexia is associated with superior spatial skills and found that individuals with dyslexia performed either equivalently to or worse than the control participants on a range of spatial tasks." The researchers found their results puzzling because it is widely believed (as we have noted) that there is often a connection between verbal difficulties and visual-spatial talents. They observe that "the failure to find spatial talents in dyslexia is surprising given the high frequency of individuals with dyslexia in spatial professions." Accordingly, in order "to reconcile these two findings," the researchers "consider two hypothesis" which they call "the default hypothesis" and "the channeling hypothesis." However, they explain that "both hypotheses predict higher spatial interests in individuals with dyslexia." The researchers consider that (in spite of their relative lack of spatial ability in relation to people who are not dyslexic) people with dyslexia may still select visual-spatial related occupations to avoid reading occupations. Their visual talents may be inferior to those who are not dyslexic, but they are still relatively better than their own reading abilities.

However, this study shows that in one area—impossible figures—the people with dyslexia did appear to do better than those without. Some have suggested that this is, in fact, a most important finding because the people with dyslexia seemed to be able to see the impossibility of the figure because they can perceive the whole picture (and the visual trick) more readily than the those who were not dyslexic. Others have suggested that the traditional tests of spatial abilities may be, in fact, ill suited to assessing the abilities of those well-trained in three dimensional skills (Parkinson 1999).

Reconsidering Associations

It is commonly observed in the history of science that it is often a great advantage to have early studies give unexpected and puzzling results. The results tend to show that the actual situation is different, or at least more complex, than we had originally expected. This is a time to step back and reconsider what we thought we knew. Perhaps these results provide an occasion for developing different tools of measurement or a very different research design. The possibilities need to be carefully considered in future investigations. However, it may be useful to briefly list here some of the possibilities.

First, we need to consider the possibility that we were entirely wrong in our initial expectations and there really exists no relationship between the sets of attributes that we have been considering. That is, we might suppose that people with dyslexia have just about the same level of visual-spatial abilities as those with no dyslexia (or even that they might have lower levels, as indicated above). Or, as already noted, we might suspect that conventional tools for assessing visual and spatial ability and talent may need to be redesigned, perhaps using new technologies, as suggested by the Johns Hopkins researchers. Sample size may also be a complicating factor. When dealing with a population that is expected to be unusually heterogeneous in distribution and attribute, it may be necessary to have a larger sample, or use a different sample selection method. We might look at the problem from the other direction. Perhaps researchers could start with individuals already known to be highly talented in several visual-spatial fields. Then they might look for numbers of individuals with dyslexia within this group (as the art school study noted above).

Inadvertent referral bias and self-selection need to be considered. Thus, we might speculate that people with dyslexia who have especially high visual talents may be unlikely to show up in a population selected at a college. Instead, perhaps they are more likely to be found elsewhere—for example, as art students at the Rhode Island School of Design; or as trainees at Christie's art auction house in New York or London; or at the Julliard School of Music; or at Caltech or MIT and its Media Lab; or working as poorly educated but brilliant and highly paid programmers creating video games at Namco, animated cartoons at Pixar, or scientific visualizations at the National Center for Supercomputing Applications; or as rock musicians; or as young drop-outs with endless body piercing and orange hair; or as young entrepreneurs with their own new internet startup companies; or as Cisco engineers installing and maintaining Internet routers and systems in companies, cities, and whole nations (creating a vibrant, youthful subculture similar to the one the young Thomas Edison entered in the early days of the telegraph).

Given the growing awareness of technological change, it is perhaps not surprising that there is at this time a renewed debate concerning kinds of visual-spatial abilities and the best way to assess them. It is also not entirely surprising that some of the new ideas seem to be coming from outside academic disciplines traditionally most interested. Now the interest also comes from computer graphics programmers and designers, or from traditionally trained artists who have become more and more familiar with the complex links between art and dyslexia. Alternatively, new interest comes from researchers who have backed into innovative forms of assessment—by dealing with extremely gifted students and discovering the need to use new technologies to measure the visual-spatial talents so closely linked to creative science.

VISUAL THINKERS, VISUAL TOOLS

Although new technologies may now make visual talents more broadly appreciated, these talents have always been supremely important for at least a small group of highly creative people, whether or not they happened to be dyslexic. In this context, it is useful to have a look at one strong visual thinker to see how very different these modes of thought are when compared with individuals who mainly use conventional non-visual approaches. It is considered most valuable to look at a profile of one remarkable person in order to gain a deeper understanding of what we should be looking for in a research context.

James Gleick's book about the late Nobel laureate physicist, Richard Feynman, *Genius*, provides classic illustrations of the tension between two very different ways of approaching a problem. Over and over again, Glieck's portrait of Feynman provides us with wonderful examples of the working and thinking style of the strong visual thinker. We are shown how different his way of working is from that of his colleagues and competitors who follow the more conventional verbal, logical, and mathematical approaches—approaches that have largely dominated physics and other fields. Where others used mainly mathematics, Feynman (like Albert Einstein, James Clerk Maxwell, and Michael Faraday) relied mainly on diagrams, pictures, and mental models. Indeed, Feynman once told an associate that "Einstein's great work had sprung from physical intuition and that when Einstein stopped creating it was because 'he stopped thinking in concrete physical images and became a manipulator of equations' " (quoted in Gleick 1992).

Feynman's style of thinking was, in most respects, different from another important physicist, Murray Gell-Mann. As Gleick observes,

> In so many ways these two scientific icons had come to seem like polar opposites. . . . Gell-Mann loved to know things' names and to pronounce them correctly. . . . Feynman . . . despised nomenclature of all kinds. Gell-Mann was an enthusiastic bird watcher; . . . Feynman's [belief] was that the name of a bird did not matter. . . .

Repeatedly, we see Feynman making the point that simply nam-ing a thing does not demonstrate that you really understand it in any meaningful way—a fundamental idea that is in opposition to basic ed-ucation and testing at all levels, especially in the sciences. He was furi-ous that his own young children were being taught not real science, as he saw it, but "mere definitions" (Gleick 1992).

Gleick cites comparisons of the visual Feynman and the verbal Gell-Mann at some length.

> Physicists kept finding new ways to describe the contrast between them. Murray makes sure you know what an extraordinary person he is, they would say, while Dick is not a person at all but a more advanced life form pretending to be human to spare your feelings.

Their use of the body is important.

> Feynman talked with his hands—with his whole body, in fact—whereas Gell-Mann, as [one] physicist and science writer . . . observed, 'sits calmly behind his desk . . . hands folded, never lifting them to make a gesture. . . . Information is exchanged by words and numbers, not by hands or pictures.'
>
> 'Their personal styles spill over into their theoretical work, too. Gell-Mann insists on mathematical rigor in all his work, often at the expense of comprehensibility. . . . Where Gell-Mann disdains vague, heuristic models that might only point the way toward a true solution, Feynman revels in them. He believes that a certain amount of imprecision and am-biguity is *essential* to communication.'

It is important for us to note that for Feynman, and others like him, what was needed was not only or entirely visual. It was some-thing just beyond the visual—as it extends naturally into the physical. These kinds of thinkers needed "a kind of seeing and feeling" grounded in "physical intuition." (It is noteworthy that Albert Einstein made similar observations; he pointed out that in his own thought processes, part of his "vague play" with "signs and more or less clear images" were "elements" which were "of visual and some of muscular type" (West 1997). As Gleick observed,

> . . . intuition was not just visual but auditory and kinesthetic. Those who watched Feynman in moments of intense concentration came away with a strong, even disturbing sense of the physicality of the process, as though his brain did not stop with the grey matter but extended through every muscle in his body. A Cornell dormitory neighbor opened Feynman's door to find him rolling about on the floor beside his bed as he worked on a problem. When he was not rolling about, he was mur-muring rhythmically or drumming with his fingers. In part the process of scientific visualization is a process of putting oneself in nature: in an imagined beam of light, in a relativistic electron. . . .

Feynman tried to explain how his approach was not entirely or exclusively visual. " 'What I am really trying to do is bring birth to clarity, which is really a half-assedly thought-out pictorial semi-vision thing. I would see the jiggle-jiggle-jiggle or the wiggle of the path. . . .'" Gleick notes that "in seeking to analyze his own way of visualizing the unvisualizable [Feynman] had learned an odd lesson. The mathematical symbols he used every day had become entangled with his physical sensations of motion, pressure, acceleration. . . ." And Feynman observed,

> 'When I start describing the magnetic field moving through space, I speak of . . . fields and wave my arms and you may imagine that I can see them. I'll tell you what I see. I see some kind of vague, shadowy, wiggling lines . . . and perhaps some of the lines have arrows on them—an arrow here or there which disappears when I look too closely. . . . I have a terrible confusion between the symbols I use to describe the objects and the objects themselves' (quoted in Gleick 1992).

Cheap Illusions-A Successor to Plato's Cave

Anyone who has experienced high-quality immersive-virtual-reality environments can see immediately the close relevance of Feynman's descriptions to the kinds of tools we now have at our fingertips. The information visualization tools, which became available only a short time ago to a small group of senior scientists and supercomputer users, are now available to almost anyone who owns a personal computer. Soon, the question will be not the power of the tool, but the capability of the user to employ effectively these powerful tools and techniques, to discover new patterns and see new trends—or, at least, to maintain their relative position in a competitive world.

With Feynman's reference to "wiggling lines" and disappearing arrows, we can compare our own immersion in the data. An example of such immersion is a display of wind currents over Florida at a demonstration of the "CAVE" virtual reality system (Raloff 1999). The computer images are projected onto the walls of a small, dark room and special light-weight glasses provide a strong 3D illusion. Users seem quite realistically and effortlessly to be walking inside and through the data. (The quality of the images, covering whole walls, is much finer than ever could be produced by heavy helmet-mounted eye pieces or even TV-sized monitors.) As viewers move, yellow lines with arrows at about waist height show wind direction and speed. When viewers crouch down, they see all the streaming lines coursing over their head like a layer of thin yellow clouds. (In passing, it may be no small surprise that one of the two inventors of this highly successful virtual reality device—the CAVE—is a dyslexic physicist, based at the Electronic Visualization Laboratory, University of Illinois, Chicago.)

Such whole-body interaction with very high-quality imagery can have effects far beyond what might expected. As we know, airline pilots emerge perspiring and shaken from their simulated near misses and crashes. And car designers now know never to allow visitors to take coffee cups into their simulators, because they are so likely to put their cups down on surfaces that are not really there. Remarkably, in such a display as the CAVE there is a persuasive illusion of concreteness and physicality that we might not expect. Visual material presented in the right way, at the right speeds and resolutions may go far toward activating and mimicking the kinesthetic along with the visual and the auditory senses. (We must also be aware, however, that beyond certain limits, our bodies and brains sometimes do not take well to a confusing incomplete message—as with the strange symptoms and brief neurological shutdowns fighter pilots sometimes suffer as a consequence of simulator sickness, as they get all the right visual information with only a small fraction of the appropriate "G" forces [West 1997].)

3-D Moving to Center Stage

The rapid spread and wide impact of these technologies may have been much accelerated recently by a major milestone of sorts: In March 1999, the New York Stock Exchange incorporated three-dimensional virtual reality (VR) systems as major components of its trading floor transactions and operations. Thus, at one stroke, visually oriented VR systems, which have often been considered academic or experimental, are now center stage in one of the largest and fastest-moving capital markets in the world.

> On March 16, the Dow closed over 10,000, the S&P 500 ended at 1310.17, and the 747.6 million shares changed hands on the New York Stock Exchange.

> And it all could be easily monitored

> on the NYSE's new 3-D trading floor—a VRML data world of network performance, order flow, price movement, and a dozen other systems that keep the tickers ticking. Launched in March, the virtual trading floor project was conceived several years ago when NYSE execs saw an eye-popping demo of 3-D visualization by SGI [Silicon Graphics]. With the basic idea in mind, the exchange enlisted . . . New York-based Asymptote Architecture. Create a space, the NYSE charged, that shows the correlation of Dow stocks affected by a crisis in the Brazilian market, and links trading data to related news and company announcements. . . . Set on the ramp between the two main rooms on the exchange floor[,] sixty flat-

screen monitors display network information, trading data and live news feeds. Operations managers can fly through a representation of the NYSE systems, quickly scan the virtual floor to gauge trading activity, or zoom in for a view of, say, the exact workstations that will be affected by a network quirk. 'The difference is how fast we can identify a problem, grasp the business implications and account for the situation,' says [a NYSE vice president] (Scanlon 1999).

There can be little doubt that these systems can provide a major opportunity for data visualization technologies to sell themselves to the world at large—especially if it is shown, through day-to-day operations, that traders and operators are better informed and can make better and faster decisions.

NEW TOOLS, NEW TALENTS

Dr. Norman Geschwind pointed out that what we consider talents and disabilities depends greatly on the needs for particular abilities at particular times—within a changing economic and technological context. Perhaps it is time to recognize that many of the problems that people with dyslexia have are, in reality, artifacts of an old print-based technological culture whose prime has past. Perhaps it is time to recognize that many of the talents that many of those with dyslexia exhibit are, in reality, strikingly appropriate for a new image-based technological culture whose prime is yet to come.

As visualization technologies and new ways of working and thinking spread throughout the economy, in time, we should expect to see increased tension and a widening divide, at least in the short run. Of course, the wider use of visualization technologies should be expected to help everyone, regardless of their preferred modes of thought. However, as these techniques become increasingly sophisticated, a certain measure of talent and natural propensity toward the techniques are likely to be a factor of growing importance. These changes may make traditional, non-visual talents less valued, while they make traditional methodological approaches less relevant. In the end, both sides and both kinds of approaches will always be needed. But it may be some time before we have moved beyond all of this to circle back once again to an awareness and a genuine appreciation for a broad range of approaches and thinking styles.

However, as the changes progress, we should expect that moving from one strategy to the other will have powerful consequences. Without being fully aware of the deep importance of what we are doing, we are now learning to use the tools and technologies that support the simultaneous strategy of the human brain—linked to images.

In the past, developing a major part of our culture around the sequential strategy of the human brain served us well, if imperfectly. It seems now is the time to employ these new tools to fully develop the other strategy and make it a major part of our culture—balancing the two. Very possibly, this could be the most important change in the foundation (and balancing) of human culture for a very long time. And we are now only at the beginning.

As we proceed along the way, however, we should expect the pace and direction to be set by strong visual thinkers and creative people with dyslexia who will often ignore conventional verbal descriptions—instead, putting themselves into their own mental models, talking with their hands. And, perhaps a broader understanding of the importance of rediscovered spatial abilities, coupled with the greater use of sophisticated spatial assessment tools, might help prevent conventional educational systems from dropping many of those who are especially well suited to emerging new visual and spatial tasks—whether in creating grand computer graphic illusions for Oscar-winning feature films, or using scientific visualization and newly developed analytic techniques to understand patterns in an elusive stock market or, in many-layered ecological systems. It is time to take a long, hard look at visual thinkers and creative people who are dyslexic and begin to see how these individuals and our larger culture can benefit from new understandings about what we used to see mainly as problems.

EDITOR'S COMMENTS

No one knows dyslexia like a person with dyslexia does at least his or her brand of dyslexia. West lists a long line of successful persons who are either dyslexic or have unusual visuo-spatial powers, or other talents. The question is: When a special talent co-exists with a disability (dyslexia), is the one causal and necessary to the other? Thus West raises several interesting questions about defining the favorable trade-off when nature endows an individual with dyslexia with special gifts. It may be that the subtype question, when answered, will hold a key to that association. Perhaps further investigation of these trade-offs will provide a new system of subtyping dyslexias.

—DDD

REFERENCES

Note: some parts of this chapter have appeared previously in different form in *In the Mind's Eye* as well as in talks, columns, and articles by Thomas G. West.

Agence France Press. 1996. Why Lee Kuan Yew Was Lost for Words. *South China Morning Post*, Hong Kong, January.

Bass, T. A. 1995. Being Nicholas. *Wired* 3(11):146ff.

Benbow, C. P. 1993. Personal communication, The Orton Dyslexia Society Conference. Iowa.

Branson, Richard. 1998. *Losing My Virginity: How I've Survived, Had Fun, and Made a Fortune Doing Business My Way.* New York: Times Business.

Channel Four Television. 1999. Dyslexia. Three 30-minute television programs produced by 20/20 for Channel Four Television; broadcast in the United Kingdom, July 1999. Persons interviewed include Richard Branson, Sally Shaywitz, Paula Tallal and Thomas West.

Churchill, Winston S. 1932. Painting As A Pastime. In *Amid These Storms: Thoughts and Adventures.* London: Butterfield.

Delahaye, Valerie. 1997, 1998. Personal communications and interviews, Los Angeles, CA, and Ottawa, Canada.

Dreyer, William. 1997, 1998. Personal communications, California Institute of Technology, Pasadena, CA, August 1997 and January 1998.

The Economist. 1995. Technology, the Future of Your Job and Other Misplaced Panics, February 11-17, p. 13.

Everatt, John. 1998. Personal communication, email message of June 17, 1998, Psychology Department, Surrey University, United Kingdom.

Frey, Walter. 1990. Schools Miss Out on Dyslexic Engineers. *IEEE Spectrum. December* p. 6.

Galaburda, Albert M. (ed.), 1993. *Dyslexia and Development: Neurobiological Aspects of Extra-Ordinary Brains.* Cambridge, Mass.: Harvard University Press.

Gardner, Howard 1983. *Frames of Mind: The Theory of Multiple Intelligences.* New York: Basic Books.

Geschwind, Norman. 1982. Why Orton Was Right. *The Annals of Dyslexia* 32. The Orton Dyslexia Society Reprint No. 98.

Geschwind, Norman. 1984. The Brain of a Learning-Disabled Individual. *Annals of Dyslexia* 34: 319-27.

Geschwind, Norman, and Galaburda, Albert M. 1987. *Cerebral Lateralization: Biological Mechanisms, Associations and Pathology.* Cambridge, MA: MIT Press.

Gleick, James. 1992. *Genius—The Life and Science of Richard Feynman.* New York, NY: Pantheon Books.

Hussin, Aziz. 1996. S[enior] M[inister] Donates Royalties to Dyslexia Body. *The Straits Times* (Singapore), January 18:3.

Independent, The. 1997. The Art of Being Dyslexic. (London, England), Education Supplement, February 27:4-5.

Institute for the Academic Advancement of Youth (IAAY), Perspectives: Dr. Heinrich Stumpf and His Spatial Test. *Imagine*, Institute for the Academic Advancement of Youth, Johns Hopkins Press. (The list of suggested further reading provided by the IAAY includes: Carrol, J. B. 1993. *Human Cognitive Abilities* (Cambridge University Press); Eliot, J. 1987. *Models of Psychological Space* (Springer-Verlag); Gardner, H. 1983. *Frames of Mind* (Basic Books); Nelson, R. B. 1993. *Proofs Without Words: Exercises in Visual Thinking* (Mathematical Association of America); Stumpf, H. 1995. *Development of a Talent Search and Related Programs for Scientific Innovation Among Youth* (IAAY, CTY, Technical Report No. 12); West, T. G. 1991. *In the Mind's Eye* (Prometheus Books).)

Institute for the Academic Advancement of Youth. 1997. *IAAY Research: Spatial Ability*, unpublished overview, Institute for the Academic

Advancement of Youth, Center for Talented Youth, Center for Academic Advancement, Johns Hopkins University.

Jackson, Tim. 1994. *Virgin King: Inside Richard Branson's Business Empire.* London: HarperCollins Publishers.

K., J. 1997, 1998. Personal communications, Washington, DC, of senior State Department official describing his personal experience of visually oriented problem solving in politics—so useful to himself and so puzzling to most of his associates.

Kaufmann, William J, and Larry L. Smarr. 1993. *Supercomputing and the Transformation of Science.* New York: The Scientific American Library.

Kupfer, Andrew. 1996. Craig McCaw Sees an Internet in the Sky. *Fortune*, May 27:64ff.

McDonald, Kim A. 1994. The Iconoclastic Fossil Hunter. *The Chronicle of Higher Education.* November 16:A9-A17.

Miles, T. R. 1993. *Dyslexia: The Pattern of Difficulties*, Second Edition. London: Whurr Publishers.

Mills, Carol. 1998. Personal communication, (Carol J. Mills, Head of IAAY Research), May 1998.

Mitchell, Russell et al. 1995. The Schwab Revolution. *Business Week*, December 19.

Morgan, W. Pringle. 1896. A Case of Congenital Word Blindness. *British Medical Journal*, November 7:1378.

Negroponte, Nicholas. 1995. *Being Digital.* New York: Alfred A. Knopf. (The MIT disease remark was made during Negroponte's appearance on the "Diane Rehm Show," WAMU-FM, Washington, D.C., March 1995.)

Parkinson, Susan. 1999. Personal Communication. Letter from Susan Parkinson, ARCA, General Secretary, Arts Dyslexia Trust, Great Britain, February 16, 1999.

Petzinger, Thomas. 1998. A Banc One Executive Credits His Success to Mastering Dyslexia. The Front Lines, *The Wall Street Journal*, April 24:B1. (Thanks for this citation are extended to Delos Smith, The Conference Board, New York City.)

Raloff, Janet. 1999. Souping Up Supercomputing—Retooling the Underpinnings of High-Performance Computing. *Science News*, February 27:136-38.

Robins, Cynthia. 1992. One Man's Battle Against Dyslexia—How Financier Charles Schwab is Helping Others Whose Kids Have Learning Disabilities. *San Francisco Examiner*, March 8:D-3, D-10.

Scanlon, Jessie. 1999. Ride the Dow. *Wired*, June:176-79.

Semansky, Anna C. 1999. Charles Schwab, More than Just Discount Brokerage. *Red Herring*, June:136.

Smarr, Larry. 1994. Personal communication, National Center for Supercomputing Applications, University of Illinois, Urbana, IL, email message. (See Kaufmann and Smarr, above.)

Strong, Morgon. 1998. Richard Branson. *Icon Magazine*, December:88ff. (Thanks for this citation are extended to Benjamin West, Washington, D.C.)

Stumpf, H., and E. Klieme. 1989. Sex-Related Differences in Spatial Ability: More Evidence for Convergence. *Perceptual and Motor Skills* 69:915-21.

Weiner, Norbert. 1948, 1961. *Cybernetics: Or Control and Communication in the Animal and the Machine.* Cambridge, MA: MIT Press.

West, Thomas G. 1992. A Future of Reversals—Dyslexic Talents in a World of Computer Visualization. *Annals of Dyslexia* 42:124-39.

West, Thomas G. 1997. *In the Mind's Eye: Visual Thinkers, Gifted People with Dyslexia and Other Learning Difficulties, Computer Images, and the Ironies of*

Creativity. Updated edition with new Preface, Epilog and Notes. Amherst, N.Y.: Prometheus Books.

West, Thomas. 1998. Brain Drain. One of a series of columns titled Images and Reversals, for *Computer Graphics*, a quarterly publication of ACM SIG-GRAPH, the International Association for Computer Graphics Professionals August:15.

Winner, Ellen, French, Lisa, Seliger, Colleen, von Karolyi, Catya, Ross, Erin, Weber, Christina, and Malinsky, Daphna. 1999. *Dyslexia and Spatial Talents: Is There a Relationship?* Pre-publication, January 12:59.

Wszeborowska-Lipinska, Bozena and Singleton, Chris. 1998. Learning Styles in Developmental Dyslexia. (Thesis, University of Gdansk, Poland and the University of Hull, UK; University of Hull, UK.)

Yeo, Geraldine. 1996. Dyslexia: S[enior M[inister]'s Case Gives Parents Hope—They Are Motivated, Encouraged by His Example. *The Straits Times* (Singapore), January 19, p. 25. . (Thanks for this citation and story are extended to Leslie Coull, Vancouver, British Columbia, Canada.)

Index